Frommer's®

Miami & the Keys

day BY day™

1st Edition

by Lesley Abravanel

WILEY

Wiley Publishing, Inc.

Contents

Published by:

Wiley Publishing, Inc.

111 River St.
Hoboken, NJ 07030-5774

ISBN 978-0-470-47407-5
Editor: Anuja Madar
Production Editor: Jana M. Stefanciosa
Photo Editor: Richard Fox
Cartographer: Andrew Dolan
Production by Wiley Indianapolis Composition Services

For information on our other products and services or to obtain technical support, please contact our Customer Care Department within the U.S. at 877/762-2974, outside the U.S. at 317/572-3993 or fax 317/572-4002.

Wiley also publishes its books in a variety of electronic formats. Some content that appears in print may not be available in electronic formats.

Manufactured in China

5 4 3 2 1

A Note from the Editorial Director

Organizing your time. That's what this guide is all about.

Other guides give you long lists of things to see and do and then expect you to fit the pieces together. The Day by Day guides are different. These guides tell you the best of everything, and then they show you how to see it *in the smartest, most time-efficient way*. Our authors have designed detailed itineraries organized by time, neighborhood, or special interest. And each tour comes with a bulleted map that takes you from stop to stop.

Looking to rub shoulders with the beautiful people on South Beach, play dominoes with senior citizens in Little Havana, or capture the city's Art Deco buildings with your camera? Want to swim with dolphins in the turquoise waters of the Keys or hike the trails of Bahia Honda State Park? Whatever your interest or schedule, the Day by Days give you the smartest routes to follow. Not only do we take you to the top attractions, hotels, and restaurants, but we also help you access those special moments that locals get to experience—those "finds" that turn tourists into travelers.

The Day by Days are also your top choice if you're looking for one complete guide for all your travel needs. The best hotels and restaurants for every budget, the greatest shopping values, the wildest nightlife—it's all here.

Why should you trust our judgment? Because our authors personally visit each place they write about. They're an independent lot who say what they think and would never include places they wouldn't recommend to their best friends. They're also open to suggestions from readers. If you'd like to contact them, please send your comments our way at feedback@frommers.com, and we'll pass them on.

Enjoy your Day by Day guide—the most helpful travel companion you can buy. And have the trip of a lifetime.

Warm regards,

Kelly Regan, Editorial Director

Frommer's Travel Guides

About the Author

Lesley Abravanel is a freelance journalist living in Miami Beach. When she isn't combing Florida for the latest hotels, restaurants, and attractions, she's on the lookout for vacationing celebrities, about whom she writes in her thrice weekly nightlife and gossip columns and blog, Scene in the Tropics and Velvet Underground for the *Miami Herald*. She is a contributor to *Time Out* and most of the illustrious supermarket tabloids. She is the author of *Frommer's Florida, Frommer's South Florida, Frommer's Portable Miami,* and *Florida For Dummies*.

Acknowledgments

Thanks to my husband, parents, Winston, and Anuja for putting up with me during the birthing of this new book.

An Additional Note

Please be advised that travel information is subject to change at any time—and this is especially true of prices. We therefore suggest that you write or call ahead for confirmation when making your travel plans. The authors, editors, and publisher cannot be held responsible for the experiences of readers while traveling. Your safety is important to us, however, so we encourage you to stay alert and be aware of your surroundings.

Star Ratings, Icons & Abbreviations

Every hotel, restaurant, and attraction listing in this guide has been ranked for quality, value, service, amenities, and special features using a **star-rating system.** Hotels, restaurants, attractions, shopping, and nightlife are rated on a scale of zero stars (recommended) to three stars (exceptional). In addition to the star-rating system, we also use a **kids icon** to point out the best bets for families. Within each tour, we recommend cafes, bars, or restaurants where you can take a break. Each of these stops appears in a shaded box marked with a coffee-cup-shaped bullet.

The following **abbreviations** are used for credit cards:

AE	American Express	DISC	Discover	V	Visa
DC	Diners Club	MC	MasterCard		

Travel Resources at Frommers.com

Frommer's travel resources don't end with this guide. **Frommers.com** has travel information on more than 4,000 destinations. We update features regularly, giving you access to the most current trip-planning information and the best airfare, lodging, and car-rental bargains. You can also listen to podcasts, connect with other Frommers.com members through our active-reader forums, share your travel photos, read blogs from guidebook editors and fellow travelers, and much more.

A Note on Prices

In the "Take a Break" and "Best Bets" sections of this book, we have used a system of dollar signs to show a range of costs for 1 night in a hotel (the price of a double-occupancy room) or the cost of an entree at a restaurant. Use the following table to decipher the dollar signs:

Cost	Hotels	Restaurants
$	under $125	under $15
$$	$125–$300	$15–$30
$$$	$300–$450	$30–$45
$$$$	$450–$600	$45–$60
$$$$$	over $600	over $60

How to Contact Us

In researching this book, we discovered many wonderful places—hotels, restaurants, shops, and more. We're sure you'll find others. Please tell us about them, so we can share the information with your fellow travelers in upcoming editions. If you were disappointed with a recommendation, we'd love to know that, too. Please write to:

Frommer's Miami & the Keys Day by Day, 1st Edition
Wiley Publishing, Inc. • 111 River St. • Hoboken, NJ 07030-5774

ARK CENTRAL HOTEL
Quinn's
Quinn's

16 Favorite **Moments**

16 Favorite **Moments**

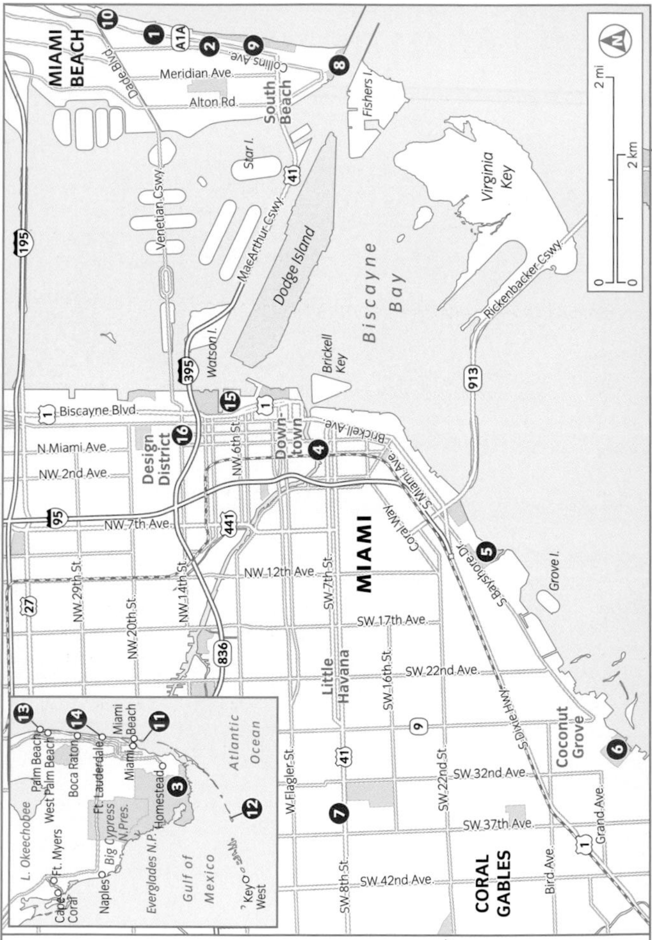

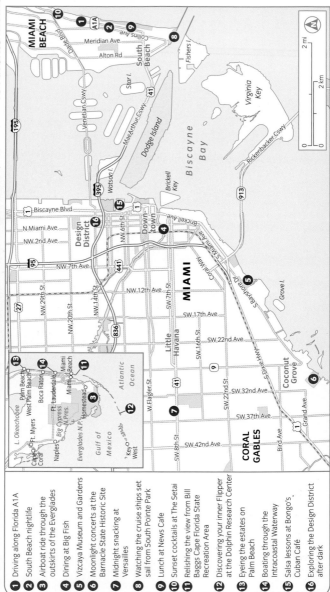

1. Driving along Florida A1A
2. South Beach nightlife
3. Airboat ride through the outskirts of the Everglades
4. Dining at Big Fish
5. Vizcaya Museum and Gardens
6. Moonlight concerts at the Barnacle State Historic Site
7. Midnight snacking at Versailles
8. Watching the cruise ships set sail from South Pointe Park
9. Lunch at News Cafe
10. Sunset cocktails at The Setai
11. Relishing the view from Bill Baggs Cape Florida State Recreation Area
12. Discovering your inner Flipper at the Dolphin Research Center
13. Eyeing the estates on Palm Beach
14. Boating through the Intracoastal Waterway
15. Salsa lessons at Bongo's Cuban Café
16. Exploring the Design District after dark

Previous page: The lively night scene along Ocean Drive.

Miami is a city where the paparazzi camp out for days hoping to catch a glimpse of something, or someone, fabulous; where former presidents pick at stone crabs while pop stars party until dawn; where Old Cuba meets the 21st century with a techno soundtrack; where you can do everything or nothing—and that's just a small sampling of the surreal, Felliniesque world that exists here.

The A1A stretches north through Miami.

❶ **Driving along Florida A1A.** This oceanfront route runs north up Miami Beach and embodies the essence of South Florida. This is one of the most heavily trafficked roads in the state, and time-warped hotels steeped in Art Deco kitsch and multimillion-dollar modern high-rises dot its path. The A1A travels through Sunny Isles, Hollywood, and into Fort Lauderdale, starting at Ocean Drive and First Street in Miami and merging onto Collins Avenue before running north.

❷ **South Beach nightlife.** Miami's got countless clubs and lounges where you can boogie down until the sun comes up. SET and Mokai, where the likes of Justin Timberlake, Scarlett Johansson, Tom Cruise, Paris Hilton, and Sting mix with a colorful crowd of local and international hipsters, are just two of a long list of world-class hotspots that include Skybar, Prive, Mansion, Opium, The Setai, and The Forge. *See p 89.*

❸ **Airboat ride through the outskirts of the Everglades.** Unfettered by jet skis, cruise ships, and neon bikinis, the Everglades are Florida's outback, resplendent in their swampy nature. The Everglades are best explored either by slow-moving canoes, which really get you acquainted with your surroundings, or an airboat that can quickly navigate its way through the most stubborn of saw grass while providing you with an up-close and personal (as well as fun) view of the land's inhabitants, from alligators and manatees to raccoons and Florida panthers. *See p 138.*

Crowds line up outside the latest hotspot, LIV.

Explore the Everglades via airboat.

4 Dining at Big Fish. Some consider dining on the Miami River to be industrial chic; others consider it seedy in a *Miami Vice* sort of way. However you choose to look at it, by all means do look at it; the sleepy Miami River is nestled below the sweeping downtown Miami skyline, reminding you that even though you're in a major metropolis, things in this often-frenetic city are capable of slowing down to a more soothing pace. *See p 74.*

5 Vizcaya Museum and Gardens. Built in 1916, this Italian Renaissance–style manse on Biscayne Bay features 34 rooms of antiques, art, and tapestries; 10 acres (4 hectares) of Italian gardens, statues, and fountains; a new orchid display; and a picture-perfect view of the skyline and Key Biscayne. *See p 68.*

Statues line the paths in the Vizcaya Gardens.

6 Moonlight concerts at the Barnacle State Historic Site. Once a month, on or near the full moon (except during July and Aug), the Barnacle State Historic Site hosts a concert in the backyard of their charming 1908 Coconut Grove bungalow, built on 5 acres (2 hectares) of waterfront property. Listeners are welcome to picnic and bask in this sublime setting for a mere $5. *See p 22, 9.*

7 Midnight snacking at Versailles. This iconoclastic, gaudy Cuban diner in the heart of Miami's Little Havana is humming with the buzz of old-timers reminiscing about pre-Castro Cuba, local politicos trying to appease them, and a slew of detached people only there for the fantastically cheap and authentic Cuban fare. Much like its French namesake, whose image it mirrors, Miami's Versailles provides a palatial view of Miami's ever-changing Cuban landscape. *See p 88.*

8 Watching the cruise ships set sail from South Pointe Park. Unless you're already on a boat, you can't get a better view of the monstrous cruise ships leaving the Port of Miami than from South Pointe Park, located at the southern tip of South Beach. If you stare long enough, you will feel like you're moving, which is almost as much fun as being on board.

❾ **Lunch at News Cafe.** The quintessential South Beach experience, lunching at News Cafe is more of a spectator sport than a dining experience. Its Ocean Drive location is one of the best sidewalk spots from which to observe the wacky, colorful mix of pedestrians on parade. *See p 84.*

❿ **Sunset cocktails at The Setai.** The most luxe and expensive hotel on South Beach may not be in everyone's budget, but the Friday-night cocktail parties are—and should not be missed. *See p 125.*

⓫ **Relishing the view from Bill Baggs Cape Florida State Recreation Area.** You haven't truly seen South Florida until you've checked out the view from the southern point of Key Biscayne. Whether it's the turquoise water or the sight of Stiltsville—seven still-inhabited aquatic cabins dating back to the 1930s, perched smack in the middle of the Biscayne Channel—it may take a little coercing to get you to leave. *See p 69.*

Versailles is a favorite any time of day or night.

⓬ **Discovering your inner Flipper at the Dolphin Research Center.** Learn to communicate with and touch, swim, or play with the mammals at the nonprofit Dolphin Research Center in Marathon Key, home to a school of approximately 15 dolphins. *See p 150.*

Giant cruise ships dock at the Port of Miami.

Prime people-watching along Ocean Drive can be had at News Cafe.

⓭ Eyeing the estates on Palm Beach. The winter playground for the *Lifestyles of the Rich and Famous* set, Palm Beach is lined with jaw-dropping palatial estates. Though many of them are hidden behind towering shrubbery, head south on South County Road, from Brazilian Avenue, where you will see some of the most opulent homes ever built. *See p 134.*

⓮ Boating through the Intracoastal Waterway. The waterway that connects the natural bays, lagoons, and rivers along Florida's East Coast snakes around from the Florida-Georgia border all the way to the Port of Miami. A ride through the Fort Lauderdale Intracoastal provides a sublime view of million-dollar waterfront houses.

⓯ Salsa lessons at Bongo's Cuban Café. If the only salsa you're familiar with is the kind you eat with tortilla chips, get over to Bongo's, the hottest salsa club north of Havana, where you can learn from Miami's most talented salsa dancers. *See p 97.*

⓰ Exploring the Design District after dark. After waiting patiently for this arty, funky area to hit its peak, Miami's hipsters have finally been rewarded with cool bars, lounges, and restaurants. *See p 38.*

The Design District is alive and hopping even after the sun sets.

1 The Best **Full-Day Tours**

The Best **in One Day**

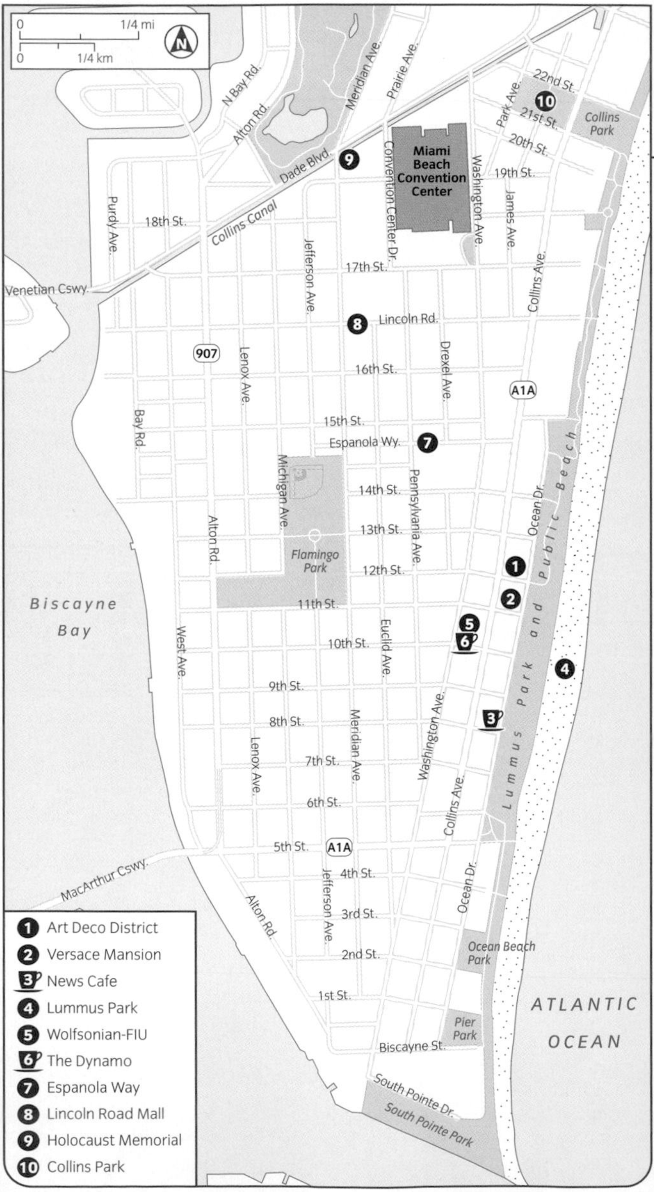

Previous page: Kenneth Triester's Sculpture of Love & Anguish *at the Holocaust Memorial.*

With one day to spend in Miami, focus on the city's media darling—South Beach, aka the American Riviera. South Beach isn't just a stretch of sand, but rather a collection of Kodak moments, from museums and models to cafes and celebrities. Here you'll find historic Art Deco buildings, whose pristine preservation rivals that of many of South Beach's saline, silicone, and Botox-saturated denizens. **START: Art Deco Welcome Center.**

The Colony Hotel's distinct Art Deco signage.

1 ★★★ Gawk at the original supermodel—the Art Deco District. Take a self-guided walking and audio tour around Ocean Drive's Art Deco District, where sleek and chic streamlined, neon-lit, pastel-hued buildings are ready for their close-ups. *90 min. Set your own pace and walk on, but it's best to do so early morning or late afternoon to avoid crowds and heat. ☎ 305/672-2014. www.mdpl.org. Tickets $15 adults, $10 seniors & children.*

2 Versace Mansion. Morbid curiosity has led hordes of people—tourists and locals—here, once the only private home (now a country club and resort for those in the upper brackets) on Ocean Drive. If you can get past the fact that the late designer, Gianni Versace, was murdered on the steps of this palatial estate, you will observe the intricate Italian architecture that makes this house stand out from its streamlined deco neighbors. Built in the 1930s as a replica of Christopher Columbus's son's palace in Santo Domingo, the house was originally called Casa Casuarina (House of the Pine), but was rechristened the Amsterdam Palace in 1935 when George Amsterdam purchased it. While there were rumors that the mansion was to be turned into a Versace museum, it was, instead, purchased by a private citizen from Texas. They offer tours from time to time, so call ahead and check. There's also a restaurant inside that's open to the public if you're hungry—and in the market for a pricey snack. *5 min.–2 hr. (if you want to eat). 1114 Ocean Dr.*

The ornate pool at the Versace Mansion.

☎ *305/672-6604. www.casacasuarina.com. Tours offered seasonally; $65 per person, includes 1 mimosa.*

Quench your thirst at **3 News Cafe,** the catalyst to South Beach's late-'80s revival and the quintessence of the beach's cafe society. *800 Ocean Dr.* ☎ *305/538-6397. $.*

4 Lummus Park. This *is* South Beach. Past the dunes and the beach-volleyball courts is this stellar stretch of sand, sunbathers, and photogenic, colorful lifeguard stands. If you're not in the mood to lie under an umbrella and laze away, take a break on the bike path to take in the scenery. *5 min.–1hr. Ocean Dr. between 5th & 14th sts.*

Colorful lifeguard stands line Lummus Park.

5 ★★★ Wolfsonian-FIU. This 1927 converted storage facility is a treasure trove of Art Deco artifacts, including an original deco mailbox from NYC's Grand Central Station, pre-Castro Cuban movie posters, and all sorts of propaganda art. *1–2 hrs. 1001 Washington Ave. at 10th St.* ☎ *305/531-1001. www.wolfsonian.org. $7. Open Mon–Wed & Sat–Sun noon–6pm; Thurs–Fri noon–9pm.*

After satisfying your hunger for knowledge, stop by the Wolfsonian's museum store cum cafe, **6 The Dynamo,** where a side of Fellini with your panini is complimentary. *1001 Washington Ave.* ☎ *305/535-2680. $.*

7 ★ Espanola Way. A few blocks north of the Wolfsonian and Art Deco District is South Beach's sublime, if not somewhat touristy, Espanola Way, a block-long Spanish Mediterranean village where galleries, boutiques, street vendors, and cafes line the streets, and a youth hostel now occupies a building that once served as Al Capone's gambling headquarters. Will Smith filmed the music video for his homage to the

Magic City, "Miami," on these streets. 🕒 *30 min. Corner of Washington Ave. & 15th St.*

❽ ★★ kids **Lincoln Road Mall.** This "road" is well traveled by locals who bike, blade, board, or stroll up and down this popular pedestrian thoroughfare. Designed by architectural icon Morris Lapidus, the road is full of cafes, boutiques, requisite Starbucks (two of them so far), art galleries, and theaters. Although most of the stores here are of the chain variety, the people who hang here are hardly cookie-cutter. Stroll, shop, and make sure to stop to gawk at some of the area's most pampered pooches. If you have a sweet tooth, don't miss one of Oprah's favorite places for pies and cakes, **The Ice Box Café,** 1657 Michigan Ave. (☎ 305/538-8448). 🕒 *1 hr.*

❾ ★★★ kids **Holocaust Memorial.** Kenneth Triester's *Sculpture of Love & Anguish* depicts victims of the concentration camps crawling up a giant yearning hand stretching up to the sky, marked with an Auschwitz number tattoo. Along the reflecting pool is the story of the Holocaust, told in cut marble slabs. Inside the center of the memorial is a tableau that is one of the most solemn and moving tributes to the millions of Jews who lost their lives in the Holocaust. 🕒 *1 hr. 1933 Meridian Ave. (at Dade Blvd.).* ☎ *305/538-1663. www.holocaustmmb.org. Free admission. Daily 9am–9pm.*

❿ ★★★ kids **Collins Park.** Collins Park Cultural Center comprises a trio of arts buildings on Collins Park and Park Avenue (off Collins Ave.), bounded by 21st to 23rd streets—the newly expanded Bass Museum of Art, the new home of the Miami City Ballet, and the Miami Beach Regional Library, an ultramodern building with a special focus on the arts. The Library Café is on the library's first

Pre-Castro Cuban movie posters at the Wolfsonian-FIU.

floor, serving coffee and pastries. Collins Park, the former site of the Miami Beach Library, returned to its original incarnation as an open space extending to the Atlantic, but it is also now the site of large sculpture installations and cultural activities planned jointly by the organizations that share the space. 🕒 *1–3 hrs. 2121 Park Ave.* ☎ *305/673-7530. www.bassmuseum.org. Admission $8 adults, $6 students & seniors, free for children 6 & under. Free 2nd Thurs of the month 6–9pm. Tues–Wed & Fri–Sat 10am–5pm; Thurs 10am–9pm; Sun 11am–5pm.*

Lincoln Road Mall is big with dog walkers and window shoppers.

The Best **in Two Days**

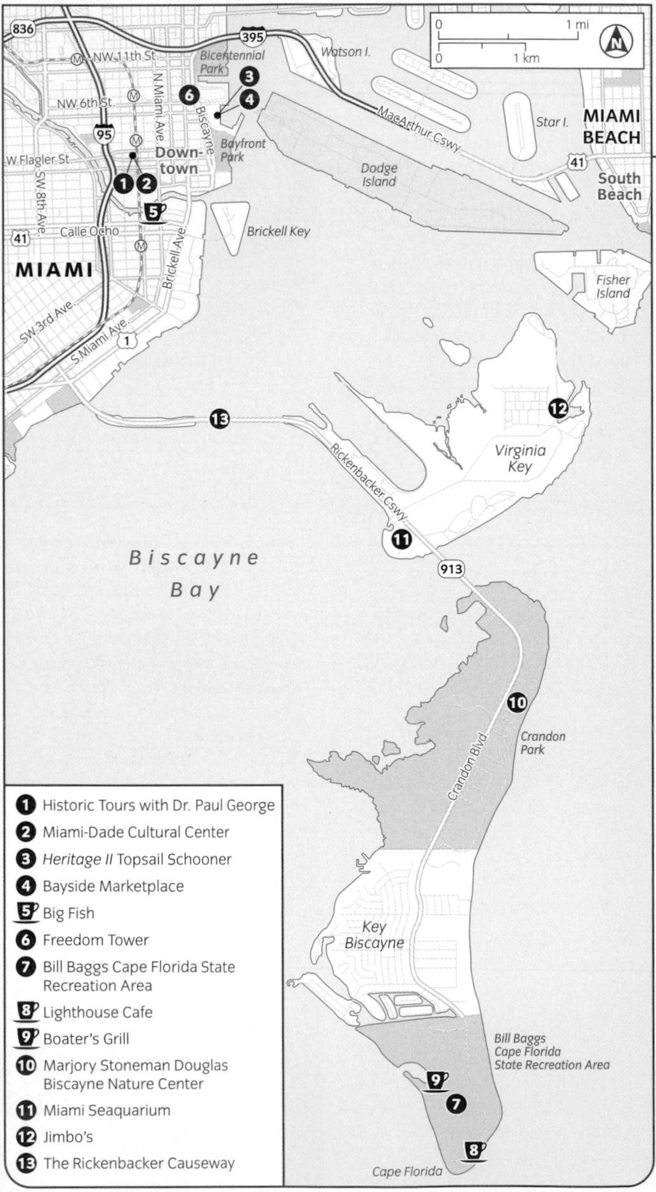
0 1 mi
0 1 km
N
836
395
NW 11th St.
Bicentennial Park
Watson I.
NW 6th St.
N. Miami Ave.
Biscayne
MacArthur Cswy.
Star I.
MIAMI BEACH
95
W Flagler St.
Down-town
Bayfront Park
Dodge Island
41
South Beach
SW 8th Ave.
Calle Ocho
Brickell Ave.
Brickell Key
41
MIAMI
Fisher Island
SW 3rd Ave.
S Miami Ave.
1
Rickenbacker Cswy.
Virginia Key
Biscayne Bay
913
Crandon Park
Crandon Blvd.
Key Biscayne
Bill Baggs Cape Florida State Recreation Area
Cape Florida
1 Historic Tours with Dr. Paul George
2 Miami-Dade Cultural Center
3 Heritage II Topsail Schooner
4 Bayside Marketplace
5 Big Fish
6 Freedom Tower
7 Bill Baggs Cape Florida State Recreation Area
8 Lighthouse Cafe
9 Boater's Grill
10 Marjory Stoneman Douglas Biscayne Nature Center
11 Miami Seaquarium
12 Jimbo's
13 The Rickenbacker Causeway

On your second day in Miami, take a tour with Dr. Paul George, the city's best tour guide, and gain insight into the people, places, and events that shaped the city's tabloid reputation, among other things. Explore the city beyond the beaches and the Hiltons—as in Paris—hit the water with a great boat tour, and finish up back on the beach, this time on Key Biscayne. **START: Historical Museum, 101 W. Flagler St.**

1 ★★★ Historic Tours With Dr. Paul George. Dr. George, a history teacher at Miami-Dade Community College and a historian at the Historical Museum of Southern Florida, offers a variety of tours. The "Mystery, Mayhem, and Vice Crime Bus Tour" explores Miami-Dade's most celebrated crimes and criminals from the 1800s to the present, including sites where the '80s TV series *Miami Vice* was filmed. Tours focus on neighborhoods such as Little Havana, Brickell Avenue, or Key Biscayne, and on themes such as Miami cemeteries and the Miami River. There are also eco-history coach, walking, and bike tours. The often long-winded discussions can be a bit much for those who just want a quick look around, but Dr. George certainly knows his stuff. *3 hrs. 101 W. Flagler St. ☎ 305/375-1621. www.hmsf.org/programs-adult.htm. Tickets $5–$44.*

2 ★ Miami-Dade Cultural Center. The Phillip Johnson–designed Miami-Dade Cultural Center, located downtown, is a Mediterranean-style complex housing the Miami-Dade Public Library, Historical Museum of Southern Florida, and Miami Art Museum. If you're not in the mood to spend a sunny day indoors, just hang out in the complex's splendid courtyard and watch the arty folk and the skyline above. *30 min. 101 W. Flagler St., at NW 1st Ave. ☎ 305/375-1700.*

3 *Heritage II* Topsail Schooner. This relaxing ride aboard Miami's only tall ship is a fun way to see the city and is the only tour company that takes you out on a schooner rather than a cruising boat. The 2-hour cruise passes by Villa Vizcaya, Coconut Grove, and Key Biscayne, and puts you in sight of Miami's spectacular skyline and

An exhibit at the Miami-Dade Cultural Center.

The Heritage II *is the only tour of its kind in the city.*

island homes. 🕘 *2 hrs. Bayside Marketplace, 401 Biscayne Blvd.* ☎ *305/442-9697. www.heritageschooner.com. Two-hr. trips at 1:30 & 4pm daily. $20 adults, $15 children. Evening trips are 1 hr. at 6:30 & 8pm daily. $15 adults, $10 children.*

4 kids Bayside Marketplace. Touristy? Yes. But for some of the best views in the entire city, Bayside's sprawling shopping, dining, and entertainment complex is the place to be, with live salsa bands playing by the water. Despite what locals say, it's still, for better or worse, very Miami. 🕘 *30 min. 401 Biscayne Blvd.* ☎ *305/577-3344. www.baysidemarketplace.com. Open Mon–Thurs 10am–10pm (Fri–Sat until 11pm); Sun 11am–9pm.*

5 Big Fish, one of downtown Miami's most scenic lunch spots, offers prime views of the hustle and bustle of the Miami River as well as fresh pasta and seafood dishes. Popular happy hours make Big Fish a major player for cocktails at sunset. *55 SW Miami Ave. Rd.* ☎ *305/373-1770. www.thebigfishmiami.com. $$$.*

6 Freedom Tower. The most dramatic presence on the heavily trafficked stretch of Biscayne Boulevard downtown is the Freedom Tower, built in 1925 and modeled after the Giralda Tower in Spain. Once home to the now-defunct *Miami Daily News* and *Metropolis* newspapers, the Freedom Tower was sold in 1957 to the U.S. General

The Freedom Tower is modeled after Spain's Giralda Tower.

Services Administration, which used the building to process more than 500,000 Cubans fleeing the island once Castro took over. Considered the Ellis Island of the Cuban Exile community, Miami's Freedom Tower has remained largely vacant over the years (the government left the building in 1974) despite hopes and unfulfilled plans to turn it into a museum reflecting its historical significance. Most recently, the building was donated to Miami-Dade College by the Terra Group, a condo development company, for use as a museum, cultural center, and classroom space—as long as they allow them to build a 62-story condo behind it. *5 min. 600 Biscayne Blvd. at NE 6th St.*

7 ★★★ kids Bill Baggs Cape Florida State Recreation Area. At the southern tip of Key Biscayne, about 20 minutes from downtown Miami, you can explore the unfettered wilds and enjoy some of the most secluded beaches in the city. There's also a historic lighthouse that was built in 1825, which is the oldest lighthouse in South Florida. The lighthouse was damaged during the Second Seminole War (1836) and again in 1861 during the Civil War. Out of commission for a while, it was restored to working condition in 1978 by the U.S. Coast Guard. A rental shack leases bikes, hydrobikes, kayaks, and many more water toys. It's a great place to picnic. Just be careful that the raccoons don't get your lunch—the furry black-eyed beasts are everywhere. Bill Baggs has been consistently rated as one of the top 10 beaches in the U.S. for its 1¼ miles (2km) of wide, sandy beaches and its secluded, serene atmosphere. *2–4 hr. 1200 S. Crandon Blvd. ☎ 305/361-5811. www.floridastateparks.org/capeflorida. Admission $5 per car with up to 8 people; $3 for a car with only 1 person; $1 to enter by foot or bicycle. Daily 8am–sunset. Tours of the lighthouse available Thurs–Mon at 10am & 1pm. Arrive at least 30 min. early to sign up—there is room for only 10 people on each tour. Take I-95 to the Rickenbacker Causeway, and take that all the way to the end.*

Inside Bill Baggs Cape Florida State Recreation Area, the **8 Lighthouse Cafe** (☎ 305/361-8487; $) is a good option for some quick refreshment. For a snack with a view, try the waterfront **9 Boater's Grill** (☎ 305/361-0080; $), a well-kept secret offering cold beer, fried fish, and even frogs' legs.

10 kids ★★★ Marjory Stoneman Douglas Biscayne Nature Center. Named after the late champion of the Everglades, the Marjory Stoneman Douglas Biscayne Nature Center is housed in a $4 million facility and offers hands-on marine exploration, hikes through coastal hammocks, bike trips, and beach walks. Local environmentalists and historians lead intriguing trips through the local habitat. Call to reserve a spot on a regularly scheduled weekend tour or program. Be sure to wear comfortable, closed-toe shoes for hikes through wet or rocky terrain. *1–3 hrs. 6767 Crandon Blvd. ☎ 305/361-6767. www.biscaynenaturecenter.org. Daily 10am–4pm. Admission to the park $4 per person; admission to the nature center free. Special programs & tours $10 per person. Call for weekend programs. Take I-95 to the Rickenbacker Causeway (Exit 1),* *and take the causeway all the way until it becomes Crandon Blvd. The center is on the east side of the street (the Atlantic Ocean side) and about 25 min. from downtown Miami.*

⑪ kids Miami Seaquarium. If you've been to Orlando's SeaWorld, you may be disappointed with Miami's version, which is considerably smaller and not as well maintained. It's hardly a sprawling seaquarium, but you will want to arrive early to enjoy the effects of its mild splash. The 35-acre (14-hectare) oceanarium has four daily shows starring a number of showy ocean mammals. You can cut your visit short if you limit yourself to the better, albeit corny, Flipper and Killer Whale shows. The highly regarded Dolphin Encounter allows visitors to touch and swim with dolphins in the Flipper Lagoon; the program is available for an extra charge, and reservations are necessary. *3 hrs. 4400 Rickenbacker Causeway (south side), en route to Key Biscayne. ☎ 305/361-5705. www.miamiseaquarium.com. Admission $36 adults, $27 children 3–9, free for children 2 & under. Daily 9:30am–6pm (ticket booth closes at 4pm). Parking $8.*

⑫ ★★★ kids Jimbo's. There are no napkins or utensils here ("This is a place where you eat with your hands."), but there is the best smoked fish (marlin or salmon) in town at this ramshackle seafood shack, which started as a gathering spot for fishermen. Now you'll find shrimpers, politicians, and well-oiled beach bums alongside stray dogs and chickens (this is not a place to get dressed up—you will get dirty—and the bathroom is rancid). Grab yourself a dollar beer (there's only beer, water, and soda, but you can also BYO) from the cooler and take in the view of the tropical lagoon where they shot *Flipper;* you may even see a manatee or two. The surrounding vacant shacks served as backdrops for films such as *True Lies.* There's a bocce court here, too, and the owner, Jimbo, may challenge you to a game. *Off the Rickenbacker Causeway at Sewerline Rd. ☎ 305/361-7026. Smoked fish about $8 a pound. No credit cards. Mon–Fri 6am–6:30pm; Sat–Sun 6am–7:30pm. Head south on the main road toward Key Biscayne,*

Catch a dolphin show at the Miami Seaquarium.

A bridge detail at the Rickenbacker Causeway.

make a left just after the MAST Academy (there will be a sign that says VIRGINIA KEY*); tell the person in the tollbooth you're going to Jimbo's and he'll point you in the right direction.*

⓭ **The Rickenbacker Causeway.** Take advantage of a wonderful photo opportunity at the bridge that arcs from downtown Miami to the first two Florida Keys—Virginia Key and Key Biscayne. 🕘 *5 min.*

On Location in Miami

With its warm weather, picturesque skylines, and gorgeous sunsets, Miami is the perfect setting for making movies.

Since the earliest days of the film industry, Miami has had a starring role in some of America's most celebrated celluloid classics, from the Marx Brothers' first feature, ***The Cocoanuts*** (1929), to the 1941 classic, ***Citizen Kane,*** which used the spectacular South Florida coastline as the setting for Kane's own Hearst Castle, Xanadu. As the film industry evolved and productions became more elaborate, Miami was thrice seized by a suave international man of intrigue known as Bond, James Bond, in ***Dr. No, Live and Let Die,*** and ***Goldfinger.*** Countless major motion pictures have been filmed in Miami–Dade County, including ***Miami Vice, True Lies, Any Given Sunday, There's Something About Mary, Random Hearts,*** and ***Bad Boys II.*** Recently, Jennifer Aniston and Owen Wilson romped around the city for the canine tearjerker ***Marley & Me,*** and George Clooney was also here shooting scenes for his newest flick, ***Up In the Air.***

The Best **in Three Days**

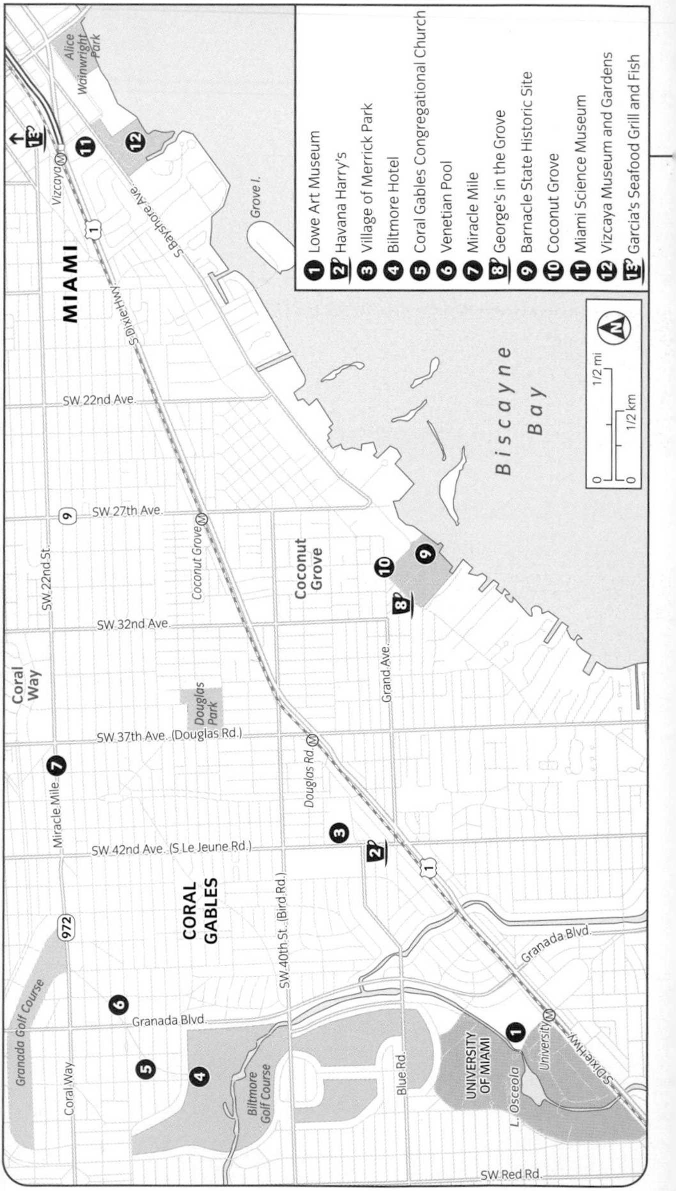
1 Lowe Art Museum
2 Havana Harry's
3 Village of Merrick Park
4 Biltmore Hotel
5 Coral Gables Congregational Church
6 Venetian Pool
7 Miracle Mile
8 George's in the Grove
9 Barnacle State Historic Site
10 Coconut Grove
11 Miami Science Museum
12 Vizcaya Museum and Gardens
13 Garcia's Seafood Grill and Fish
Biscayne Bay
1/2 mi
1/2 km
MIAMI
CORAL GABLES
Coconut Grove
Coral Way
Alice Wainwright Park
Grove I.
S. Bayshore Ave.
S. Dixie Hwy.
Vizcaya
Coconut Grove
Douglas Rd.
University
SW 22nd Ave.
SW 27th Ave.
SW 32nd Ave.
SW 37th Ave. (Douglas Rd.)
SW 42nd Ave. (S Le Jeune Rd.)
SW 22nd St.
SW 40th St. (Bird Rd.)
Miracle Mile
Grand Ave.
Douglas Park
Granada Blvd.
Granada Golf Course
Biltmore Golf Course
Blue Rd.
UNIVERSITY OF MIAMI
L. Osceola
SW Red Rd.
9
972
1

On your third day in Miami, stroll Coral Gables, The City Beautiful created by George Merrick in the early 1920s, sporting stunning Mediterranean-style homes and National Historic Landmarks along lush, tree-lined streets that open onto beautifully carved plazas, many with centerpiece fountains. The Gables is also home to some seriously stunning sightseeing, dining, and shopping. **START: Lowe Art Museum, 1301 Stanford Dr. at Ponce de León Blvd.**

1 ★★ Lowe Art Museum Located on the University of Miami campus, the Lowe Art Museum has a dazzling collection of 8,000 works that include American paintings, Latin American art, Navajo and Pueblo Indian textiles, and Renaissance and baroque art. Traveling exhibits, such as *Wine Spectator* magazine's classic posters of the Belle Epoque, also stop here. For the most part, the Lowe is known for its collection of Greek and Roman antiquities, and, as compared to the more modern MOCA, Bass, and Miami Art Museum, features mostly European and international art hailing back to ancient times. *1 hr. University of Miami, 1301 Stanford Dr. (at Ponce de León Blvd.). ☎ 305/284-3603. www.lowemuseum.org. Admission $10 adults, $5 seniors and students with ID. Donation day is 1st Tues of the month. Tues–Wed and Fri–Sat 10am–5pm; Thurs noon–7pm; Sun noon–5pm.*

2 Havana Harry's, a casual Cuban restaurant in the heart of Coral Gables, is a mom-and-pop eatery serving stellar sweet plantains, *tostones*, and *cortaditos*. *4612 LeJeune Rd. ☎ 305/661-2622. $.*

3 ★ Village of Merrick Park. Although Miracle Mile is Coral Gables' main downtown shopping area, the sprawling and picturesque Village of Merrick Park is not your average mall. The outdoor shopping mecca is a mammoth, 850,000-square-foot (78,968 sq. km) complex between Ponce de León Boulevard and LeJeune Road, just off the Mile, and is dotted with fountains, lush foliage, and gardens. It houses Nordstrom, Neiman Marcus, Armani,

Outdoor shopping at the Village of Merrick Park.

The Biltmore Hotel is Coral Gables' oldest.

Gucci, Jimmy Choo, and Yves St. Laurent, to name a few. *1 hr. 358 San Lorenzo Ave. 305/529-0200. www.villageofmerrickpark.com. Mon–Sat 10am–9pm; Sun noon–6pm.*

4 ★★ **Biltmore Hotel.** A romantic sense of old-world glamour combined with a rich history permeates the Biltmore as much as the pricey perfume of the guests who stay here. Built in 1926, it's the oldest Coral Gables hotel and is a National Historic Landmark—one of only two operating hotels in Florida to receive that designation. Rising above the Spanish-style estate is a majestic 300-foot (90m) copper-clad tower, modeled after the Giralda bell tower in Seville and visible throughout the city. The landmark 23,000-square-foot (2,137 sq. km) winding pool now has the requisite hipster accessories—private cabana, alfresco bar, and restaurant. Take advantage of a free, 55-minute Sunday walking tour; if it's available, you'll get a look at the Everglades Suite, which has hosted gangsters (Al Capone), dignitaries, heads of state, and celebrities. *1 hr. 1200 Anastasia Ave. 305/445-1926. www.biltmorehotel.com. Free admission. Tours Sun at 1:30, 2:30 & 3:30pm.*

5 **Coral Gables Congregational Church.** This Mediterranean revival building is a stunning photo op, designed as a replica of a Costa Rican church. Completed in 1924, the church not only hosts religious ceremonies, but also popular jazz, classical, and folk music concerts and big-name book readings.

The Coral Gables Congregational Church is modeled after a church in Costa Rica.

The Venetian Pool is open to the public for swimming.

10 min. 3010 DeSoto Blvd. at Anastasia Ave. ☎ 305/448-7421.

6 ★★★ kids Venetian Pool. Miami's most beautiful and unusual swimming pool, dating from 1924, is hidden behind pastel stucco walls and is honored with a listing in the National Register of Historic Places. Underground artesian wells feed the free-form lagoon, which is shaded by three-story Spanish porticos and has both fountains and waterfalls. It can be cold in the winter months. During summer, the pool's 800,000 gallons of water are drained and refilled nightly, thanks to an underground aquifer, ensuring a cool, clean swim. Visitors are free to swim and sunbathe here, just as Esther Williams and Johnny Weissmuller did decades ago. *2 hrs. 2701 DeSoto Blvd. (at Toledo St.). ☎ 305/460-5356. www.coralgablesvenetianpool.com. Admission Nov–Mar $5.50 for those 13 & older, $3.50 for children 12 & under; Apr–Oct $10 for those 13 & older, $6.75 for children 12 & under. Children must be at least 3 years old and provide proof of age with birth certificate, or 38 in. (1m) tall to enter. Daily hours are at least 11am–4:30pm but are often longer.*

7 Miracle Mile. Actually only a ½-mile (.8km) long, this central shopping street was an integral part of George Merrick's city plan. Originally it encompassed property within the designated geographic area—Douglas Road to LeJeune Road (east–west), and Aragon Avenue to Andalusia Avenue (north–south). In November 2007, the geographic area was expanded to include 1 more block north, making the northern boundary Giralda Avenue. Today the strip still enjoys popularity, especially for its boutiques and upscale restaurants. Recently, newer chain stores, such as Barnes & Noble, Old Navy, and Starbucks, have been appearing on the Mile. *30 min. ☎ 305/569-0311.*

8 George's in the Grove is a modern French bistro, with sleek decor and a sleeker champagne-sipping clientele. Entrees range from classics such as ratatouille and steak frites to a very Miami mango *tart tartin.* Food is good, but the ambience is better. As the night goes on, music gets louder and a party scene ensues. *3145 Commodore Plaza. ☎ 305/444-7878. $$.*

9 ★★★ kids **Barnacle State Historic Site.** The former home of naval architect and early settler Ralph Middleton Munroe is now a museum in the heart of Coconut Grove. It's the oldest house in Miami and rests on its original foundation, which sits on 5 acres (2 hectares) of natural hardwood forest and landscaped lawns. The house's quiet surroundings, wide porches, and period furnishings illustrate how Miami's first snowbird lived in the days before condo mania and luxury hotels. Enthusiastic and knowledgeable state park employees provide a wealth of historical information. The site also hosts sunset yoga (Wed 6–7:30pm) and monthly moonlight concerts (picnicking is encouraged). *1 hr. 3485 Main Hwy. (1 block south of Commodore Plaza). ☎ 305/448-9445. Admission $1. Concerts $5; free for children 9 & under. Fri–Mon 9am–4pm. Tours Fri–Mon 10am, 11:30am, 1pm & 2:30pm. From downtown Miami, take U.S. 1 south to 27th Ave., make a left, and continue to S. Bayshore Dr.; then make a right, follow to the intersection of Main Hwy., and turn left.*

10 **Coconut Grove.** An arty, hippie hangout in the psychedelic '60s, Coconut Grove once had residents who dressed in swirling tie-dyed garb. Nowadays, they prefer the uniform color schemes of the Gap. Chain stores, theme restaurants, a megaplex, and bars galore make Coconut Grove a commercial success, but this gentrification (plus the Ritz-Carlton Coconut Grove and the Mayfair hotels) has pushed most alternative types out. The intersection of Grand Avenue, Main Highway, and McFarlane Road pierces the area's heart. Right in the center of it all is CocoWalk, filled with boutiques, eateries, and bars. Sidewalks here are often crowded, especially at night, when University of Miami students come out to play. *2 hrs.*

11 kids **Miami Science Museum.** Science is fascinating, yes, but even better at this museum

Barnacle State Historic Site hosts sunset yoga on Wednesday evenings.

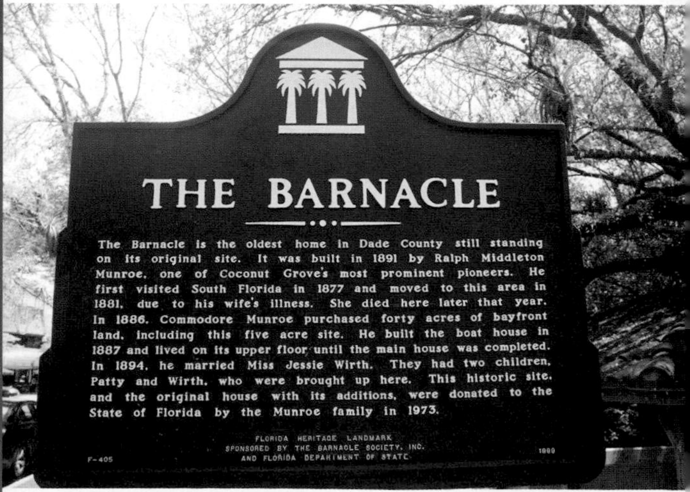
THE BARNACLE
The Barnacle is the oldest home in Dade County still standing on its original site. It was built in 1891 by Ralph Middleton Munroe, one of Coconut Grove's most prominent pioneers. He first visited South Florida in 1877 and moved to this area in 1881, due to his wife's illness. She died here later that year. In 1886, Commodore Munroe purchased forty acres of bayfront land, including this five acre site. He built the boat house in 1887 and lived on its upper floor until the main house was completed. In 1894, he married Miss Jessie Wirth. They had two children, Patty and Wirth, who were brought up here. This historic site, and the original house with its additions, were donated to the State of Florida by the Munroe family in 1973.
FLORIDA HERITAGE LANDMARK
SPONSORED BY THE BARNACLE SOCIETY, INC.
AND FLORIDA DEPARTMENT OF STATE
F-405

Interactive exhibits at the Miami Science Museum.

is its Wildlife Center, featuring more than 175 live reptiles and birds of prey. There are also more than 140 hands-on exhibits that explore the mysteries of the universe. Live demonstrations and collections of rare natural history specimens make a visit here fun and informative. ⌚ *1 hr. 3280 S. Miami Ave. (just south of the Rickenbacker Causeway).* ☎ *305/646-4200. www.miamisci.org. Admission $18 adults, $16 seniors & students, $13 children 3–12, free for children 2 & under. Daily 10am–6pm; 1st Fri of every month 10am–10pm; call for show times (last show is at 4pm weekdays & 5pm on weekends).*

Digging Miami

During a routine investigation at the mouth of the Miami River in September 2008, archaeologists discovered a circular structure cut into the bedrock, 38 feet (11m) in diameter, with intentional markings of the cardinal directions, as well as a 5-foot-long (1.5m) shark and two stone axes. These suggested the circle had ceremonial significance to Miami's earliest inhabitants—the Tequesta Indians. Radiocarbon tests confirmed the circle to be about 2,000 years old. Most scholars believe that the discovery represents the foundation of a circular structure, perhaps a council house or a chief's house. Local preservationists formed an organization, Save the Miami Circle, to ensure that developers don't raze the circle to make way for condominiums. For now, the circle remains put, albeit surrounded by cranes constructing mega-condos. See www.miamicircle.org for more information.

Hispanic Heritage Tour

For those looking to immerse themselves in Miami's rich Latin-American culture, the **Herencia Hispana Tour** is the ideal way to explore it all. Hop on a bus and zoom past such hotbeds of Latin activity as downtown's Flagler Street, the unavoidable Elian Gonzalez house, and Little Havana's Domino Park and Tower Theater, among others. Not just a sightseeing tour, this one includes two very knowledgeable, albeit corny, guides who know just when to infuse a necessary dose of humor into the Elian saga, a segment of history that some people may not consider so amusing. Tours depart at 9, 9:30, and 10am every Saturday in October from the Steven P. Clark Government Center, 111 NW 1st St. ☎ 305/770-3131. www.co.miami-dade.fl.us/transit/hispanicher.asp. Tours (in Spanish or English, but you must specify which one you require) are free, but advanced reservations are required.

⓬ ★★★ kids **Vizcaya Museum and Gardens.** Sometimes referred to as the "Hearst Castle of the East," this magnificent villa was built in 1916 as a winter retreat for James Deering, cofounder and former vice president of International Harvester. The industrialist was fascinated by 16th-century art and architecture, and his ornate mansion, which took 1,000 artisans 5 years to build, became a celebration of that period. It's packed with European relics and works of art from the 16th to the 19th centuries. Most of the original furnishings, including dishes and paintings, are still intact. A free guided tour of the 34 furnished rooms on the first floor takes about 45 minutes. The second floor, which consists mostly of bedrooms, is open to tour on your own. The villa surrounds a central courtyard, and lush formal gardens, accented with statuary, balustrades, and decorative urns, front an enormous swath of Biscayne Bay. ⌚ *2–3 hr. 3251 S. Miami Ave. (just south of Rickenbacker Causeway).* ☎ *305/250-9133. www.vizcayamuseum.com. Admission $15 adults, $10 seniors, $6 children 6–12, free for children 5 & under. Villa daily 9:30am–5pm (ticket booth closes at 4:30pm); gardens daily 9:30am–5:30pm.*

⓭ **Garcia's Seafood Grill and Fish,** on the banks of the Miami River, has a fairly simple yet tasty menu of fresh fish and a great, gritty ambience that takes you away from neon, neo-Miami in favor of the old seafaring days. *398 NW N. River Dr.* ☎ *305/375-0765. $.* ●

2 The Best Special-Interest Tours

Art Deco to MiMo

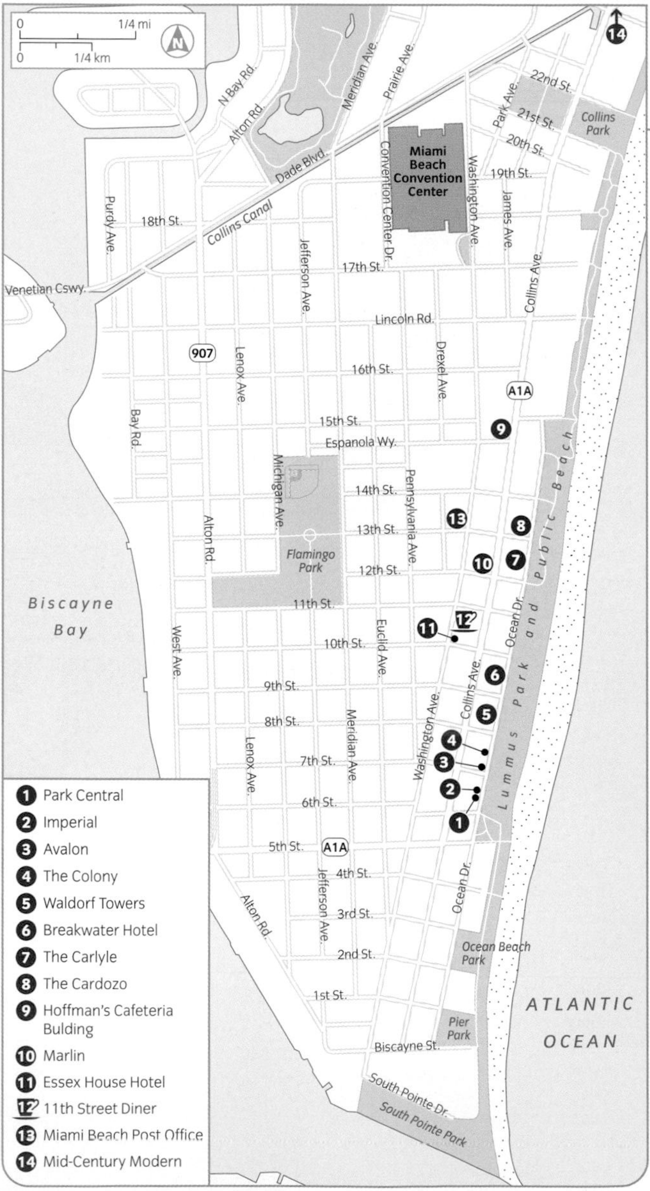
0 1/4 mi
0 1/4 km
N
14
Miami Beach Convention Center
Collins Park
22nd St.
21st St.
20th St.
19th St.
18th St.
17th St.
Lincoln Rd.
16th St.
15th St.
Espanola Wy.
14th St.
13th St.
12th St.
11th St.
10th St.
9th St.
8th St.
7th St.
6th St.
5th St.
4th St.
3rd St.
2nd St.
1st St.
Biscayne St.
South Pointe Dr.
South Pointe Park
N Bay Rd.
Alton Rd.
Meridian Ave.
Prairie Ave.
Park Ave.
Dade Blvd.
Collins Canal
Convention Center Dr.
Washington Ave.
James Ave.
Collins Ave.
Purdy Ave.
Jefferson Ave.
Venetian Cswy.
907
Lenox Ave.
Drexel Ave.
A1A
Bay Rd.
Michigan Ave.
Pennsylvania Ave.
Flamingo Park
Euclid Ave.
West Ave.
Ocean Dr.
Biscayne Bay
Lummus Park and Public Beach
Ocean Beach Park
Pier Park
ATLANTIC OCEAN
1 Park Central
2 Imperial
3 Avalon
4 The Colony
5 Waldorf Towers
6 Breakwater Hotel
7 The Carlyle
8 The Cardozo
9 Hoffman's Cafeteria Bulding
10 Marlin
11 Essex House Hotel
12 11th Street Diner
13 Miami Beach Post Office
14 Mid-Century Modern

Previous page: Galerie Bertin-Toublanc.

Miami Beach has the highest concentration of Art Deco in the world, but there's more to Miami architecture than candy-colored buildings, Philippe Starck–designed boutique hotels, and your grandma's retirement home. Enter MiMo: Mid-Century Modern or, if you ask locals who claim the moment as their own, Miami Modern. **START: Ocean Drive at 6th Street, South Beach.**

❶ **Park Central.** Architect Henry Hohauser created this 1937 masterpiece, featuring bold vertical bands and what's known in Deco-speak as window "eyebrows." *5 min. 630 Ocean Dr.*

❷ **Imperial.** The Park Central's neighbor and fellow Hohauser creation, the Imperial features circles that were inspired by a ship's portholes. *5 min. 650 Ocean Dr.*

❸ **Avalon.** One of the finest examples of what's known as Streamline Moderne, the Avalon features angular edges that exemplify the influence of Cubism. *5 min. 700 Ocean Dr.*

❹ **The Colony.** One of Hohauser's best-known hotels, not to mention the most photographed in town, The Colony features Streamline Moderne racing stripes, porthole windows, and that famous neon sign that kick-started the neon epidemic on Ocean Drive. Be sure to step inside for a glimpse of the hotel's original 1935 green Vitriolite fireplace. *5 min. 736 Ocean Dr.*

❺ **Waldorf Towers.** In addition to those ubiquitous Deco window "eyebrows," the Waldorf features an ornamental lighthouse, earning the building the design label "Nautical Moderne." *5 min. 860 Ocean Dr.*

❻ **Breakwater Hotel.** A classic Streamline Moderne hotel by Anton Skislewicz, the Breakwater features a soaring central tower reminiscent of a ship's funnel, railings emulating those on ship decks, and one of Ocean Drive's original terrazzo floors. *5 min. 940 Ocean Dr.*

❼ **The Carlyle.** The quintessence of Miami Beach Deco, The Carlyle sports three vertical columns, curvaceous corners, and a reputation as the place where Robin Williams unleashed his inner diva as a gay club owner in the 1996 film *The Birdcage.* *5 min. 1250 Ocean Dr.*

❽ **The Cardozo.** Deco preservationist Barbara Capitman's favorite hotel, The Cardozo is currently owned by pop star and Miami resident Gloria Estefan, and screams of Streamline Deco with beautifully rounded corners and a stunning terrazzo floor in the bar area composed of stone chips and mortar. Walk inside the hotel's lobby or

The Colony's 1935 Vitriolite fireplace.

Hoffman's Cafeteria Building now serves up sandwiches and more as Jerry's Famous Deli.

enjoy a drink or snack at the Estefan-owned Asian/Cuban eatery, Oriente. *5 min–1hr. 1300 Ocean Dr.*

9 Hoffman's Cafeteria Building. Competing with the building's central turret are its sweeping "angel wings," designed by Hohauser in 1939. Today, Hoffman's is known as Jerry's Famous Deli, but it's perhaps best known as the long-gone, much-lamented Warsaw, a gay nightclub that saw the likes of Madonna and Calvin Klein in the nascent days of South Beach's early '90s renaissance. *5 min.–1hr. 1450 Collins Ave.*

The Carlyle starred in The Birdcage *alongside Robin Williams.*

10 Marlin. Once one of South Beach's hottest hotels, today the Marlin's claim to fame is its design—a 1939 L. Murray Dixon masterpiece inspired by the colorful sci-fi serials of the era. *5 min. 1200 Collins Ave.*

11 Essex House Hotel. Another Hohauser masterpiece, the Essex features porthole windows and a smokestack-esque neon tower. *5 min. 1001 Washington Ave.*

Ideal for a pick-me-up, the retro-fab **12 ★★★ 11th Street Diner** is a greasy spoon housed in the original 1948 structure, which was uprooted from its Wilkes-Barre, Pennsylvania, foundation and rebuilt in the heart of the Deco district. *1065 Washington Ave. ☎ 305/534-6373. $.*

13 Miami Beach Post Office. Dating back to 1939, the post office earned itself its own designation as a classic example of what's known as Deco Federal. The post office's

Mid-Century Modern

Inspired by Bauhaus and Frank Lloyd Wright, MiMo is the antithesis of Deco in that it's austere and adheres to strict angles. That said, Miami brought out a more flamboyant version with wacky motifs, campy cheese-hole cutouts, and assorted pre-Jetsonian space-age details. Morris Lapidus was the Don Corleone of MiMo, as evidenced in the recently renovated but mostly preserved **Fontainebleau,** 4441 Collins Ave. at 44th Street (☎ 305/538-2000; www.fontainebleau.com). Although the hotel has succumbed to the trappings of 21st century modern, it still retains some of the original Lapidus details, including the bowtie-dotted flooring and famous "stairs to nowhere." Next door is another Lapidus masterpiece, the **Eden Roc,** 4525 Collins Ave. (☎ 305/531-0000; www.boldnewedenroc.com), also renovated but still a sterling example of MiMo's 1950s Rat Pack glam. For a fabulous view of some of Miami's best examples of MiMo, take a **Miami Beach Architecture Cruise,** departing from 65th Street and Indian Creek Drive (☎ 305/865-4147). The 90-minute cruise on a 32-foot (9.6m) catamaran costs $30. Cruises leave at 5:30pm Fridays in the summer and 4pm in the winter.

main feature is its central rotunda and minimalist facade, but for those waiting in line for stamps inside, it's perhaps best known for its stellar starburst ceiling and brass detailing, giving a much more pleasant meaning to the ominous term of "going postal." ⌚ ***5 min. (unless you need stamps, in which case your entire day is shot). 1300 Washington Ave.***

Art Deco Weekend

The Miami Design Preservation League (☎ 305/672-2014; www.mdpl.org) hosts the 33rd annual **Art Deco Weekend** January 15 to 17, 2010. This year's festival celebrates the technology and design of the motorcar, with more than 85 events ranging from films, guided tours, and lectures to live music, dance, and theater performances, classic automobiles, and a parade. Ocean Drive, between 5th and 15th streets.

The central rotunda at the Miami Beach Post Office.

Little Havana

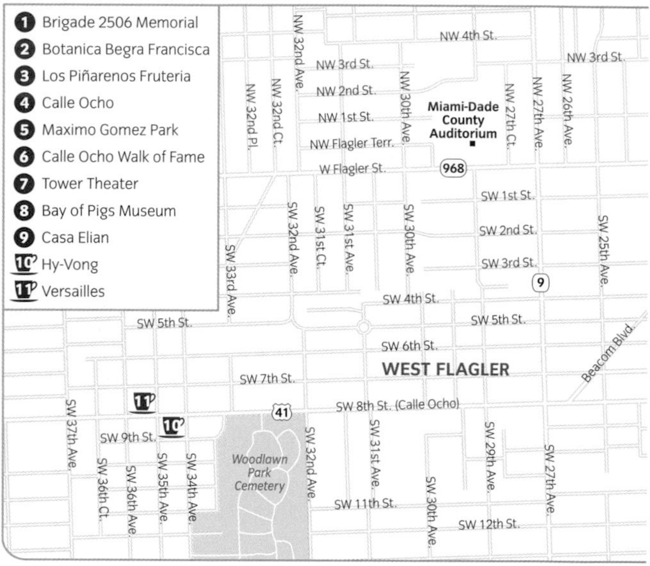

The hub of Miami's Cuban community, Little Havana and its main thoroughfare, SW 8th Street, or Calle Ocho, is a cultural explosion of pre- and (in the hopes of many) post-Castro Cuba. A mix of old-school and new-school Cuban culture thrives here, from cigar stores with rollers dating back to Havana's halcyon days to music stores, restaurants, and shops helmed by a younger generation of neo-Cuban Americans. **START: Memorial Boulevard at SW 13th Avenue.**

1 ★ Brigade 2506 Memorial. Located at the entrance of Memorial Boulevard is this eternal flame burning in memory of those killed in the Bay of Pigs invasion. Also check out the bronze map of Cuba and statue of the Virgin Mary, which is revered by many in the largely Catholic Cuban-American community. ◷ *20 min. Memorial Blvd. at SW 13th Ave.*

2 Botanica Begra Francisca. Don't freak out if you happen to notice chicken bones left under a large tree right in the center of the boulevard. It's just a sacred offering by practitioners of Santeria, a religion that originated in the Caribbean and is based on the Yoruba culture of West Africa. This store, or *botanica,* caters to its followers and sells oils and candles and offers spiritualist readings by local practitioners. ◷ *20 min. 1323 SW 8th St. at SW 13th Ave.* ☎ *305/860-9328.*

3 Los Piñarenos Fruteria. While you'll have a full-fledged Cuban meal later in Versailles, you'll need something to hold you over until then. Try a fresh-squeezed *guarapo* (sugar cane) juice at this venerable fruit and vegetable stand

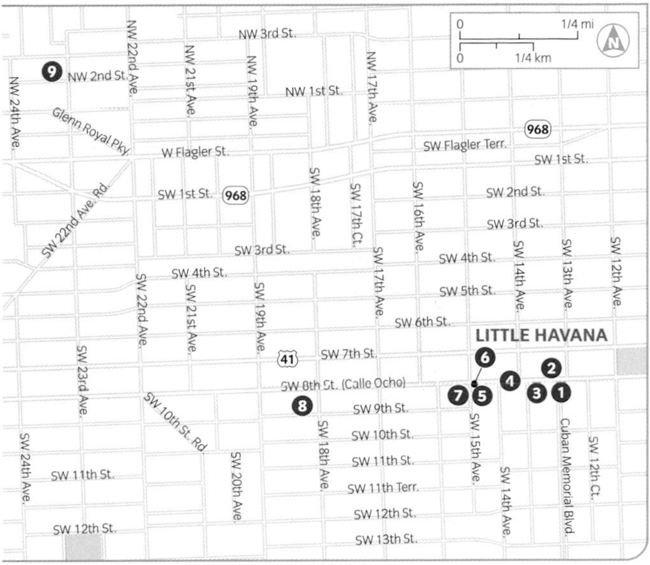

serving all sorts of Cuban treats, juices, and local color. 🕘 *20 min. 1334 SW 8th St.* ☎ *305/285-1135.*

❹ ★★★ **Calle Ocho.** Everything from cigars to *guyaberas* (men's shirts popular in Latin America) can be found in the shops on Calle Ocho. Those who are really stoked on stogies will like the show at **El Credito Cigars** (1100 SW 8th St.; ☎ 305/856-4162), where veteran rollers knock out torpedoes and other varieties. For more pre-Castro retro Cuba, browse around **Little Havana To Go,** 1442 SW 8th St. (☎ 305/857-9720), where you can

Recharge with fresh fruit juices at Los Piñarenos Fruteria.

Calle Ocho brings Cuba to Miami. Don't miss a cup of fresh Cuban coffee.

flip through (and purchase) a Havana phonebook from 1958 or Fidel Castro playing cards complete with an X through his face.

5 ★★ Maximo Gomez Park. This landmark Little Havana park is command central for Cuban retirees who sit here all day playing dominoes, hence its popular name "Domino Park," and drinking coffee. They're sometimes tough about letting in anyone under the age of 55, but if you're lucky, you might be invited to get a closer look. 🕘 *10 min. 801 SW 15th Ave. at the corner of SW 14th Ave.* ☎ *305/285-1684.*

Cuban stars are honored on Calle Ocho's Walk of Fame.

6 ★ Calle Ocho Walk of Fame. Just like in Hollywood, only the stars here are for legendary Cuban celebrities including Celia Cruz, the first to receive a star on the Walk of Fame back in 1987. 🕘 *5 min. SW 8th St.*

7 ★★ Tower Theater. The only movie theater in Miami showing English-language flicks with Spanish subtitles back in the day, the Tower Theater today is a cultural institution showcasing a plethora of Spanish-language films (no English subtitles), concerts, and performances. 🕘 *5 min. 1508 SW 8th St. at SW 15th Ave.* ☎ *305/649-2960.*

8 ★★★ Bay of Pigs Museum. A small but impressive collection dedicated to the 1961 invasion, this museum includes some interesting memorabilia commemorating the event, including a flag held up by President John F. Kennedy during a speech at the now demolished Orange Bowl in 1962. *30 min. 1821 SW 9th St. at SW 18th Ave.* ☎ *305/649-4719. Free admission. Mon–Sat 9am–4pm.*

9 Casa Elian. This house hosted then 6-year-old Elian Gonzalez (and the media frenzy that followed him) and his Miami family after he was rescued from a raft at sea in November 1999. He was eventually removed by the feds and returned to his father back in Cuba, but the house has become a shrine and a monument to the plight of the Cuban exile movement. Exhibits include Elian's toys, letters, and photos. *10 min. 2319 NW 2nd St. at SW 23rd Ave. No phone. Free admission. Sun 10am–6pm.*

Bay of Pigs Museum's collection commemorates the 1961 invasion.

10 ★ **Hy Vong,** arguably Miami's best Vietnamese restaurant, is an unlikely landmark in Little Havana. But if you're craving expertly prepared *bánh bao*, get in line, as the place has only 35 seats, and they're always full. *3458 SW 8th St. at SW 34th Ave.* ☎ *305/446-3674.* On the opposite corner is 11 ★ **Versailles,** command central for Miami's most vocal and political Cubans serving an unabridged selection of Cuban cuisine, not to mention some seriously powerful Cuban coffee. Much like its Parisian namesake, this is a local landmark. *3555 SW 8th St.* ☎ *305/444-0240. $.*

Old-timers spend the day playing dominoes and chess at Maximo Gomez Park.

Miami with Kids

1. Coral Castle
2. Miami Metrozoo
3. Monkey Jungle
4. Matheson Hammock Park Beach
5. Red Fish Grill
6. Jungle Island
7. Miami Children's Museum
8. Big Pink
9. Miami Duck Tours

Although it's not Disney World, Miami is a veritable playground, with a slew of child (and child at heart) -friendly attractions (some wackier than others), parks, museums, and even a few beaches where you won't have to cover the little ones' eyes. **START: Coral Castle.**

1 ★ **Coral Castle.** There's plenty of competition, but Coral Castle is probably the strangest attraction in Florida. In 1923, the story goes, a 26-year-old crazed Latvian, suffering from the unrequited love of a 16-year-old who left him at the altar, immigrated to South Miami and spent the next 25 years of his life carving huge boulders into a prehistoric-looking roofless "castle." Rocker Billy Idol's "Sweet 16" was said to be inspired by the castle. An interesting 25-minute audio tour guides you through the spot, now on the National Register of Historic Places. *1–2 hrs. 28655 S. Dixie Hwy. ☎ 305/248-6345. www.coralcastle.com. Admission $9.75 adults, $6.50 seniors, $5 children 7–12. Group rates available. Daily 7am–8pm. Take 836 West (Dolphin Expwy.) toward Miami International Airport. Merge onto 826 South (Palmetto Expwy.) and take it to the Florida Tpk. toward Homestead. Take the 288th St. exit (#5) and then take a right on South Dixie Hwy., a left on SW 157th Ave., and then a sharp left back onto South Dixie Hwy. Coral Castle is on the left side of the street.*

2 ★★★ **Miami Metrozoo.** This 290-acre (116-hectare) complex is quite a distance from Miami proper and the beaches—about 45 minutes—but worth the trip. Isolated and never really crowded, it's also completely cageless—animals are kept at bay by cleverly designed moats. This is a fantastic spot to take younger kids; there are wonderful play areas and safari cycles for rent, and the zoo offers several daily programs designed to educate and entertain. Mufasa and Simba (of Disney fame) were modeled on a couple of Metrozoo's lions. The air-conditioned monorail and tram tours offer visitors an overview of the park. Opened in December 2008, Amazon & Beyond features jaguars, anacondas, giant river otters (one of its keystone species), harpy eagles, a stingray touch tank,

Coral Castle's hulking boulders took one man 25 years to carve.

and two interactive water features, The Flooded Forest, with a display of a forest before and during flood times, and Cloud Forest, which houses reptiles. Private tours and overnights are also available. Keep in mind that the distance between animal habitats can be great, and it can be miserably hot during summer months. *1–4 hrs. 12400 SW 152nd St. 305/251-0400. www.miamimetrozoo.com. Admission $16 adults, $12 children 3–12, plus tax. Daily 9:30am–5:30pm (ticket booth closes at 4pm). Free parking. From U.S. 1 south, turn right on SW 152nd St. and follow signs about 3 miles (4.8m) to the entrance. From FL Tpk. S., take Exit 16 west to the entrance.*

3 ★ Monkey Jungle. Unless you're a lover of primates, it will be hard to look past the fact that this place smells bad, the monkeys are either sleeping or in heat, and it's really far from the city, even farther than the zoo. If you are a fan, though, you'll see rare Brazilian golden lion tamarins and Asian macaques. There are no cages, but screened-in trails wind through acres of "jungle." An interesting archaeological exhibition excavated from a sinkhole displays 10,000-year-old artifacts, including human teeth and animal bones. At the Wild Monkey Swimming Pool, you can watch monkeys diving for food. *2 hrs. 14805 SW 216th St. 305/235-1611. www.monkeyjungle.com. Admission $26 adults, $24 seniors & active-duty military, $20 children 4–12. Daily 9:30am–5pm (tickets sold until 4pm). Take U.S. 1 south to SW 216th St., or from Florida Tpk., take Exit 11 and follow the signs.*

4 ★★★ Matheson Hammock Park Beach. Because of its man-made lagoon, which is fed naturally by the tidal movement of the adjacent Biscayne Bay, the waters of **Matheson Hammock Park Beach** are extremely calm, not to mention safe and secluded enough for families to keep an eye on the kids. Clean bathrooms are a plus. *1–4 hrs. 9610 Old Cutler Rd. 305/665-5475.*

Housed in a coral-rock building in the midst of Matheson Hammock Park is **5 ★ Red Fish Grill,** a seafood spot with views that are better than the food. If you didn't pack a picnic, this is the place to recharge after or during a day at the beach. *9610 Old Cutler Rd. 305/668-8788.*

6 ★★★ Jungle Island. Not exactly an island and not quite a

Feeding giraffes at the Miami Metrozoo.

jungle, this is an excellent diversion for the kids and for animal lovers. While the island doubles as a protected bird sanctuary, the very pricey 19-acre (7.6-hectare) park features an Everglades exhibit, a petting zoo, and several theaters, jungle trails, and aviaries; hundreds of parrots, macaws, peacocks, cockatoos, and flamingos can be seen flying around. Be sure to check out the Crocosaurus, a 20-foot-long (3m) saltwater crocodile that hangs out in the park's Serpentarium. Highlights include the Ichimura Miami Japan Garden; shows such as Tale of the Tiger and Gator X-treme; the only African penguins in South Florida; a Liger (part lion, part tiger); and a rare albino alligator. *3 hrs. 1111 Parrot Jungle Trail, Watson Island (on the north side of MacArthur Causeway/ I-395). ☎ 305/372-3822. www.parrotjungle.com. Admission $30 adults, $28 seniors & military, $24 children 3–10. Parking $7 per vehicle. Daily 10am–6pm. From I-95, take I-395 E. (MacArthur Causeway); make a right on Parrot Jungle Trail, which is the first exit after the bridge. Follow the road around and under the causeway to the parking garage on the left side.*

7 ★★★ Miami Children's Museum. This modern, albeit odd-looking, 56,500-square-foot (5,249 sq. m) facility includes 14 galleries, classrooms, a parent/teacher resource center, a gift shop, a 200-seat auditorium, a Subway restaurant, and an outdoor interactive play area. The museum offers hundreds of bilingual, interactive exhibits as well as programs, classes, and learning materials related to arts, culture, community, and communication. Check out the mini versions of Bank of America and Publix Supermarket; re-creations of the NBC 6 television studio and a Carnival cruise ship; and a gallery of teddy bears from around the world. The coolest attraction is the World Music Studio, in which aspiring rock stars can lay down a few tracks and play instruments. *2 hrs. 980 MacArthur Causeway, across from Jungle Island. ☎ 305/ 373-5437. www.miamichildrensmuseum.org. Admission $12 adults & children over 12 months. Daily 10am–6pm.*

Jungle Island houses the only African penguins in South Florida.

Over the bridge on South Beach, **8 Big Pink** is the panacea for a picky child, featuring a huge menu of kids' favorites including mac and cheese and chicken fingers. For big kids, the restaurant has a grownup version of a Hungry Man dinner, complete with compartments and dessert. *157 Collins Ave. ☎ 305/ 532-4700. $.*

9 ★★★ Miami Duck Tours. This is the "quackiest" way to visit Miami and the beaches. The Watson Willy is the first of several Miami Duck Tours' "vesicles," a hybrid that's part vessel, part vehicle and looks like a duck. Tours leave from Watson Island behind Jungle Island, traveling through downtown Miami and South Beach, through Biscayne Bay and past all the swanky houses. *90 min. 1665 Washington Ave. ☎ 877/ DUCK-TIX. www.ducktoursmiami.com. Tickets $32 adults, $26 seniors & military, $18 children 12 & under.*

Miami's Art & Design Districts

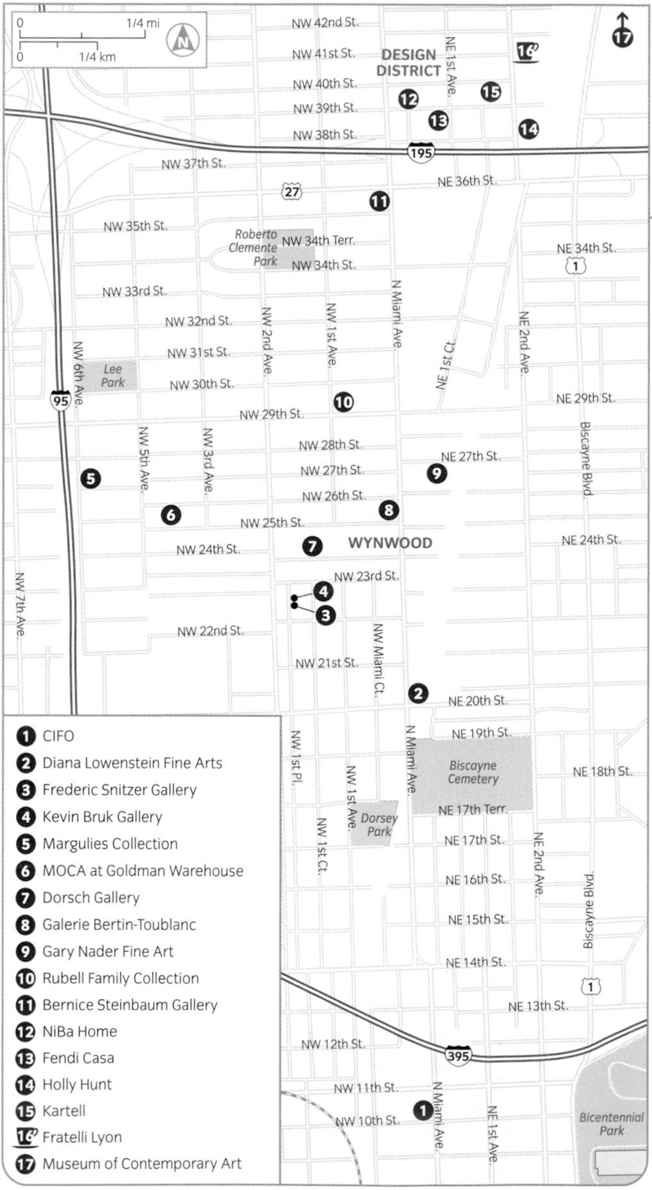

The Design District is, as locals say, the new South Beach. The district, formerly one of ill-repute, is a hotbed for furniture-import companies, interior designers, architects, and artists, and is loosely defined as the area bounded by NE 2nd Avenue, NE 5th Avenue East and West, and NW 36th Street to the south. Just south of the Design District is yet another burgeoning arts district, a sketchy strip of Miami bounded by NE 2nd Avenue to the east and NE 36th Street to the north, known as Wynwood. Explore at your own risk, preferably during the day. **START: CIFO.**

1 ★★★ CIFO. An outstanding nonprofit gallery established by Ella Fontanals Cisneros and her family to foster cultural exchange among the visual arts, CIFO is dedicated to the support of emerging and mid-career contemporary multidisciplinary artists from Latin America. *30 min. 1018 N. Miami Ave. at NW 10th St. ☎ 305/455-3380. www.cifo.org. Thurs–Sun 10am–4pm during exhibitions or by appointment.*

2 ★★★ Diana Lowenstein Fine Arts. One of Miami's preeminent modern art collectors, Lowenstein's gallery in the burgeoning Wynwood area of downtown Miami is a hot spot for serious collectors and admirers. *30 min. 2043 N. Miami Ave. at NE 20th St. ☎ 305/576-1084. www.dlfinearts.com. Tues–Sat 10:30am–6pm.*

Serious art collectors should check out Diana Lowenstein Fine Arts.

Frederic Snitzer Gallery features works by local and Cuban artists.

3 ★★ Frederic Snitzer Gallery. The catalyst to the explosion of the Wynwood arts scene, this warehouse pays homage to works by local stars and New World School of the Arts grads, as well as artists from Cuba's legendary '80s Generation. *15 min. 2247 NW 1st Place at N. Miami Ave. ☎ 305-448-8976. www.snitzer.com. Tues–Sat 11am–5pm.*

4 ★ Kevin Bruk Gallery. Up-and-coming sculptors, photographers, and painters from around the world aspire to be featured in this excellent gallery of international art. *15 min. 2249 NW 1st Place at N. Miami Ave. ☎ 305/576-2000. www.kevinbrukgallery.com. Tues–Fri 10am–6pm; Sat noon–5pm.*

Margulies Collection is said to be the best in the city.

5 ★★★ Margulies Collection. This massive, 45,000-square-foot (4,181 sq. m) Wynwood warehouse is the city's crown jewel, showcasing contemporary and vintage photography, video, sculpture, and installations in various genres including pop art, minimalism, and expressionism. *15 min–1 hr. 591 NW 27th St at 6th Ave. ☎ 305/576-1051. www.marguliesswarehouse.com. Wed–Sat 11am–4pm.*

6 ★★★ MOCA at Goldman Warehouse. An annex of the Museum of Contemporary Art featuring funky pieces from the museum's permanent collection and from up-and-comers. *15 min. 404 NW 26th St. at 5th Ave. ☎ 305/893-6211. www.mocanomi.org. Wed–Sat noon–5pm; second Sat of every month 7–10pm.*

7 ★ Dorsch Gallery. An expansive gallery known for hosting some fabulous parties for the who's-who in the art world and some seriously funky exhibitions. *15 min. 151 NW 24th St. at N. Miami Ave. ☎ 305/576-1278. www.dorschgallery.com. Thurs–Sat 1–5pm or by appointment.*

8 ★ Galerie Bertin-Toublanc. This Parisian import has a soothing Zen garden and exhibition spaces featuring worldwide edginess in the form of India's Baba Anand and France's Philippe Chevalier. *15 min. 2534 N. Miami Ave. at 25th St. ☎ 305/573-3554. www.galeriebertin.fr. Tues–Sat 10am–6pm; second Sat of every month 11am–6pm.*

9 Gary Nader Fine Art. If you're into Latin American art by the likes of Botero, Matta, and Lam, this is the place for you. In addition, there are monthly exhibits of emerging artists. *15 min. 62 NE 27th St. at N. Miami Ave. ☎ 305/576-0256. www.garynader.com. Mon–Sat 10am–6pm.*

10 ★★★ Rubell Family Collection. This impressive collection, owned by the Miami hotelier family the Rubells, is housed in a two-story,

Rubell Family Collection's hulking space allows for large, and plentiful, showcases.

40,000-square-foot (3,716 sq. m), former Drug Enforcement Agency warehouse in a sketchy area north of downtown Miami. The building looks like a fortress, which is fitting: Inside is a priceless collection of more than 1,000 works of contemporary art by the likes of Keith Haring, Damien Hirst, Julian Schnabel, Jean-Michel Basquiat, Paul McCarthy, Charles Ray, and Cindy Sherman. *30 min. 95 NW 29th St. at NW 1st Ave. 305/573-6090. www.rubellfamilycollection.com. Wed–Sun 10am–6pm; second Sat of every month 10am–10pm.*

⓫ ★★ **Bernice Steinbaum Gallery.** Check out the modern multimedia exhibits here by contemporary artists including Hung Liu, Glexis Novoa, and Maria Gonzalez. *15 min. 3550 N. Miami Ave. 305/573-2700. www.bernicesteinbaumgallery.com. Open Mon–Sat 10am–6pm.*

⓬ ★★ **NiBa Home.** Fabulous home accessories including glass, furniture, lighting, and pretty much anything else you'd expect to see in a photo shoot in a trendy decor magazine. *15 min. 39 NE 39th St. at N Miami Ave. 305/573-1939.*

Colorful accessories can be found at NiBa Home.

Fendi Casa carries the designer's fashionable home accessories.

www.nibahome.com. Mon–Fri 9am 6pm; Sat 11am–5pm.

⓭ ★ **Fendi Casa.** The posh purse purveyor delves into furniture at this swanky showroom featuring butter leather couches, sofas, and coffee tables at designer prices. *15 min. 90 NE 39th St. at NE 2nd Ave. 305/438-1660. www.fendicasa.com. Mon–Fri 9am–5pm; Sat noon–4pm.*

⓮ ★★★ **Holly Hunt.** One of the most stylish furniture showrooms in the entire country, Holly Hunt's Design District outpost is a must-see if not for the furniture, textiles, and lighting, then for the space itself. *15 min. 3833 NE 2nd Ave. 305/571-2012. www.hollyhunt.com. Mon–Sat 10am–6pm.*

⓯ ★ **Kartell.** Who knew plastic could be so pricey? Kartell showcases furniture from sleek to kitsch—all in plastic. The merchandise may be uncomfortable and pricey, but it sure looks good. *15 min. 170 NE 40th St. 305/573-4010. www.kartell.com. Mon–Fri 10am–6pm; Sat 11am–5pm.*

Bernice Steinbaum Gallery champions modern multimedia artists.

Stop for a late lunch or early dinner at 16 ★★★ **Fratelli Lyon,** a stylish Italian trattoria cum furniture store where, for $24, you'll feast on an appetizer, entree, dessert, and house wine. *4141 NE 2nd Ave. ☎ 305/572-2901. $–$$$.*

Holly Hunt's space is just as beautiful as the pieces it houses.

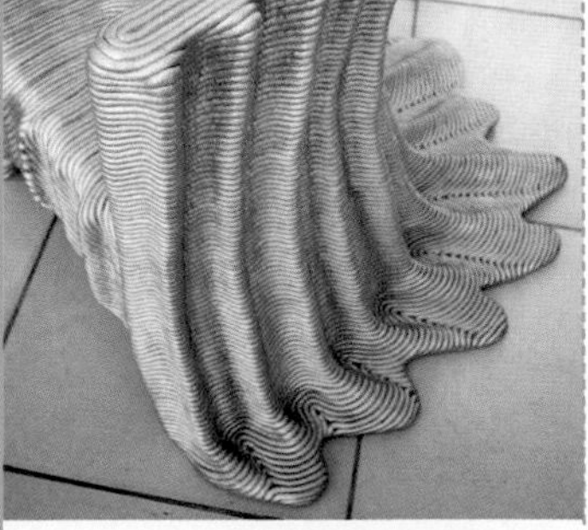

17 Museum of Contemporary Art (MOCA). Here you'll see an impressive collection of internationally acclaimed art with a local flavor. The museum is also known for discovering and highlighting new artists. A high-tech screening facility allows for film presentations. You can see works by Roy Lichtenstein, Larry Rivers, and Claes Oldenburg; plus, there are special exhibitions by such artists as Sigmar Polke, John Baldessari, and Goya. Guided tours are offered in English, Spanish, French, Creole, Portuguese, German, and Italian. *770 NE 125th St. ☎ 305/893-6211. www.mocanomi.org. Admission $5 adults, $3 seniors & students with ID, free for children 12 & under. Tues by donation. Tues–Sat 11am–5pm; Sun noon–5pm.* ●

3 The Best **Shopping**

Shopping Best Bets

Best Place for **Cigars**
★★★ El Credito Cigars, *1100 SW 8th St. (p 49)*

Best for **Miami Beach Meets Ibiza-chic**
★★ Base, *939 Lincoln Rd. (p 50)*

Best for **Label Whores**
★★ The Webster, *1220 Collins Ave. (p 51)*

Best **Home Furnishings**
★★★ NiBa, *39 NE 39th St. (p 52)*

Best **Furniture Showroom**
★★★ Holly Hunt, *3833 NE 2nd Ave. (p 51)*

Biggest **Jewelry Bargains**
★★★ The Seybold Building, *36 NE 1st St. (p 52)*

Best **Latin Record Store**
★★★ Casino Records, *2990 SW 8th St. (p 54)*

Best **Art Gallery on Someone Else's Budget**
★★★ Kevin Bruk Gallery, *2249 NW 1st Place (p 48)*

Best **Vintage Store**
C. Madeleine's, *13702 Biscayne Blvd. (p 50)*

Best **Kids' Store**
★★ Genius Jones, *49 NE 39th St. (p 49)*

Best **Shoe Store**
Morgan Miller, *In the Aventura Mall, 19575 Biscayne Blvd. (p 54)*

Best Place for **Unisex Urban Chic**
Y-3, *150 NE 40th St. (p 51)*

Best **Trendy Baubles**
Turchin Jewelry, *130 NE 40th St. (p 52)*

Best **Indie Music Store**
★★ Sweat Records, *5505 NE 2nd Ave. (p 54)*

Best **Museum Shop**
★★ Wolfsonian-FIU, *1001 Washington Ave. (p 52)*

Best **Mall**
★★★ Aventura Mall, *19575 Biscayne Blvd. (p 53)*

Best **High-End Mall**
★★★ Bal Harbour Shops, *9700 Collins Ave. (p 53)*

Best **Gourmet Food Store**
★★★ Marky's, *687 NE 79th St. (p 51)*

Best **Latin Gourmet Market**
★★★ La Estancia Argentina, *17870 Biscayne Blvd. (p 51)*

Previous page: Japanese designer Yohji Yamamoto's funky urban designs are at Y-3. This page: Crabtree & Evelyn at Aventura Mall.

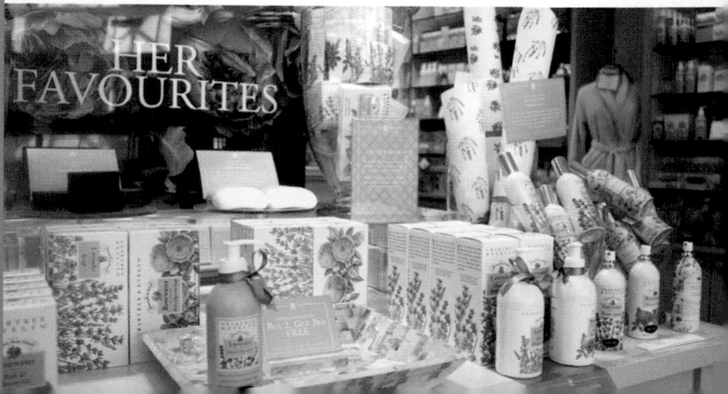

South Beach Shopping

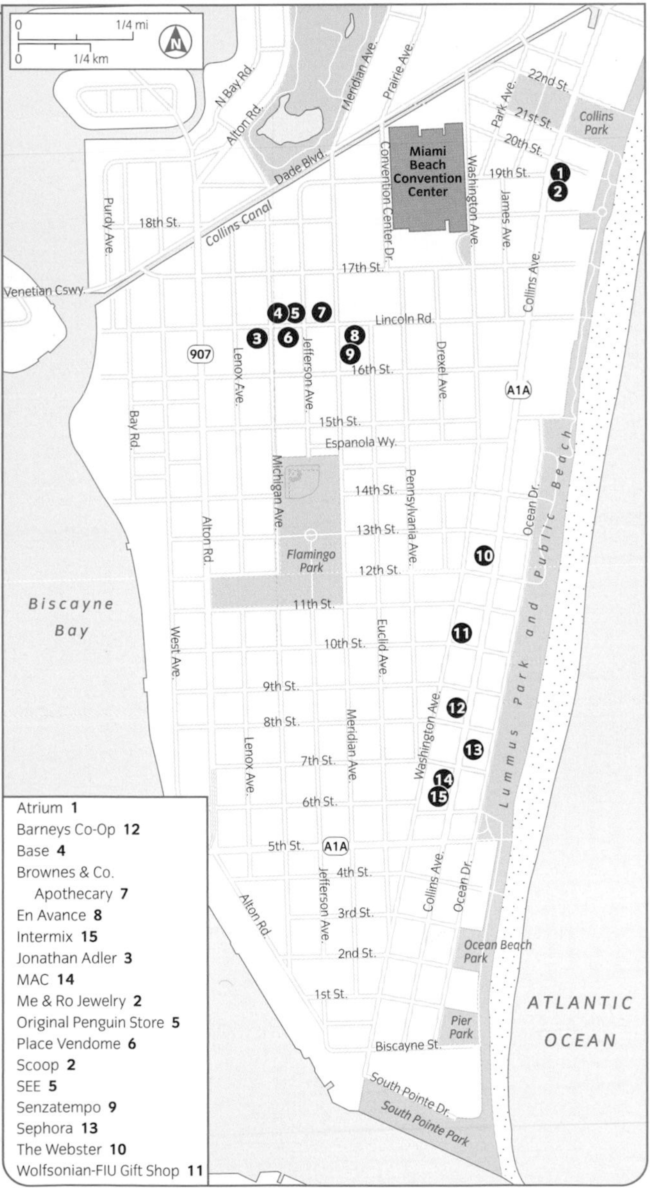

Atrium **1**
Barneys Co-Op **12**
Base **4**
Brownes & Co. Apothecary **7**
En Avance **8**
Intermix **15**
Jonathan Adler **3**
MAC **14**
Me & Ro Jewelry **2**
Original Penguin Store **5**
Place Vendome **6**
Scoop **2**
SEE **5**
Senzatempo **9**
Sephora **13**
The Webster **10**
Wolfsonian-FIU Gift Shop **11**

Miami Shopping

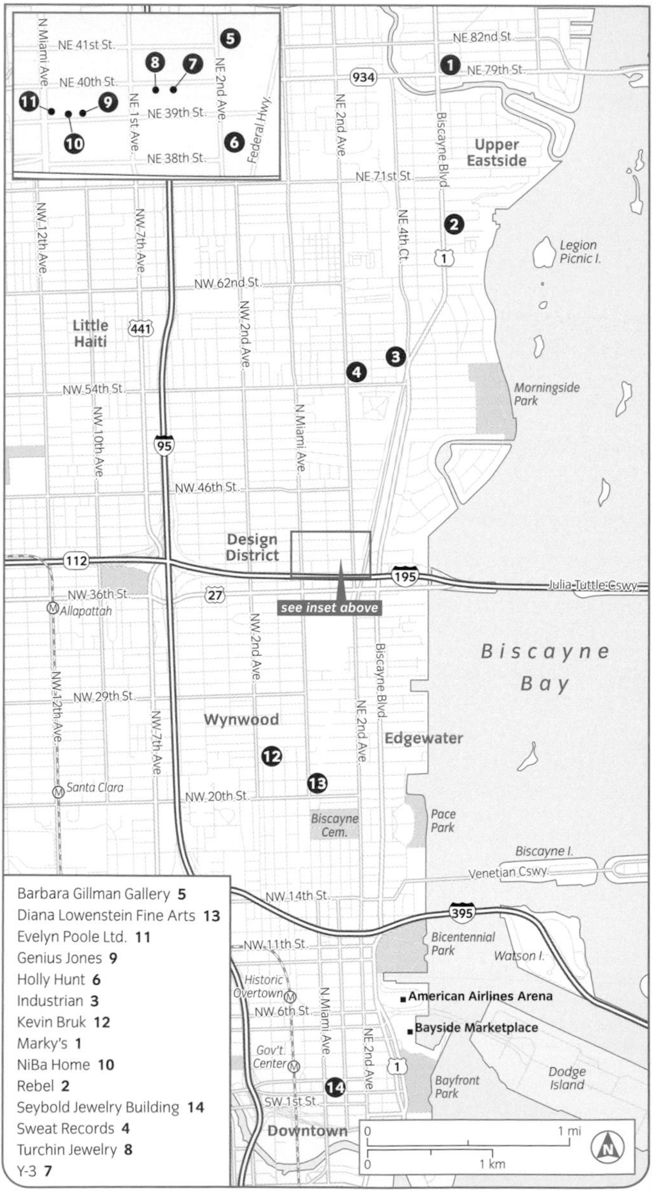

Barbara Gillman Gallery **5**
Diana Lowenstein Fine Arts **13**
Evelyn Poole Ltd. **11**
Genius Jones **9**
Holly Hunt **6**
Industrian **3**
Kevin Bruk **12**
Marky's **1**
NiBa Home **10**
Rebel **2**
Seybold Jewelry Building **14**
Sweat Records **4**
Turchin Jewelry **8**
Y-3 **7**

Miami Metro Shopping

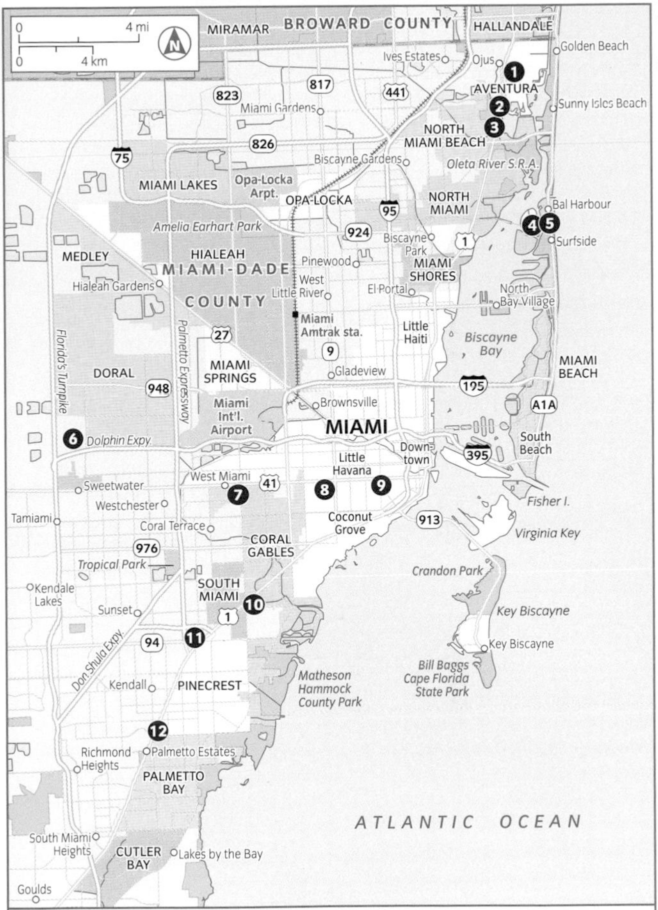

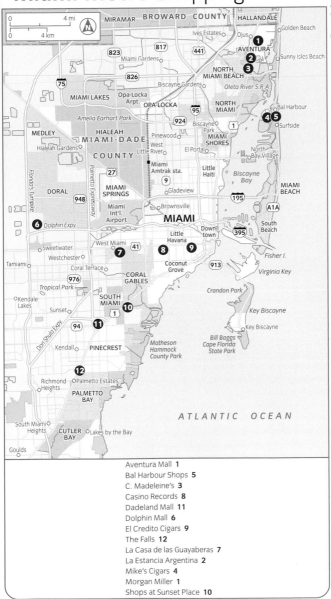

- Aventura Mall **1**
- Bal Harbour Shops **5**
- C. Madeleine's **3**
- Casino Records **8**
- Dadeland Mall **11**
- Dolphin Mall **6**
- El Credito Cigars **9**
- The Falls **12**
- La Casa de las Guayaberas **7**
- La Estancia Argentina **2**
- Mike's Cigars **4**
- Morgan Miller **1**
- Shops at Sunset Place **10**

Miami Shopping A to Z

Antiques

Evelyn Poole Ltd. DESIGN DISTRICT The Poole houses the finest assortment of European 17th-, 18th-, and 19th-century decorative furniture and accessories in 5,000 square feet (465 sq. m) of space. *3925 N. Miami Ave. ☎ 305/573-7463. www.evelynpooleltd.com. AE, MC, V. Map p 46.*

Industrian BISCAYNE CORRIDOR Here, a retro-fabulous Charles Eames chair can sit harmoniously alongside an ultra-modern, 21st-century Jetsonian piece of furniture. *5580 NE 4th Court. ☎ 305/754-6070. www.industrian.us.com. AE, MC, V. Map p 46.*

Senzatempo LINCOLN ROAD If the names Charles Eames, George Nelson, or Gio Ponti mean anything to you, then you'll want to stop here. There's retro, Euro-fabulous designer furniture and decorative arts from 1930 to 1960, as well as collectible watches, timepieces, and clocks. *1655 Meridian Ave. ☎ 305/534-5588. www.senzatempo.com. AE, MC, V. Map p 45.*

Art

Barbara Gillman Gallery DESIGN DISTRICT This gallery's ongoing exhibit of jazz photographer Herman Leonard's fantastic black-and-white photographs of legends such as Billie Holiday and Frank Sinatra has been so popular it hasn't changed in years. The gallery also displays works by artists such as Andres Serrano, Andy Warhol, and James Rosenquist, as well as new local talent. *4141 NE 2nd Ave. ☎ 305/573-1920. www.barbaragillmangallery.com. AE, MC,V. Map p 46.*

Diana Lowenstein Fine Arts WYNWOOD One of Miami's preeminent modern art collectors, Lowenstein's gallery is a hot spot for serious collectors and admirers. *2043 N. Miami Ave. ☎ 305/576-1804. www.dlfinearts.com. AE, MC, V. Map p 46.*

★★★ **Kevin Bruk** WYNWOOD Some of the edgiest works from artists from around the world are at this hip gallery, including Jesse Bransford, Alyson Shotz, and Su-En Wong. *2249 NW 1st Place. ☎ 305/576-2000. www.kevinbrukgallery.com. AE, MC, V. Map p 46.*

Find handmade soaps and more at Browne's and Co. Apothecary.

Parents can spend a pretty penny for tykes at Genius Jones.

Beauty Products & Cosmetics

★★★ **Brownes & Co. Apothecary** LINCOLN ROAD Designed to look like an old-fashioned apothecary, this recently expanded beauty emporium combines the best selection of makeup and hair products—MAC, Shu Uemura, Kiehl's, Stila, Molton Brown, Francois Nars, Dr. Hauschka—with lots of delicious-smelling bath and body stuff, plus a full-service beauty salon. Browse on your own, or ask the expert staff for help. Upstairs is Browne's Beauty Lounge and the store's renowned salon, Some Like It Hot. *841 Lincoln Rd. ☎ 305/532-8703. www.brownesbeauty.com. AE, MC, V. Map p 45.*

MAC COLLINS AVENUE Play with the bright colors of this innovative brand of makeup, or if you're lucky, get a free makeover. *650 Collins Ave. ☎ 305/604-9040. www.maccosmetics.com. AE, MC, V. Map p 45.*

Sephora COLLINS AVENUE Sephora offers a dizzying array of cosmetics, perfumes, and styling products. Unlike Brownes & Co., however, personal service and attentiveness is at a minimum. Because there are so many products, shopping here can be a harrowing experience. *721 Collins Ave. ☎ 305/532-0904. www.sephora.com. AE, DISC, MC, V. Map p 45.*

Children

★★ **Genius Jones** DESIGN DISTRICT In addition to the requisite, adorable, and pricey kids' threads, Genius Jones has high-end kids' furniture by the likes of Agatha Ruiz de la Prada, David Netto, and other brands that will set you back some serious bucks. *49 NE 39th St. ☎ 305/571-2000. www.geniusjones.com. AE, DC, DISC, MC, V. Map p 46.*

Cigars

★★★ **El Credito Cigars** LITTLE HAVANA This tiny storefront shop employs about 45 veteran Cuban rollers who sit all day rolling the very popular torpedoes and other critically

See expert rollers at El Credito Cigars.

Celebs go to C. Madeleine's for their vintage fix.

acclaimed blends. They're usually back-ordered, but it's worth stopping in: They will sell you a box and show you around. ***1100 SW 8th St.*** ☎ ***305/856-4162. AE, DC, MC, V. Map p 47.***

Mike's Cigars BAY HARBOR ISLANDS One of the oldest and best smoke shops in town. Since 1950, Mike's has been selling the best from Honduras, the Dominican Republic, and Jamaica, as well as the very hot local brand, La Gloria Cubana. Many say it has the best prices, too. Mike's has the biggest selection of cigars in town, and the employees speak English. ***1030 Kane Concourse.*** ☎ ***305/866-2277. www.mikescigars.com. AE, DC, MC, V. Map p 47.***

Fashion

Atrium COLLINS AVENUE Young Hollywood always makes Atrium a stop on their South Beach shopping list. With designer brands at designer prices, don't be surprised if you see that $200 white t-shirt featured in *Us Weekly*. ***1925 Collins Ave.*** ☎ ***305/695-0757. www.atriumnyc.com. AE, MC, V. Map p 45.***

Barneys Co-Op COLLINS AVENUE Finally, an outpost of posh Barneys New York opens on South Beach, only this time, it's more "affordable." ***832 Collins Ave.*** ☎ ***305/421-2010. www.barneys.com. AE, MC, V. Map p 45.***

★★ **Base** LINCOLN ROAD A hipster hangout featuring Ibiza–meets London's Ministry of Sound–meets Miami clothing that's fashionable and, of course, pricey. Base, which bills itself as a "lifestyle" store, is also known for its funky CD collection (all for sale of course), coffee-table books, and nice-smelling candles. ***939 Lincoln Rd.*** ☎ ***305/531-4982. www.baseworld.com. AE, MC, V. Map p 45.***

C. Madeleine's NORTH MIAMI This is the best vintage store in town with brands such as Gucci, Chanel, and Balenciaga. Celebrities such as Jessica Simpson and Lenny Kravitz call this fashion emporium home. ***13702 Biscayne Blvd.*** ☎ ***305/945-0010. www.cmadeleines.com. AE, MC, V. Map p 47.***

En Avance LINCOLN ROAD If you couldn't get into SET or Mokai last night, consider plunking down some major pocket change for the *au courant* labels that En Avance is known for. One outfit bought here, and the doormen have no ground to stand on when it comes to high-fashion dress codes. ***734 Lincoln Rd.*** ☎ ***305/534-0337. AE, MC, V. Map p 45.***

Intermix COLLINS AVENUE Pretty young things can get all dolled up thanks to Intermix's fun assortment of hip women's fashions. ***634 Collins Ave.*** ☎ ***305/531-5950. AE, DC, MC, V. Map p 45.***

La Casa de las Guayaberas LITTLE HAVANA Miami's premier purveyor of the traditional yet retro-hip Cuban shirt known as the *guayabera*—a loose-fitting, pleated, button-down shirt—was founded by

Ramon Puig, who emigrated to Miami more than 40 years ago. He still uses the same scissors he did back then, only now he's joined by a team of seamstresses who hand-sew 20 shirts a day in all colors and styles. Prices range from $15 to $375. *5840 SW 8th St. ☎ 305/266-9683. AE, MC, V. Map p 47.*

Original Penguin Store LINCOLN ROAD This hip, retro men's line features sweaters, polo shirts, and t-shirts sporting the trademark penguin logo. *925 Lincoln Rd. ☎ 305/673-0722. AE, MC, V. Map p 45.*

Place Vendome LINCOLN ROAD Cheap clubwear perfect for those messy nights out. *934 Lincoln Rd. ☎ 305/673-4005. AE, MC, V. Map p 45.*

Rebel BISCAYNE CORRIDOR Fashionable and funky clothing for mom and daughter is what you'll find in this boutique, which carries labels not found anywhere else. Super-friendly help is a bonus. *6669 Biscayne Blvd. ☎ 305/758-2639. AE, MC, V. Map p 46.*

Scoop COLLINS AVENUE This is the Shore Club hotel's boutique and is the shop of choice for celebs such as Cameron Diaz looking for the latest from Diane Von Furstenberg, Helmut Lang, Marc Jacobs, Paul Smith, Malo, and Jimmy Choo. *In the Shore Club Hotel, 1901 Collins Ave. ☎ 305/532-5929. AE, DC, DISC, MC, V. Map p 45.*

★★ **The Webster** COLLINS AVENUE A Parisian-style couture emporium, Webster features runway-ready *prêt-à-porter* for men and women by all those bold-faced names you read in the fashion magazines. *1220 Collins Ave. ☎ 305/674-7899. AE, MC, V. Map p 45.*

Y-3 DESIGN DISTRICT Japanese designer Yohji Yamamoto collaborated with Adidas to create this line of urban funkster wear, shoes, and accessories. *150 NE 40th St. ☎ 305/573-1603. AE, MC, V. Map p 46.*

Gourmet Food

★★★ **La Estancia Argentina** NORTH MIAMI The best of edible Buenos Aires is found at this small but comprehensive gourmet Argentine and Latin market. *17870 Biscayne Blvd. ☎ 305/932-6477. www.laestanciaweb.com. AE, DISC, MC, V. Map p 47.*

★★★ **Marky's** BISCAYNE CORRIDOR Shopping here is sort of like shopping at the deli owned by the Sopranos, only in Russian. Here, you'll find the finest caviar, cheeses, and pretty much anything else you can't get in Miami that's edible; make sure to ask about the secret back room. *687 NE 79th St. ☎ 305/758-9288. www.markys.com. AE, DC, MC, V. Map p 46.*

Interior Design & Furniture

★★★ **Holly Hunt** DESIGN DISTRICT Straight out of a design magazine, this furniture showroom is the area's most fabulous, if not for

Fashion meets furnishings at Holly Hunt.

NiBa Home has home accessories in every color of the rainbow.

the furniture inside, for the space alone. *3833 NE 2nd Ave.* ☎ *305/571-2012. www.hollyhunt.com. AE, MC, V. Map p 46.*

Jonathan Adler LINCOLN ROAD Campy and whimsical home accessories, from cushy pillows and throw rugs to swanky mood lighting. *1024 Lincoln Rd.* ☎ *305/534-5600. www.jonathanadler.com. AE, MC, V. Map p 45.*

★★★ **NiBa Home** DESIGN DISTRICT Color is the new black at this hipster's home decor spot, where everything, and we mean everything, has an actual hue. *39 NE 39th St.* ☎ *305/573-1939. www.nibahome.com. AE, DC, MC,V. Map p 46.*

★★ **Wolfsonian-FIU Gift Shop** WASHINGTON AVENUE This is the best museum gift shop in town, selling everything from coffee-table books and clocks, all of it retro, mod, or wacky. *1001 Washington Ave.* ☎ *305/531-1001. www.wolfsonian.org. AE, MC, V. Map p 45.*

The Dynamo, at the Wolfsonian-FIU, has a large library and cafe.

Jewelry and Accessories

Me & Ro Jewelry COLLINS AVENUE This store carries fun and funky baubles (not cheap) as seen on Debra Messing, Sarah Jessica Parker, and Julia Roberts. *In the Shore Club, 1901 Collins Ave.* ☎ *305/672-3566. AE, MC, V. Map p 45.*

SEE LINCOLN ROAD This fantastic eyewear store features an enormous selection of stylish specs, all priced between $169 and $239, including your prescription. The staff is patient and knowledgeable. *921 Lincoln Rd.* ☎ *305/672-6622. AE, MC, V. Map p 45.*

★★★ **Seybold Jewelry Building** DOWNTOWN Jewelers who specialize in an assortment of goods (diamonds, gems, watches, rings, and so on) gather here daily to sell diamonds and gold. With 300 jewelry stores located inside this independently owned and operated multilevel treasure chest, the glare is blinding as you enter. You'll be sure to see handsome and up-to-date designs, but not too many bargains unless you're good at haggling. *36 NE 1st St.* ☎ *305/374-7922. www.seyboldbldg.com. AE, DC, DISC, MC, V. Map p 46.*

Turchin Jewelry Local Teresa Turchin fancies exotic places such as Tibet, Nepal, India, and Africa, and travels all over the world for inspiration and materials. Her pricey, stylish baubles are crafted on the premises in the store's very own studio. *130 NE 40th St.* ☎ *305/573-7117. http://loveandlightjewelry.com. Map p 46.*

Malls

★★★ **Aventura Mall** AVENTURA A multimillion-dollar makeover has made this spot one of the premier places to shop in South Florida. With more than 2.3 million square feet (214,000 sq. m) of space, this airy, Mediterranean-style mall has a 24-screen movie theater and more than 250 stores, including megastores JCPenney, Nordstrom, Macy's, Bloomingdale's, Sears, and Burdines. *19501 Biscayne Blvd.* ☎ *305/935-1110. www.shopaventuramall.com.* *Map p 47.*

★★★ **Bal Harbour Shops** BAL HARBOUR One of the most prestigious fashion meccas in the country, Bal Harbour offers the best-quality goods from the finest names. Giorgio Armani, Dolce & Gabbana, Christian Dior, Fendi, Harry Winston, Brooks Brothers, Waterford, Cartier, H. Stern, Tourneau, and many others are sandwiched between Neiman Marcus and a newly expanded Saks Fifth Avenue. *9700 Collins Ave.* ☎ *305/866-0311. www.balharbourshops.com.* *Map p 47.*

Dadeland Mall KENDALL Dadeland features more than 175 specialty shops, anchored by four large department stores: Macy's, JCPenney, Nordstrom, and Saks Fifth Avenue. The mall also boasts the country's largest Limited/Express store. *7535 N. Kendall Dr.* ☎ *305/665-6226.* *Map p 47.*

Dolphin Mall WEST MIAMI This $250 million megamall is similar to Broward County's monstrous Sawgrass Mills outlet, albeit without the luxury stores. The 1.4-million-square-foot (130,000 sq. m) outlet mall features stores such as Off Fifth (Saks Fifth Avenue), plus several discount shops and a 28-screen movie theater. *Florida Tpk. at SR 836.* ☎ *305/365-7446. www.shopdolphinmall.com.* *Map p 47.*

The Falls KENDALL Traffic to this mall borders on brutal, but once you get here, you'll feel a slight sense of serenity. Tropical waterfalls are the setting for this outdoor shopping center, with dozens of moderately priced and slightly

Seybold Jewelry Building houses 300 different jewelry stores.

St. John at the Bal Harbour Shops.

upscale shops. Miami's first Bloomingdale's is here, as are Macy's, Ralph Lauren, Caswell-Massey, and more than 60 other specialty shops. *8888 Howard Dr. ☎ 305/255-4570. www.shopthefalls.com. Map p 47.*

Shops at Sunset Place SOUTH MIAMI A sprawling outdoor mall featuring the usual suspects—Victoria's Secret, Gap, Pottery Barn, Forever 21, Urban Outfitters, and more. *5701 Sunset Dr. ☎ 305/663-0482. Map p 47.*

Casino Records has a vast array of Latin music.

Music

Casino Records LITTLE HAVANA The young, hip salespeople here speak English and tend to be music buffs. This store has the largest selection of Latin music in Miami, including pop icons such as Willy Chirino, Gloria Estefan, Albita, and local boy Nil Lara. Their slogan translates to: "If we don't have it, forget it." Believe me, they've got it. *2990 SW 8th St. ☎ 305/856-6888. Map p 47.*

★★ **Sweat Records** BISCAYNE CORRIDOR This is not your father's eight-track spot, but rather an indie, electronic, underground, and esoteric music shop. *5505 NE 2nd Ave. ☎ 305/758-5862. www.sweatrecordsmiami.com. MC, V. Map p 46.*

Shoes

Morgan Miller AVENTURA A dream come true for shoe lovers, Morgan Miller is a design-your-own shoe boutique where you pick everything from heel to toe—Swarovski crystals, gold chains, bamboo rings—and the experts put it together for you. Prices range from $150 to $500. *In the Aventura Mall, 19575 Biscayne Blvd. ☎ 305/932-3451. www.morganmillershoes.com. AE, DISC, MC, V. Map p 47.* ●

4 The Best of the **Outdoors**

Beaches Best Bets

Most **Peaceful**
Matheson Hammock Park Beach, *9610 Old Cutler Rd. (p 59)*

Best **Beach Party**
Crandon Park Beach, *4000 Crandon Blvd. (p 57)*

Best for **People-Watching**
Lummus Park Beach, *Ocean Dr. between 5th & 14th sts. (p 58)*

Best for **Communing with Nature**
Bill Baggs Cape Florida State Park, *1200 Crandon Blvd. (p 69)*

Best for **Swimming**
85th Street Beach, *along Collins Ave. (p 57)*

Best for **Windsurfing**
Hobie Beach, *Rickenbacker Causeway (p 58)*

Best for **Shell-Hunting**
Bal Harbour Beach, *96th St. & Collins Ave. (p 57)*

Best for **"All-Around" Tanning**
Haulover Beach, *10800 Collins Ave. (p 58)*

Best for **Surfing**
Haulover Beach, *10800 Collins Ave. (p 58)*

Most **Scenic**
Matheson Hammock Park Beach, *9610 Old Cutler Rd. (p 59)*

Best **Family Beach**
Matheson Hammock Park Beach, *9610 Old Cutler Rd. (p 59)*

Most **Secluded**
Virginia Key, *North of Rickenbacker Causeway (p 59)*

Best for **Gay Beachgoers**
12th Street Beach, *Ocean Dr. & 12th St. (p 59)*

Surfers hit the waves at Haulover Beach.

Previous page: Fairchild Tropical Garden is home to plants, animals, and birds.

Miami's Best **Beaches**

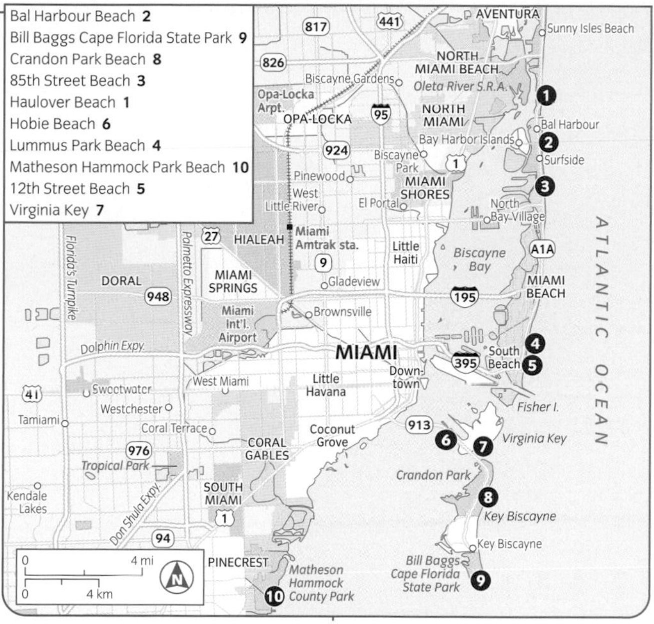

Bal Harbour Beach You'll find plenty of colorful shells here. There's also an exercise course and good shade—but no lifeguards, bathrooms, or changing facilities. *96th St. & Collins Ave. ☎ 305/866-4633. Daily 8am–sunset.*

Bill Baggs Cape Florida State Park The pot of gold at the end of Key Biscayne, with more than a mile (1.6km) of unfettered beach, a historic lighthouse, and nature trails that take you back to the days when South Florida was a tropical wilderness. *1200 Crandon Blvd. ☎ 305/361-5811. Daily 8am–sunset.*

Crandon Park Beach This beach has a diverse crowd of dedicated beach bums and lots of leisure-seeking families, set to a soundtrack of salsa, disco, and reggae music blaring from a number of competing stereos. With 3 miles (4.8km) of oceanfront beach, bathrooms, changing facilities, 493 acres (200 hectares) of park, 75 grills, three parking lots, several soccer and softball fields, and a public 18-hole championship golf course, Crandon is like a theme park on the sand. More recently, they added Eco-Adventure Tours, including kayaking and snorkeling. *4000 Crandon Blvd. ☎ 305/365-3018. Daily 8am–sunset.*

85th Street Beach This beach, along Collins Avenue, is the best place to swim away from the maddening crowds. It's one of Miami's only stretches of sand with no condos or hotels looming over sunbathers. Lifeguards patrol the area throughout the day and bathrooms are available, though they are not exactly the benchmark of cleanliness. *85th St. & Collins Ave.*

Good winds make Hobie Beach a favorite with wind and kite surfers.

Haulover Beach Join nudists from around the world in a top-to-bottom tanning session. Should you choose to keep your swimsuit on, however, there are changing rooms and bathrooms. Haulover Beach, just over the causeway from Bal Harbour, seems to get Miami's biggest swells. Go early to avoid getting mauled by the aggressive young locals prepping for Maui. Rancid bathrooms are available if you absolutely must. Surfers also like the southern tip of South Beach, not necessarily for the waves, but for the surfers themselves. *10800 Collins Ave.* ☎ *305/944-3040. Daily 8am–sunset.*

Hobie Beach Located on the side of the causeway leading to Key Biscayne, this is not really a beach, but an inlet with predictable winds and a number of places where you can rent windsurf boards. Bathrooms are available but not the cleanest. *Rickenbacker Causeway,* ☎ *305/361-2833.*

Lummus Park Beach Also known as Glitter Beach, Lummus is the best place to go if you're seeking entertainment as well as a great tan. On any day of the week, you might spy models primping for a photo shoot, nearly naked (topless is legal here) sun-worshippers

From Desert Island to Fantasy Island

Miami Beach wasn't always a beachfront playground. In fact, it was a deserted island until the late 1800s, when a developer started a coconut farm there. That action sparked an interest in many other developers, including John Collins (for whom Collins Ave. is named), who began growing avocados. Other visionaries admired Collins's success and eventually joined him, establishing a ferry service and dredging parts of the bay to make the island more accessible. In 1921, Collins built a 2½-mile bridge linking downtown Miami to Miami Beach, creating excellent accessibility and the longest wooden bridge in the world. Today, Miami Beach has six links to the mainland.

avoiding tan lines, and an assembly line of washboard abs. Bathrooms and changing facilities are available on the beach. *Ocean Dr. between 5th & 14th sts.* ☎ *305/673-7714. Daily 8am–sunset.*

Matheson Hammock Park Beach This beach is the epitome of tranquility, and while it's scenic, it's not much of a scene, so it's great for those seeking "alone time." It's also fab for families thanks to a manmade lagoon whose calm waters are fed naturally by the tides of Biscayne Bay. Clean bathrooms and changing facilities are available. *9610 Old Cutler Rd.* ☎ *305/665-5475. Daily 8am–sunset. Admission $5 per vehicle.*

12th Street Beach South Beach's 12th Street Beach is the place to be for Miami's best gay beach scene. Here you'll see strutting, kibitzing, and gossiping among some of Miami's most beautiful gay population. You might even find yourself lucky enough to happen upon a feisty South Beach party while you're soaking up some rays here. Skip the public bathroom and use the one at the Palace on Ocean Drive. *Ocean Dr. & 12th St.* ☎ *305/673-7714. Daily 8am–sunset.*

Virginia Key Here, on Key Biscayne, is where people go when they don't want to be found. It's also incredibly picturesque. Bathrooms are decent. *North of Rickenbacker Causeway.* ☎ *305/575-5256. Daily 8am–sunset.*

Miami's gay community gets together at 12th Street Beach.

Matheson Hammock Park Beach features a manmade lagoon.

Miami's Best **Golf Courses**

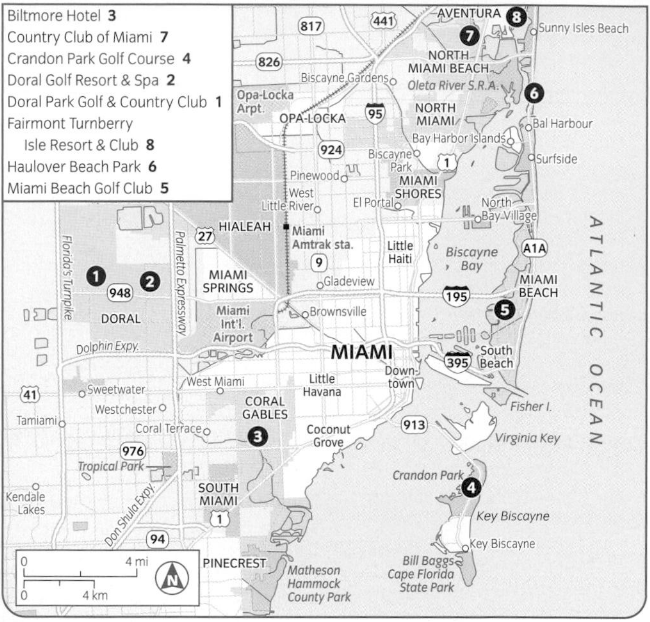

There are more than 50 private and public golf courses in the Miami area. Contact the Greater Miami Convention and Visitor's Bureau (☎ 800/933-8448; www.miamiandbeaches.com) for a list of courses and costs.

★★★ Biltmore Hotel This is our pick for best public golf course because of its modest greens fees and an 18-hole, par-71 course located on the hotel's spectacular grounds. Former president Bill Clinton prefers teeing off at this course more than any other in Miami. *1210 Anastasia Ave. ☎ 305/460-5364. www.biltmorehotel.com. Greens fees $115–$140.*

Country Club of Miami Known as one of the best in the city, with three 18-hole courses of varying degrees of difficulty. You'll encounter lush fairways and rolling greens. *6801 Miami Gardens Dr. ☎ 305/829-8456. www.golfmiamicc.com. Daily 7am–sunset. Cart and greens fees $23–$43 depending on season and tee times. Special twilight rates available.*

Crandon Park Golf Course This is the number-one-ranked municipal course in the state and one of the top five in the country. The park is situated on 200 bayfront acres (81 hectares) and offers a pro shop, rentals, lessons, carts, and a lighted driving range. *6700 Crandon Blvd. ☎ 305/361-9129. www.crandongolfclub.com. Daily dawn–dusk. Greens fees (including cart) $59 nonresidents. Special twilight rates available.*

Crandon Park Golf Course.

Doral Golf Resort and Spa The best hotel courses in Miami are found here: the legendary Blue Monster; Gold; Great White Shark; and Silver. *4400 NW 87th Ave. ☎ 800/713-6725. www.doralresort.com. Greens fees $175–$325.*

Doral Park Country Club No relation to the Doral Hotel and Spa, this is one of the most popular courses among real enthusiasts. Call to book in advance, since this challenging, semiprivate 18-holer is extremely popular with locals. *5001 NW 104th Ave. ☎ 305/591-8800. Winter daily 6:30am–6pm; summer until 7pm. Cart and greens fees vary; call ☎ 305/592-2000, ext. 2104 for information.*

Fairmont Turnberry Isle Resort & Club This resort course has two Robert Trent Jones, Sr.–designed courses for guests and members. *19999 W. Country Club Dr. ☎ 866/612-7739 or 786/279-6770. www.fairmont.com. Greens fees (including cart) range from $40–$250.*

Haulover Beach Park Golfers looking for some cheap practice time in a pretty bayside location will appreciate Haulover Beach Park. The longest hole on this par-27 course is 125 yards. *10800 Collins Ave. ☎ 305/940-6719. Daily winter 7:30am–6pm; summer until 7:30pm. Greens fees $7 per person.*

Miami Beach Golf Club This club is home to a gorgeous, 79-year-old course that received a $10 million face-lift. *2301 Alton Rd. ☎ 305/532-3350. www.miamibeachgolfclub.com. Greens fees $100–$200, depending on the season.*

Miami Beach Golf Club.

Miami by Sea

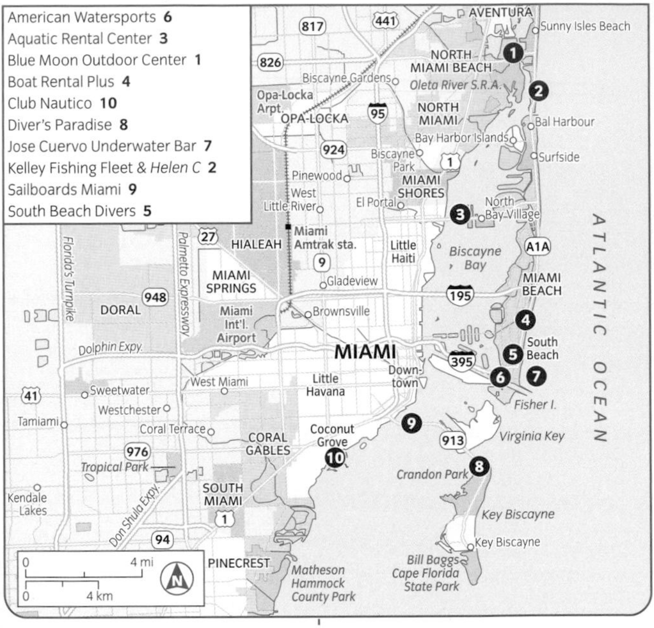

Boating

Boat Rental Plus Here 50-horsepower, 18-foot (5.4m) powerboats rent for some of the best prices on the beach. Cruising is permitted only in and around Biscayne Bay (ocean access is prohibited), and renters must be 21 or older to rent a boat. The rental office is at 23rd Street, on the inland waterway in Miami Beach. If you want a specific type of boat, call ahead to reserve. Otherwise, show up and take what's available. ***2400 Collins Ave. ☎ 305/534-4307. 2-hr. minimum. $100–$500 (including taxes and gas); Sun specials. Daily 10am–sunset.***

Club Nautico High-quality powerboats for fishing, water-skiing, diving, and cruising in the bay or ocean are available here. All boats are Coast Guard–equipped, with VHF radios and safety gear. Visit their website for information on other locations. ***2560 S. Bayshore Dr. ☎ 305/858-6258. www.clubnauticousa.com. Rates $359–$469; $125 per hour. Daily 8am–6pm (weather permitting).***

Fishing

Fishing licenses are required in Florida. If you go out with one of the fishing charter boats listed below, you are automatically accredited because the companies are. If you go out on your own, however, you must have a Florida fishing license, which costs $17 for 3 days and $30 for a week. Call ☎ 888/FISH-FLO, or visit www.wildlifelicense.com. In addition to the below, Key Biscayne offers deep-sea fishing to those willing to get their hands dirty and pay a bundle. The competition among the boats is fierce, but the prices are basically the same. The going rate is about $400 to $450 for a half-day and $600 to $700 for a full day of fishing. Some of the best surf casting in the city can be had at **Haulover Beach Park,** Collins Avenue and 105th Street, where there's a bait-and-tackle shop right on the pier. **South Pointe Park,** at the southern tip of Miami Beach, is another popular fishing spot and features a long pier, comfortable benches, and a great view of the ships passing through Government Cut, the deep channel made when the port of Miami was dug. You can also do some deep-sea fishing in the Miami area.

One bargain outfitter, the **Kelley Fishing Fleet** (10800 Collins Ave.; ☎ 305/945-3801; www.miamibeachfishing.com), has half-day, full-day, and night fishing aboard diesel-powered "party boats." The fleet's emphasis on drifting is geared toward trolling and bottom fishing for snapper, sailfish, and mackerel. Prices range from $22 to $49, and departures are daily at 9am and 1:45 and 8pm. Reservations are recommended.

Also at the Haulover Marina is the charter boat ***Helen C*** (10800 Collins Ave.; ☎ 305/947-4081; www.fishmiamibeach.com). Although there's no shortage of private charter boats here, Captain Dawn Mergelsberg is a good pick, since she puts individuals together to get a full boat. The *Helen C* is a twin-engine 55 footer (17m), equipped for big-game fish such as marlin, tuna, mahi-mahi, shark, and sailfish. Cost is $150 per person, and daily trips depart at 8am and 1pm. Private trips are also available.

For a serious fishing charter, Captain Charlie Hotchkiss's ***Sea Dancer*** (☎ 305/733-5126; www.seadancercharter.com) offers a first-class experience on a 38-foot (11m) Luhrs boat complete with tuna tower and air-conditioned cabin. If you're all about big game—marlin, dolphin, tuna, wahoo, swordfish, and sailfish—this is the charter for you. Catch and release or fillet your catch to take home. The *Sea Dancer* also offers a 6-hour Bar Cruz, covering the finest watering holes in Miami and Fort Lauderdale, or a Sandbar Cruz, where the boat drops anchor out by Biscayne Bay's

Haulover Beach has a bait-and-tackle shop on its pier.

Miami Beach Marina.

historic Stiltsville, where you'll swim, bounce on a water trampoline, and play sports—all in the middle of the bay. Auto transportation is available to wherever the boat may be docked. Rates are half-day $700, full day $1,100, and tours $500.

Jet Skis/Waverunners

American Watersports, at the Miami Beach Marina, 300 Alton Rd. (☎ 305/538-7549; www.jetskiz.com), is the area's most popular spot for jet-ski rental. Rates begin at $75 for a half-hour and $140 for an hour. They also offer fun jet-ski tours past celebrity homes for $160 for the first hour and $80 for the second.

Take a guided kayak tour at Oleta River State Recreation Area.

Kayaking

The **Blue Moon Outdoor Center,** 3400 NE 163rd St., in Oleta River Park (☎ 305/957-3040; www.bluemoonmiami.com), is the best kayak rental in town. The outfitters here give explorers a map to take with them and quick instructions on how to work the paddles and boats. They also operate scenic 4-hour guided tours through rivers with mangroves and islands, a 3-hour kayak and mountain-bike tour; ecotours; and full-moon tours. Prices range from $35 to $75; rentals $18 to $45. Along the route you'll pass Blue Marlin Fish House, where you can stop for smoked fish daily 9am to sunset.

Sailing

Aquatic Rental Center, 1275 NE 79th St., at northern Biscayne Bay in the Pelican Harbor Marina (☎ 305/751-7514 days, 305/279-7424 evenings; www.arcmiami.com), can get you out on the water in style. A

22-foot (6.6m) sailboat rents for $85 for 2 hours, $150 for a half-day, and $225 for a full day. A Sunfish sailboat for two people rents at $30 per hour. If you've always had a dream to win the America's Cup but can't sail, the able teachers here will get you started. They offer a 10-hour course over 5 days for $350 per person or $500 for you and a friend.

Scuba Diving & Snorkeling

Diver's Paradise, 4000 Crandon Blvd. (☎ 305/361-3483; www.keydivers.com), offers one dive expedition per day during the week and two per day on the weekends to the more than 30 wrecks and artificial reefs off the coast of Miami Beach and Key Biscayne. You can take a 3-day certification course for $499, which includes all the dives and gear. If you already have your C-card, a dive trip costs about $100 if you need equipment and $60 if you bring your own gear. It's open Tuesday through Friday 10am to 6pm and Saturday and Sunday 8am to 6pm. Call ahead for times and locations of dives. For snorkeling, they will set you up with equipment and maps on where to see the best underwater sights. Rental for mask, fins, and snorkel is $50.

South Beach Divers, 850 Washington Ave. (☎ 305/531-6110; www.southbeachdivers.com), will also be happy to tell you where to go under the sea and will provide you with scuba rental equipment for $65. You can rent snorkel gear for $20. They also do dive trips to Key Largo three times a week and do dives off Miami on Sunday at $100 for a two-tank dive or $80 if you have your own equipment.

Set sail with the winds at Hobie Beach.

Jose Cuervo Underwater Bar

This has to be the most amusing and apropos South Beach diving spot, located 150 yards (135m) southeast of the Second Street lifeguard station. The 22-ton concrete margarita bar was sunk on May 5, 2000, hence nicknamed "Sinko de Mayo." There's a dive-flag roof, six barstools, and a protective wall of tetrahedrons.

Windsurfing

Sailboards Miami, Rickenbacker Causeway, Key Biscayne (☎ 305/361-SAIL; www.sailboardsmiami.com), operates out of two big yellow trucks on Windsurfer Beach, the most popular (though our pick for best is Hobie Beach) windsurfing spot in the city. For those who've never ridden a board but want to try it, they offer a 2-hour lesson for $69 that's guaranteed, or you get your money back. After that, you can rent a board for $25 to $30 an hour. If you want to make a day of it, a 10-hour prepaid card costs $220. These cards reduce the price by about $70 for the day. You can use the card year-round, until the time on it runs out. They also rent kayaks. Open Tuesday through Sunday 10am to 5:30pm. Make your first right after the tollbooth (at the beginning of the causeway—you can't miss it) to find the outfitters.

Miami by **Land**

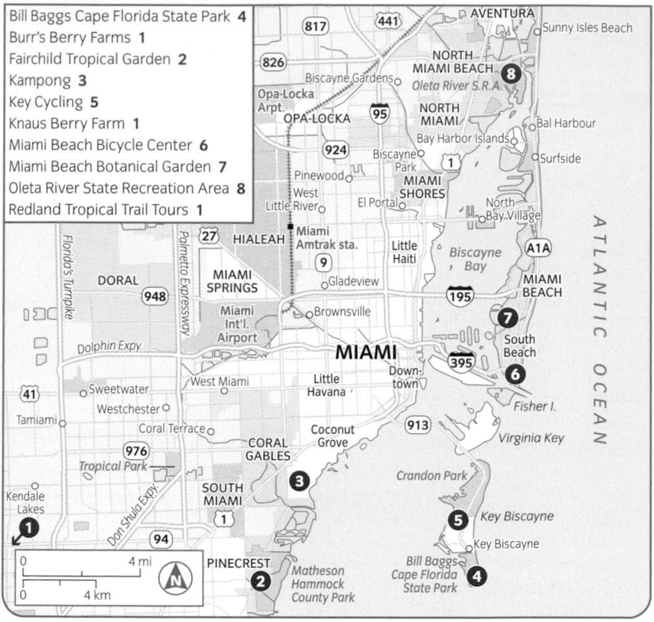

Biking

The cement promenade on the southern tip of South Beach is a great place to ride. Biking up the beach (either on the beach or along the beach on a cement pathway) is great for surf, sun, sand, exercise, and people-watching. Most of the big beach hotels rent bicycles, as does the **Miami Beach Bicycle Center** (601 5th St.; ☎ 305/674-0150; www.bikemiamibeach.com), which charges $8 per hour or $24 for up to 24 hours. Bikers can also enjoy more than 130 miles (209km) of paved paths throughout Miami. The beautiful and quiet streets of Coral Gables and Coconut Grove (several bike trails are spread throughout these neighborhoods) are great for bicyclists, where old trees form canopies over wide, flat roads lined with grand homes and quaint street markers. The terrain in **Key Biscayne** is perfect for biking, especially along the park and beach roads. If you don't mind the sound of cars whooshing by your bike lane, **Rickenbacker Causeway** is also fantastic, since it is one of the only bikeable inclines in Miami from which you get fantastic elevated views of the city and waterways. However, be warned that this is a grueling ride, especially going up the causeway. **Key Cycling** (61 Harbor Dr.; ☎ 305/361-0061; www.keycycling.com) rents mountain bikes for $15 for 2 hours or $20 a day.

Fruit Stands

Burr's Berry Farms Located in the township of Goulds, about an hour from downtown Miami, this farm has created a sensation with its fabulous strawberry milkshakes.

Burr's Berry Farms is known for its strawberry milkshakes.

12741 SW 216th St. ☎ 305/251-0145. Go south on U.S. 1 and turn right on SW 216th St. The fruit stand is about 1 mile (1.6km) west. Daily 9am–5:30pm.

Knaus Berry Farm For fresh fruit in a tasty pastry or tart, head over to this farm, in an area known as The Redlands. Some people erroneously call this farm an Amish farm, but it's run by a sect of German Baptists. The stand offers items ranging from fresh flowers to homemade ice cream, but be sure to indulge in one of their famous homemade cinnamon buns. Be prepared to wait in a long line to stock up—people flock here from as far away as Palm Beach. *15980 SW 248th St. ☎ 305/247-0668. Head south on U.S. 1 and turn right on 248th St.; farm is 2½ miles (4km) farther on the left side. Mon–Sat 8am–5:30pm.*

Gardens

★★★ Fairchild Tropical Garden This is the largest garden of its kind in the continental United States. A veritable rainforest of both rare and exotic plants, as well as 11 lakes and countless meadows, are spread across 83 acres (34 hectares). Palmettos, vine pergola, palm glades, and other unique species create a scenic, lush environment. More than 100 species of birds have been spotted at the garden (ask for a checklist at the front gate), and it's home to a variety of animals. Don't miss the 30-minute narrated tram tour (tours leave on the hour weekdays 10am–3pm and weekends 10am–4pm) to learn about the various flowers and trees on the grounds. There is also a museum, a cafe, a picnic area, and a gift shop. Fairchild often hosts major art exhibits by the likes of Dale Chihuly and Roy Lichtenstein. The 2-acre (1-hectare) rainforest exhibit, Windows to the Tropics, will save you a trip to the Amazon. Expect to spend a minimum of 2 hours here. *10901 Old Cutler Rd. ☎ 305/667-1651. www.ftg.org. Admission $20 adults, $15 seniors, $10 children 3–12, free for children under 3. Daily except Christmas 9:30am–4:30pm. Take*

I-95 south to U.S. 1, turn left onto LeJeune Rd., and follow it straight to the traffic circle; from there, take Old Cutler Rd. 2 miles to the park.

★★ Kampong The Kampong, on Biscayne Bay in Coconut Grove, is a 7-acre (3-hectare) botanical garden with a stunning array of flowering and tropical fruit trees, including mango, avocado, and pomelos. The garden's name comes from the Malaysian word "kampong," meaning "home in the garden"; the Fairchild family built a home here, which is listed on the National Register of Historic Places. It's a must-see for those interested in horticulture. *4013 Douglas Rd. www.ntbg.org/gardens/kampong.php. Admission & tours by appointment only, Mon–Fri. For tour & price information, call ☎ 305/442-7169. Take U.S. 1 to Douglas Rd. (SW 37th Ave.). Go east on Douglas Rd. for about a mile (1.6km); the Kampong is on the left.*

Miami Beach Botanical Garden Because so many people are focused on the beach itself, the Miami Beach Botanical Garden remains a secret. The lush, tropical 4½-acre (1.8-hectare) garden is a fabulous natural retreat from the hustle and bustle of the silicone-enhanced city. *2000 Convention Center Dr. ☎ 305/673-7256. Tues–Sun 9am–5pm. Admission free.*

★★★ Vizcaya Museum and Gardens This magnificent villa is more Gatsby-esque than anything else you'll find in Miami. It was built in 1916 as a winter retreat for James Deering, cofounder and former vice president of International Harvester. The industrialist was fascinated by 16th-century art and architecture, and his ornate mansion, which took 1,000 artisans 5 years to build, became a celebration of that period. If you love antiques, this place is a dream come true, packed with European relics and works of art from the 16th to the 19th centuries. A free guided tour of the 34 furnished rooms on the first floor takes about 45 minutes. The second floor, which consists mostly of bedrooms, is

Escape the city's madness at the Miami Beach Botanical Garden.

open to tour on your own. Outside, lush formal gardens, accented with statuary, balustrades, and decorative urns, front an enormous swath of Biscayne Bay. Definitely take the tour of the rooms, but immediately thereafter, you will want to wander and get lost in the resplendent gardens. *3251 S. Miami Ave. (just south of Rickenbacker Causeway), North Coconut Grove. ☎ 305/250-9133. www.vizcayamuseum.com. Admission $15 adults, $10 seniors, $6 children 6–12, free for children 5 and under. Villa daily 9:30am–5pm (ticket booth closes at 4:30pm); gardens daily 9:30am–5:30pm.*

The historic lighthouse at Bill Baggs Cape Florida State Park.

Parks & Trails

Bill Baggs Cape Florida State Park Bill Baggs has been consistently rated as one of the top 10 beaches in the U.S. for its 1¼ miles (2km) of wide, sandy beaches and its secluded, serene atmosphere. There's also a historic lighthouse, the oldest in South Florida, which was built in 1825. A rental shack leases bikes, hydrobikes, kayaks, and more. It's a great place to picnic, and the **Lighthouse Cafe** (☎ 305/361-8487) serves homemade Latin food, including great fish soups and sandwiches (they'll even pack your lunch to go). A more grown-up meal can be had at the sister restaurant **Boater's Grill** (☎ 305/361-0080); try the shrimp asopado or cuban desserts made by the owner's 80-year-old mother. *Admission $5 per car with up to 8 people (or $3 for a car with only 1 person; $1 to enter by foot or bicycle). Daily 8am–sunset. Lighthouse tours Thurs–Mon 10am & 1pm. Arrive at least a half-hour early to sign up—there is room for only 10 people on each tour. Take I-95 to the Rickenbacker Causeway and take that all the way to the end.*

★★★ Oleta River State Recreation Area This is the state's largest urban park at 993 acres (402 hectares). The beauty of the Oleta River, combined with the fact that you're essentially in the middle of a city, makes this park especially worth visiting. There are miles of bike and canoe trails, a sandy swimming beach, a kayak and mountain-bike rental shop, the Blue Marlin Fish House Restaurant, shaded picnic pavilions, and a fishing pier. Facilities include 14 air-conditioned cabins ($45 per night up to 4 people; guests are required to bring their own linens), outdoor bathrooms and showers, and a fire circle with grill. *3400 NE 163rd St. ☎ 305/919-1846; reservations ☎ 800/326-3521. Daily 8am–sunset. Admission $1 per person pedestrians & cyclists; $3 car or $5 car with up to 7 passengers. Take I-95 to Exit 17 (S.R. 826 E.) and go all the way east until just before the causeway. Park entrance on the right.*

★★★ Redland Tropical Trail Tours This tour takes you through the South Florida farmlands in an area near Homestead called The Redlands. The tour has a number of stops, tastings, and sites that include gardens, jungles, an orchid farm, and fruit stands. **Schnebly Redland's Winery** (www.schneblywinery.com) is another stop, offering live music (Sat–Sun) and tastings in its new $1.5 million tasting room. A free map (available online) allows you to follow the trail on your own, but call for pricing for certain attractions. ☎ *305/245-9180. www.redlandtrail.com.*

Tennis

Crandon Tennis Center. Hard courts cost $3 per person per hour during the day, $5 per person per hour at night. Clay courts cost $6 per person per hour during the day. There are no night hours on the clay courts. *6702 Crandon Blvd.* ☎ *305/361-5263. Mon–Fri 8am–9pm; Sat–Sun until 6pm.*

Miami Beach public courts at Flamingo Park. There are 19 clay courts that cost $4 per person an hour for Miami Beach residents and $8 per person an hour for nonresidents. It's first-come, first-served. *1001 12th St.* ☎ *305/673-7761. Mon–Fri 8am–9pm; Sat–Sun 8am–8pm.*

Surfside Tennis Center. Free for residents and same cost as Flamingo Park (above) for nonresidents. *8750 Collins Ave.* ☎ *305/866-5176.*

Preston B. Bird and Mary Heinlein Fruit and Spice Park

This park is a testament to Miami's unusual climate and harbors rare fruit trees that cannot survive elsewhere in the country. If a volunteer is available, you'll learn some fascinating things about this 30-acre (12-hectare) living plant museum, where the most exotic varieties of fruits and spices—akee, mango, Ugli fruits, carambola, and breadfruit—grow. There are also original coral-rock buildings dating back to 1912. The Strawberry Folk Festival in February and an art festival here in January are among the park's most popular—and populated—events. The best part? You're free to take anything that has naturally fallen to the ground (no picking here). You'll also find samples of interesting fruits and jellies made from the park's bounty, as well as exotic ingredients and cookbooks in the gift store. 24801 SW 187th Ave., Homestead. ☎ 305/247-5727. www.fruitandspicepark.org. Admission $6 adults, $1.50 children 12 and under. Daily 10am to 5pm; closed on Christmas. Tours included in the price of admission and offered at 11am and 1:30 and 3pm. Take U.S. 1 south, turn right on SW 248th Street, and go straight for 5 miles (8km) to SW 187th Avenue.

5 The Best **Dining**

Dining Best Bets

Best **Steakhouse**
★★★ Prime 112 $$$ *112 Ocean Dr. (p 85)*

Best **Burger**
★★ Clarke's $$ *840 1st St. (p 79)*

Best **When Someone Else Is Paying**
★★★ Casa Tua $$$ *1700 James Ave. (p 78)*

Best **Sushi**
★★★ Nobu $$$ *1901 Collins Ave. (p 85)*

Best **Kitsch(en)**
★ Barton G. The Restaurant $$$ *1427 West Ave. (p 76)*

Best **Celebrity-Chef Meal**
★★★ Michy's $$$ *6927 Biscayne Blvd. (p 84)*

Best **Special-Occasion Restaurant**
★ The Forge $$$$ *432 Arthur Godfrey Rd. (p 80)*

Best **French Bistro**
★ A La Folie $ *516 Espanola Way (p 75)*

Best **Cuban**
★★ Puerto Sagua $ *700 Collins Ave. (p 86)*

Burgers and VWs at Big Pink.

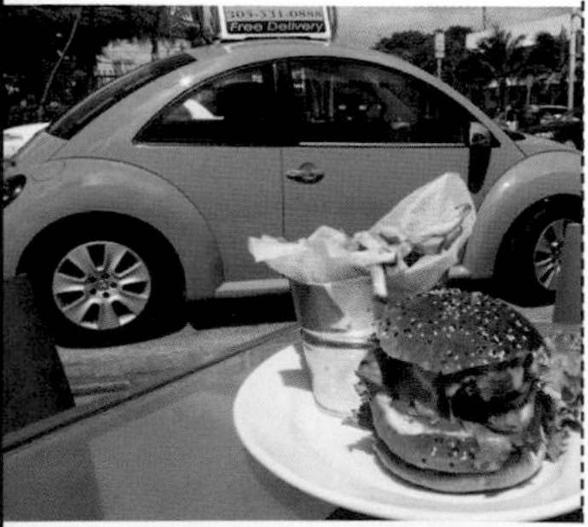

Most **Romantic**
★★★ Wish $$$ *810 Collins Ave. (p 88)*

Best **Outdoor Dining**
★ Big Fish $$ *55 SW Miami Ave. Rd. (p 76)*

Best **Italian**
★★★ Escopazzo $$ *1311 Washington Ave. (p 80)*

Best **Gourmet Organic**
★★★ Michael's Genuine Food & Drink $$$ *130 NE 40th St. (p 83)*

Best **Asian**
★ China Grill $$$ *404 Washington Ave. (p 78)*

Best **Brunch**
★★★ Blue Door at Delano $$$ *1685 Collins Ave. (p 77)*

Best **Seafood**
★★ Garcia's Seafood Grille & Fish $ *398 NW N. River Dr. (p 81)*

Best **Cakes**
★ Icebox Cafe $ *1656 Michigan Ave. (p 82)*

Best **View**
★★★ Smith & Wollensky $$$$ *1 Washington Ave. (p 87)*

Best **Late-Night Bites**
★ La Sandwicherie $ *229 114th St. (p 82)*

Best **For Picky Kids**
★ Big Pink $ *157 Collins Ave. (p 77)*

Best **For People-Watching**
★ News Cafe $ *800 Ocean Dr. (p 84)*

Best **For Cheap Eats**
★ Dogma Grill $ *7030 Biscayne Blvd. (p 79)*

Previous page: A goat cheese-infused martini at Meat Market.

South Beach Dining

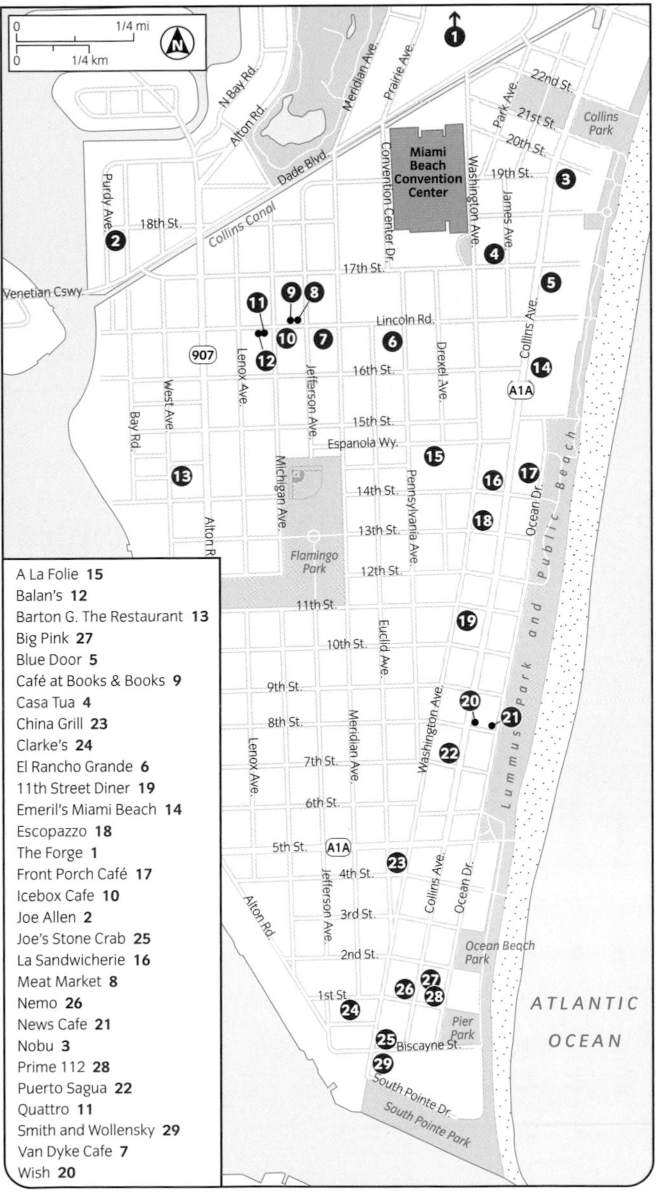

A La Folie **15**
Balan's **12**
Barton G. The Restaurant **13**
Big Pink **27**
Blue Door **5**
Café at Books & Books **9**
Casa Tua **4**
China Grill **23**
Clarke's **24**
El Rancho Grande **6**
11th Street Diner **19**
Emeril's Miami Beach **14**
Escopazzo **18**
The Forge **1**
Front Porch Café **17**
Icebox Cafe **10**
Joe Allen **2**
Joe's Stone Crab **25**
La Sandwicherie **16**
Meat Market **8**
Nemo **26**
News Cafe **21**
Nobu **3**
Prime 112 **28**
Puerto Sagua **22**
Quattro **11**
Smith and Wollensky **29**
Van Dyke Cafe **7**
Wish **20**

Miami Dining

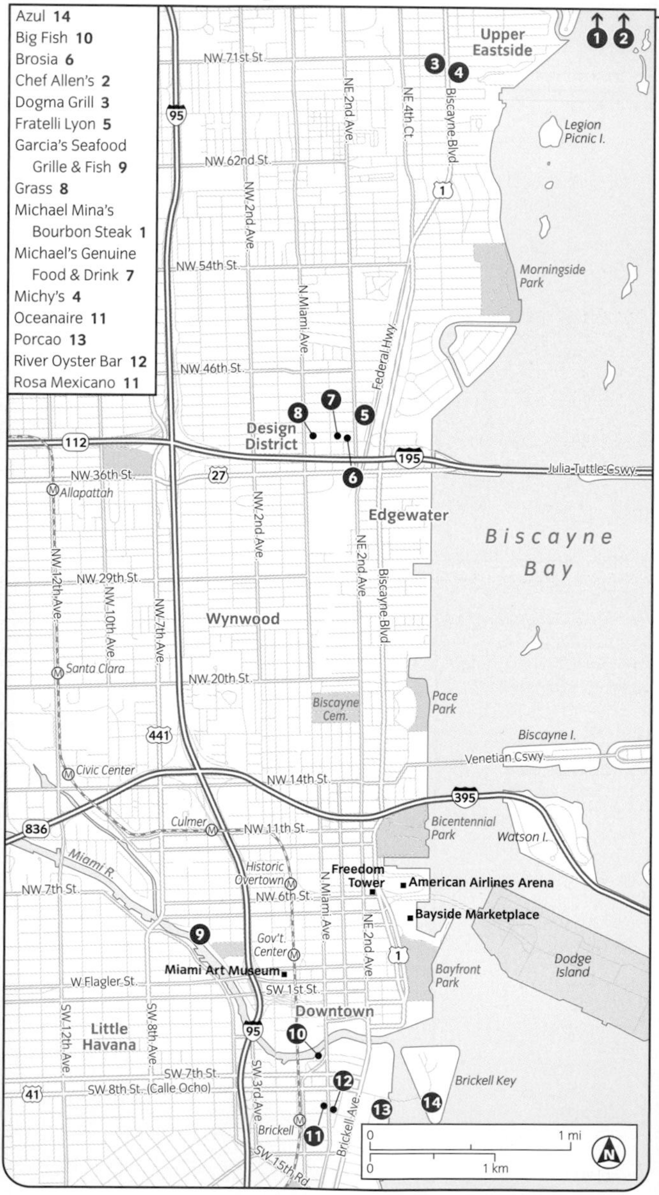

Miami **Restaurants A to Z**

★ **A La Folie** SOUTH BEACH *FRENCH* A La Folie is an authentic French cafe in which wooden booths and walls full of foreign newspapers and magazines make you take a second look at your plane ticket to make sure you're still in Miami. ***516 Espanola Way. ☎ 305/538-4484. Entrees $5–$10. MC, V. Lunch & dinner daily. Map p 73.***

★★★ **Azul** BRICKELL *FUSION* Executive Chef Clay Conley, who honed his skills with star Chef Todd English, creates a tour de force of international cuisine, inspired by Caribbean, French, Argentinean, Asian, and even American flavors. A waterfront view, high ceilings, walls burnished in copper, and silk-covered chairs are complemented by the food. Among the standouts: Moroccan-inspired lamb; a miso-marinated duck breast; and, our favorite, "A Study in Tuna": raw tuna, tempura avocado, and Asian sauces with Ossetra caviar. ***In the Mandarin Oriental, 500 Brickell Key Dr. ☎ 305/913-8254. Entrees $24–$55. AE, DC, DISC, MC, V. Dinner daily. Map p 74.***

★ **Balan's** LINCOLN ROAD *MEDITERRANEAN* A direct import from London's Soho, Balan's draws inspiration from various Mediterranean and Asian influences. With a brightly colored interior straight out of a mod '60s flick, Balan's is a favorite among the gay and arty crowds, especially on weekends during brunch hours. The moderately priced food is good: double-baked cheese soufflé with

Get your seafood with a view at Big Fish (see p 76).

Coral Gables & Coconut Grove Dining

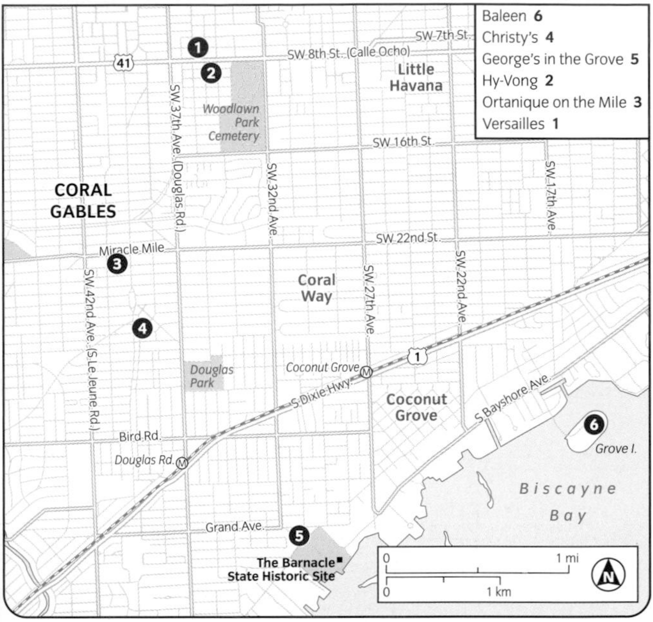

citrus-tossed mixed greens; Thai red curry; and pan-fried tilapia with Indian garbanzo-bean curry and mint yogurt. When in doubt, the restaurant's signature US1 Burger is always a good choice. *1022 Lincoln Rd. ☎ 305/534-9191. Entrees $9–$37. AE, DISC, MC, V. Breakfast, lunch & dinner daily. Map p 73.*

★ **Baleen** COCONUT GROVE *MEDITERRANEAN* The cuisine here is worth every pricey penny. Oversize crab cakes, oak-smoked diver scallops, and steakhouse-quality meats are among Baleen's excellent offerings. The lobster bisque is the best on Biscayne Bay. Everything here is a la carte, so order wisely, as it tends to add up. The restaurant's spectacular waterfront setting makes Baleen a true knockout. *4 Grove Isle. ☎ 305/858-8300. Entrees $18–$50. AE, DC, MC, V. Breakfast, lunch & dinner daily. Map above.*

★ kids **Barton G. The Restaurant** SOUTH BEACH *AMERICAN* Barton G. The Restaurant is an homage to gourmet kitsch. It looks like a trendy restaurant, but eats like a show, and presentation is paramount. *1427 West Ave. ☎ 305/672-8881. www.bartong.com. Entrees $10–$50. AE, DC, DISC, MC, V. Dinner daily. Map p 73.*

★ **Big Fish** DOWNTOWN *SEAFOOD* This scenic seafood shack on the

Miami River is hard to locate but well worth the search. The mostly seafood menu has some Italian options (added in the hopes of luring more people), and the space offers a sweeping view of the Miami skyline. *55 SW Miami Ave. Rd.* ☎ *305/373-1770. Entrees $15–$35. AE, DC, MC, V. Lunch & dinner Mon–Sat; closed Sun. Map p 74.*

★ **kids** **Big Pink** SOUTH BEACH *AMERICAN* Scooters and motorcycles line the streets surrounding this place, which is a favorite among beach bums and club kids. The fare, above average at best, includes hugely portioned pizzas, sandwiches, salads, and hamburgers. Check out their "gourmet" spin on the classic TV dinner, done perfectly, right down to the compartmentalized dessert. *157 Collins Ave.* ☎ *305/532-4700. www.bigpinkrestaurant.com. Entrees $9–$20. AE, DC, MC, V. Breakfast, lunch & dinner daily. Map p 73.*

★★★ **Blue Door** SOUTH BEACH *FRENCH BRAZILIAN* This is quintessential South Beach dining. The most recent incarnation of the restaurant begs for superlatives more flattering than the standard "fabulous." The eye candy is still here, but now you have good reason to focus your eyes on the food rather than who's eating it, thanks to award-winning Chef Claude Troisgrois (rhymes with foie gras). The menu favors a classic French approach to tropical spices and ingredients. A Sunday brunch buffet is the city's best. *1685 Collins Ave.* ☎ *305/674-6400. Entrees $31–$46. AE, DC, MC, V. Breakfast, lunch & dinner daily. Map p 73.*

★ **Brosia** DESIGN DISTRICT *MEDITERRANEAN* Brosia brings some much-needed life to its quiet Design District location with a spectacular setting (a mosaic-walled courtyard lined with hundred-plus-year-old oak trees) and outstanding cuisine. The latter includes shared plates such as the Mediterranean meze platter with Sopresatta, Manchego cheese, and an assortment of olives and fig jams; sautéed shrimp with garlic sherry wine; and mini grilled lamb chops. Save room for the grilled pork tenderloin with caperberries, cornichons, grain mustard, and sides of perfectly salted, skinny fries and roasted garlic asparagus. *163 NE 39th St.* ☎ *305/572-1400. www.brosiamiami.com. Entrees $18–$29. AE, DC, DISC, MC, V. Breakfast, lunch & dinner Mon–Fri; dinner Sat–Sun. Map p 74.*

★ **Café at Books & Books** SOUTH BEACH *AMERICAN* This is not your chain bookstore's prefab tuna sandwich. Sandwiches, salads, and burgers are good, but after 5pm Chef Bernie Matz shines with dishes such as a juicy flank steak marinated in espresso and brown sugar, seared, sliced, and served with a pineapple-and-onion salsa and a pair of plantain nests smothered in garlicky *mojo. 933 Lincoln Rd.* ☎ *305/695-8898. Entrees $5–$25. AE, MC, V. Breakfast, lunch & dinner daily. Map p 73.*

French classics get a tropical twist at Blue Door.

Casa Tua's Italian dishes are served in a variety of dining spaces.

★★★ Casa Tua SOUTH BEACH *ITALIAN* The stunning Casa Tua is a sleek, chic, country Italian–style establishment set in a refurbished 1925 Mediterranean-style house-cum-hotel. It has several dining areas, including a resplendent outdoor garden, a comfy Ralph Lauren–esque living room, and a communal eat-in kitchen. The roasted rack of lamb is stratospheric in price, upwards of $50, but sublime in taste and a bargain compared to the whole Branzino served for two at twice that price. Service is inconsistent, ranging from ultraprofessional to absurdly lackadaisical. For these prices, they should be wiping our mouths for us. ***1700 James Ave. ☎ 305/673-1010. Entrees $24–$100. AE, DC, MC, V. Dinner daily. Map p 73.***

★ Chef Allen's AVENTURA *NEW WORLD* Chef Allen, the man, is royalty around here. Chef Allen's, the restaurant, is his province, and he rules with new-world cuisine, exotic tropical fruits, spices, and vegetables. It is under Allen's magic that ordinary Key limes and mangoes become succulent salsas and sauces; organic corn meal, tamarind, shallots, and Manchego cheese are transformed into an appetizer of shrimp and grits brûlée; grouper marries with rock shrimp, leeks, mango, and coconut rum; and whole yellowtail in saffron tea, capers, and red quinoa is spectacular. ***19088 NE 29th Ave. ☎ 305/935-2900. www.chefallens.com. Entrees $19–$48. AE, DC, MC, V. Dinner daily. Map p 74.***

★ China Grill SOUTH BEACH *ASIAN* China Grill offers a dizzying array of amply portioned dishes, including crispy spinach, wasabi mashed potatoes, seared rare tuna in spicy Japanese pepper, broccoli rabe dumplings, lobster pancakes, and a sinfully delicious dessert sampler complete with sparklers. ***404 Washington Ave. ☎ 305/534-2211. www.chinagrillmgmt.com. Entrees $26–$59. AE, DC, DISC, MC, V. Lunch & dinner Mon–Thurs; dinner Fri–Sat. Map p 73.***

★★ Christy's CORAL GABLES *STEAKHOUSE* Christy's is the kind of place where conversations are at a hush and no one seems to care who they're sitting next to. The selling points here are the broiled lamb chops, prime rib of beef with horseradish sauce, teriyaki-marinated filet mignon, herb-crusted sea bass, crab cakes, and perfectly tossed Caesar salad. ***3101 Ponce de Leon Blvd.*** ☎ ***305/446-1400. www.christysrestaurant.com. Entrees $20–$48. AE, DC, DISC, MC, V. Lunch & dinner Mon–Sat; dinner Sun. Map p 76.***

★★ **Clarke's** SOUTH BEACH *IRISH* There's more to this neighborhood pub than pints of Guinness. With a warm, inviting ambience and a gorgeously rich wood bar as the focal point, Clarke's is the only true gastropub in Miami, with excellent fare that goes beyond bangers and mash and delicious burgers, and delves into the gourmet. ***840 1st St.*** ☎ ***305/538-9885. www.clarkesmiamibeach.com. Entrees $10–$27. AE, MC, V. Lunch & dinner Mon–Fri; dinner Sat; brunch & dinner Sun. Map p 73.***

★ **Dogma Grill** BISCAYNE CORRIDOR *AMERICAN* A little bit of L.A. comes to a gritty stretch of Biscayne Boulevard in the form of this very tongue-in-cheek hot-dog stand whose motto is "A Frank Philosophy." ***7030 Biscayne Blvd.*** ☎ ***305/759-3433. www.dogmagrill.com. Hot dogs $3–$5. No credit cards. Lunch & dinner daily. Map p 74.***

Clarke's offers more than the usual pub grub.

★ **El Rancho Grande** SOUTH BEACH *MEXICAN* El Rancho Grande is a local favorite, with ultrafresh fare and an unassuming ambience ("Pottery Barn meets Acapulco"). ***1626 Pennsylvania Ave.*** ☎ ***305/673-0480. Entrees $10–$20. AE, DC, MC, V. Lunch & dinner daily. Map p 73.***

Dogma brings hot dogs and humor to Miami.

Cuban Coffee

Despite the more than dozen Starbucks that dot the Miami landscape, locals still rely on the many Cuban cafeterias for their daily caffeine fix. Beware of the many establishments throughout Miami that serve espresso masked as Cuban coffee. For the real deal, go to the most popular—and most animated—Cuban cafeterias: **La Carreta** (3632 SW 8th St.; ☎ 305/444-7501) and **Versailles** (3555 SW 8th St.; ☎ 305/444-0240).

Cuban coffee is a longstanding tradition in Miami. You'll find it served from the takeout windows of hundreds of cafeterias or luncherías around town, especially in Little Havana, Downtown, and the beaches. Depending on where you are and what you want, you'll spend between 40¢ and $1.50 per cup.

The best café Cubano has a rich layer of foam on top formed when the hot espresso shoots from the machine into the sugar below. The result is the caramelly, sweet, potent concoction that's a favorite of locals of all nationalities.

To partake, you've just got to learn how to ask for it en español.

★ **11th Street Diner** SOUTH BEACH *AMERICAN* The only real diner on the beach, the 11th Street Diner is the antidote to a late-night run to Denny's. Some of Miami's most colorful characters, especially the drunk ones, convene here at odd hours, and your greasy-spoon experience can quickly turn into a three-ring circus. ***1065 Washington Ave.*** ☎ ***305/534-6373. Entrees $8–$15. AE, MC. Breakfast, lunch & dinner daily. Map p 73.***

★★★ **Emeril's Miami Beach** SOUTH BEACH *CREOLE* If you've never dined at Emeril's original restaurant(s) in New Orleans and you're craving gourmet Creole cuisine, don't miss this. The 8,000-square-foot (743 sq. m) restaurant is a bustling and cavernous hot spot with chandeliers, massive wine cellars, and an inviting open kitchen in which Emeril himself sometimes stars. ***In the Loews Hotel, 1601 Collins Ave.*** ☎ ***305/695-4550. www.emerils.com. Main courses $18–$50. AE, MC, V. Lunch & dinner daily; brunch Sun. Map p 73.***

★★★ **Escopazzo** SOUTH BEACH *ITALIAN* Should you be so lucky to score a table at this romantic local favorite, choose one in the back dining room that's reminiscent of an Italian courtyard, complete with fountain and faux windows. You'll have trouble deciding between dishes; standouts are milk-and-basil dough pasta with baby calamari, chickpeas, tomatoes, and arugula; or grass-fed hanger steak with roasted baby organic veggies in a truffle sauce. The hand-rolled pastas and risotto are near perfection. ***1311 Washington Ave.*** ☎ ***305/674-9450. www.escopazzo.com. Entrees $27–$55. AE, MC, V. Dinner daily. Map p 73.***

★ **The Forge** MIAMI BEACH *STEAKHOUSE* English oak paneling and Tiffany glass suggest high prices and haute cuisine, and that's exactly what you get at The Forge. Like the rest of the menu, appetizers are mostly classics, from Beluga caviar and baked onion soup to shrimp cocktail and escargot. When they're in season, order the stone crabs. For the main course, any of the seafood, chicken, or veal dishes are recommended, but The Forge is especially known for its award-winning steaks. Its wine selection is equally lauded—ask for a tour of the cellar. At the time of writing, The Forge was closed for renovations. It is set to reopen by fall or winter, but be sure to call ahead. ***432 Arthur Godfrey Rd. ☎ 305/538-8533. Main courses $25–$60. AE, DC, MC, V. Dinner daily. Map p 73.***

★ **Fratelli Lyon** DESIGN DISTRICT *ITALIAN* This Design District standout resides in a fabulously industrial modern furniture showroom. And while the uncomfortable-but-cool-looking chairs you sit on may be for sale at an astronomical price, when it comes to the wine and cheese, they're a bargain in comparison. Owned by a former caterer, Fratelli offers everything from a multi-tiered platter of antipasti and pizzas to salads and a delicious saffron risotto served with boneless *osso buco*. Fratelli is also popular for lunch. ***4141 NE 2nd Ave. ☎ 305/572-2901. Main courses $8–$25. AE, DC, DISC, MC, V. Lunch & dinner Mon–Sat; closed Sun. Map p 74.***

★ **Front Porch Café** SOUTH BEACH *BREAKFAST* Located in an unassuming, rather dreary-looking Art Deco hotel, the Front Porch Café is a relaxed local hangout known for cheap breakfasts. Some of the servers are attitudinal and lackadaisical, so this isn't the place to be if you're in a hurry. On weekends it's packed all day long and lines are the norm. Enjoy home-style French toast with bananas and walnuts, omelets, and fresh fruit. ***In the Penguin Hotel, 1418 Ocean Dr. ☎ 305/531-8300. Main courses $5–$18. AE, DC, DISC, MC, V. Breakfast, lunch & dinner daily. Map p 73.***

★★ **Garcia's Seafood Grille & Fish** DOWNTOWN *SEAFOOD* A good catch on the banks of the Miami River, Garcia's has a great waterfront setting and a simple yet tasty menu of fresh fish cooked in a number of ways—grilled, broiled, fried, or, the best in our opinion, in garlic or green sauce. Meals are quite a deal, served with green salad or grouper soup, and yellow rice or French fries. The complimentary fish-spread appetizer is also a nice touch. ***398 NW N. River Dr. ☎ 305/375-0765. Main courses $14–$23. AE, DC, DISC, MC, V. Lunch & dinner daily. Map p 74.***

★ **George's in the Grove** COCONUT GROVE *FRENCH* An urbane—and urban—chic French bistro, George's offers classics from ratatouille and steak frites to a very Miami mango tart tartin. Food is good, but the ambience is better; as the night goes on, music gets louder and a party scene ensues. ***3145 Commodore Plaza. ☎ 305/444-7878. Main courses $13–$40. AE, DC, MC, V. Dinner daily except Mon. Map p 76.***

★ **Grass** DESIGN DISTRICT *ASIAN/AMERICAN* At this restaurant-lounge, the priority is excellent, fresh cuisine. Signature dishes include ginger-lime-marinated grilled mahi-mahi, grass-fed grilled and smoked beef rib-eye, and wasabi-and-ginger-crusted wild salmon. The tiki-chic eatery surrounded by vines, bamboo, and cozy banquettes is all outdoors, so it's really weather-permitting, but when it's nice out, it's a stunning departure from the rest of Miami's ultra-modern restaurants. ***28 NE 40th St. ☎ 305/573-3355. Main courses $20–$80. AE, DC, MC, V. Dinner Mon–Sat. Map p 74.***

★★★ **Hy Vong** LITTLE HAVANA *VIETNAMESE* This Vietnamese cuisine combines the best of Asian and French cooking with spectacular results. Food at Hy Vong is elegantly simple and super spicy. Appetizers include small, tightly packed Vietnamese spring rolls and kimchi, a spicy, fermented cabbage. Star entrees include pastry-enclosed chicken with watercress cream-cheese sauce and fish in tangy mango sauce. ***3458 SW 8th St.*** ☎ ***305/446-3674. Main courses $7–$20. AE, DISC, MC, V. Dinner daily. Map p 76.***

★ **Icebox Cafe** SOUTH BEACH *DESSERT* Locals love this place for its homey comfort food—tuna melts, potpies, and eggs for breakfast, lunch, and dinner—but its desserts are why people really come here (Oprah Winfrey is a fan). Here you'll discover the best chocolate cake, pound cake, and banana-cream pies outside of your grandma's kitchen. ***1657 Michigan Ave.*** ☎ ***305/538-8448. Main courses & desserts $3–$10. AE, MC, V. Breakfast, lunch & dinner daily. Map p 73.***

★ **Joe Allen** SOUTH BEACH *AMERICAN* Located on the bay side of the beach, Joe Allen is conspicuously devoid of neon lights, valet parkers, and fashionable pedestrians. Inside, however, one discovers a hidden jewel: a stark yet elegant interior and no-nonsense, fairly priced, ample-portioned dishes such as meatloaf, pizza, fresh fish, and salads. The scene has a homey feel favored by locals looking to escape the hype without compromising quality. ***1787 Purdy Ave.*** ☎ ***305/531-7007. Main courses $15–$25. MC, V. Lunch & dinner daily. Map p 73.***

★★ **Joe's Stone Crab** SOUTH BEACH *SEAFOOD* Open only during stone-crab season (Oct–May), Joe's reels in the crowds with the freshest (though some disagree), meatiest stone crabs and their essential accouterments: creamed spinach and excellent sweet-potato fries. The claws come in medium, large, and jumbo. ***11 Washington Ave.*** ☎ ***305/673-0365. www.joesstonecrab.com. Entrees $8–$65. AE, DC, DISC, MC, V. Mid-Oct to mid-May lunch & dinner daily. Map p 73.***

★ **La Sandwicherie** SOUTH BEACH *SANDWICHES* This gourmet sandwich bar, open until the crack of dawn, caters to ravenous club kids, biker types, and the body artists who work in the tattoo parlor next door. For many people, in fact, no night of clubbing is complete without capping it off with a turkey sub from La Sandwicherie. ***229 14th***

Joe's Stone Crab's got claws in all sizes.

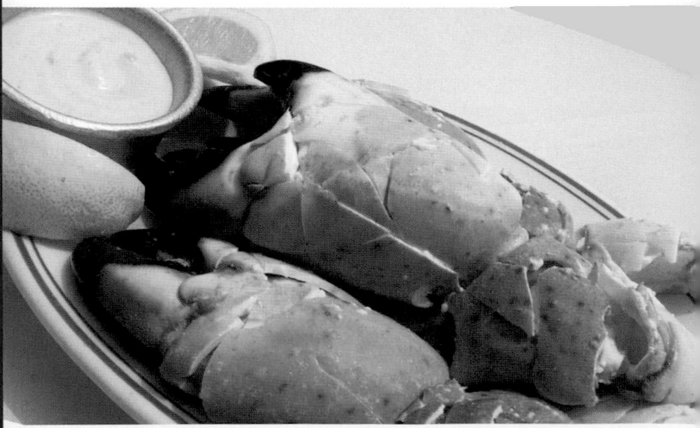

Late-night revelers are a fan of La Sandwicherie.

St. ☎ 305/532-8934. Sandwiches $6–$12. AE, MC, V. Breakfast, lunch & dinner daily. Map p 73.

★ **Meat Market** SOUTH BEACH *STEAKHOUSE* The focus at this newly opened restaurant is, as the name implies, the meat, served a la carte, but the seafood steals the show (try the sea bass or mahi-mahi). Appetizers include a heavenly Kobe tartar, and a raw bar features tuna tartar and smoked scallops. Portions are big, and the sommelier is there to help with wine selections. Service is stellar—unheard of on Lincoln Road. The space marries feminine (cream couches and pony-hair walls) and masculine touches (distressed wood), and a large Lucite light fixture bathes the room in its warmth. *915 Lincoln Rd. ☎ 305/532-0088. Entrees $25–$52. AE, DC, DISC, MC, V. Dinner daily. Map p 73.*

★★★ **Michael Mina's Bourbon Steak** AVENTURA *STEAKHOUSE* Reminiscent of something out of Las Vegas, everything here is massive, from the stunning all-glass wine cellar that takes up an entire wall to the sheer size of the place at 7,600 square feet (706 sq. m)—and then there are the prices. If you don't mind splurging, a meal at the star chef's first and only South Florida location is worth it. Start off with some oysters on the half shell—East Coast or West Coast, your choice—and then continue with the all-natural farm-raised angus beef, American Kobe beef, or actual Japanese Kobe beef—where a 6-ounce rib-eye will set you back $190. Side dishes are delicious—jalapeño creamed corn, truffled mac and cheese. Try not to fill up on the complimentary duck fat or potato focaccia bread with truffle butter and chives. *In the Fairmont Turnberry Isle & Club, 1999 W. Country Club Dr. ☎ 786/279-6600. Main courses $22–$190. AE, DC, DISC, MC, V. Dinner Mon–Sat; closed Sun. Map p 74.*

★★★ **Michael's Genuine Food & Drink** DESIGN DISTRICT *AMERICAN* The sleek yet unassuming dining room and serene courtyard seating are constantly abuzz with Design District hipsters, foodies, and celebrities thanks to chef/owner Michael Schwartz's vision for fabulous food. The food is stellar, a fresh mix of organic products, some from

Schwartz's own stash, including eggs hatched from his own hens. With an emphasis on products sourced from local growers and farmers, the menu, which changes daily, is divided into small, medium, large, and extra-large plates, all rather reasonably priced and extremely hard to choose from. *130 NE 40th St. ☎ 305/573-5550. www.michaelsgenuine.com. Main courses $14–$46. AE, DC, DISC, MC, V. Dinner Mon–Fri; dinner Sat–Sun. Map p 74.*

★★★ **Michy's** BISCAYNE CORRIDOR *LATIN* Star chef Michelle Bernstein left the fancy confines of the Mandarin Oriental Miami's Azul to open her own homey, 50-seat eatery on Miami's burgeoning Upper East Side. If you drive too fast, you'll miss the small storefront restaurant, a deceiving facade for a whimsical retro orange-and-blue interior where stellar small plates such as ham-and-blue-cheese croquettes are consumed in massive quantities. There's also a zingy ceviche; braised duck with Jerez and peaches; conch escargot-style in parsley, butter, and garlic; and sautéed sweetbreads with bacon and orange juice. There's nothing ordinary about Michy's, except for the fact that a reservation here is nearly impossible to score if not made weeks in advance. *6927 Biscayne Blvd. ☎ 305/759-2001. Reservations required. Main courses $15–$30. AE, DC, MC, V. Lunch & dinner Tues–Fri; Sat–Sun dinner. Map p 74.*

★ **Nemo** SOUTH BEACH *PAN ASIAN* Nemo is a funky, high-style eatery with an open kitchen and an outdoor courtyard canopied by trees and lined with an eclectic mix of model types and foodies. Among the reasons to eat in this restaurant: grilled Indian-spiced pork chop; grilled local mahi-mahi with citrus and grilled sweet-onion salad, kimchi glaze, basil, and crispy potatoes; and an inspired dessert menu that's not for the faint of calories. *100 Collins Ave. ☎ 305/532-4550. www.nemorestaurant.com. Main courses $26–$48. AE, MC, V. Lunch & dinner daily; brunch Sun. Map p 73.*

★ **News Cafe** SOUTH BEACH *AMERICAN* News Cafe is still *au courant,* albeit swarming with tourists. Unless it's appallingly hot or rainy out, you should wait for an outside table, where you can fully appreciate the experience. Service is abysmal and often arrogant (perhaps because the tip is included), but the menu is reliable, running the gamut from sandwiches and salads to pasta dishes and omelets. *800 Ocean Dr. ☎ 305/538-6397. Entrees $5–$20. AE, DC, MC, V. Breakfast, lunch & dinner daily. Map p 73.*

Sushi fans should not miss the famous Nobu.

It's all you can eat—and more—at Porcao.

★★★ **Nobu** SOUTH BEACH *SUSHI* Nobu has been hailed as one of the best sushi restaurants in the world, with always-packed eateries in New York, London, and Los Angeles. The Omakase, or Chef's Choice—a multi-course menu of the chef's choice—gets consistent raves. Although you won't wait long for your food to be cooked, you will wait forever to score a table. ***In the Shore Club Hotel, 1901 Collins Ave. ☎ 305/695-3232. Entrees $26–$70. AE, MC, V. Dinner daily. Map p 73.***

★★★ **Oceanaire** BRICKELL *SEAFOOD* Oceanaire is a pricey ocean liner–inspired chain known for fresh-caught fare. The elegant, streamlined dining room is always abuzz with power types and foodies looking for the freshest fish dishes in town. This is not always the case, but it's not everywhere in Miami where you can indulge in *guajillo* barbecue salmon with spicy crispy red onions or order Nairagi Marlin. Chef Sean Bernal is a rare talent (and was featured on Discovery Channel's hit reality show *The Deadliest Catch*). ***900 S. Miami Ave. ☎ 305/372-8862. Entrees $15–$30. AE, DC, MC, V. Dinner daily. Map p 74.***

★★★ **Ortanique on the Mile** CORAL GABLES *CARIBBEAN* Chef Cindy Hutson has perfected her tantalizing new-world Caribbean cuisine that also graces the menus of her two other Ortaniques in Washington, D.C., and Las Vegas. Start with the pumpkin bisque or the tropical mango salad, followed by the pan-sautéed Bahamian black grouper marinated in teriyaki and sesame oil, served with an *ortanique* (an orangelike fruit) orange-liqueur sauce and a lemon-orange boniato–sweet plantain mash. ***278 Miracle Mile. ☎ 305/446-7710. Entrees $19–$40. AE, DC, MC, V. Dinner daily. Map p 76.***

★★★ **Porcao** BRICKELL *BRAZILIAN STEAKHOUSE* The name sounds eerily like "pork out," which is what you'll be doing at this exceptional Brazilian *churrascaria* (the Portuguese translation of "steakhouse"). For about $45, you can feast on salads and meat *after* you sample the unlimited gourmet buffet, which includes such fillers as pickled quail eggs, marinated onions, and an entire pig. ***801 Brickell Bay Dr. ☎ 305/373-2777. Prix-fixe $45 adults, $22 children. AE, DC, MC, V. Lunch & dinner daily. Map p 74.***

★★★ **Prime 112** SOUTH BEACH *STEAKHOUSE* A celebrity-saturated, sleek steakhouse ambience and bustling bar (complete with dried strips of bacon in lieu of nuts) play second fiddle to the beef, which is arguably the best in the entire city. The 12-ounce filet mignon is seared to perfection and

Latin Cuisine at a Glance

In Little Havana for dinner? Many restaurants list menu items in English for the benefit of norteamericano diners. In case they don't, though, here are translations and suggestions for filling and delicious meals:

Arroz con pollo: Roast chicken served with saffron-seasoned yellow rice and diced vegetables.

Café Cubano: Very strong black coffee, served in thimble-size cups with lots of sugar. It's a real eye-opener.

Camarones: Shrimp.

Ceviche: Raw fish seasoned with spices and vegetables and marinated in vinegar and citrus to "cook" it.

Croquetas: Golden-fried croquettes of ham, chicken, or fish.

Paella: A Spanish dish of chicken, sausage, seafood, and pork mixed with saffron rice and peas.

Palomilla: Thinly sliced beef, similar to American minute steak, usually served with onions, parsley, and a mountain of french fries.

Pan Cubano: Long, white crusty Cuban bread. Ask for it tostada—toasted and flattened on a grill with lots of butter.

Picadillo: A rich stew of ground meat, brown gravy, peas, pimientos, raisins, and olives.

Plátano: A deep-fried, soft, mildly sweet banana.

Pollo asado: Roasted chicken with onions and a crispy skin.

Ropa vieja: A shredded beef stew whose name literally means "old clothes."

Sopa de pollo: Chicken soup, usually with noodles or rice.

Tapas: A general name for Spanish-style hors d'oeuvres, served in grazing-size portions.

can be enhanced with optional dipping sauces (for a price)—truffle, garlic herb, foie gras, and chipotle. *112 Ocean Dr.* ☎ *305/532-8112. www.prime112.com. Reservations a must. Entrees $20–$88. AE, DISC, MC, V. Lunch & dinner Mon–Fri; dinner Sat–Sun. Map p 73.*

★★ **Puerto Sagua** SOUTH BEACH *CUBAN* This brown-walled diner is one of the only old holdouts on South Beach. Its steady stream of regulars ranges from *abuelitos* (little old grandfathers) to local politicos to hipsters, who come for the food—good, if a little greasy. Some of the less heavy dishes are a superchunky fish soup with pieces of whole flaky grouper, seafood paella, marinated kingfish, or shrimp in garlic sauce. *700 Collins Ave.* ☎ *305/673-1115. Main courses $5–$24. AE, DC, MC, V. Breakfast, lunch & dinner daily. Map p 73.*

★ **Quattro** SOUTH BEACH *ITALIAN* Signature dishes on the menu include homemade fontina ravioli with white-truffle oil and veal wraps with melted Parmesan cheese and breadcrumbs. The wine list is all Italian and reasonably priced. The room is gorgeous, with dramatic lighting, chandeliers, and an all-glass bar. *1014 Lincoln Rd.* ☎ *305/531-4833. www.quattromiami.*

Puerto Sagua attracts colorful local characters.

com. Main courses $31–$50. AE, DC, MC, V. Lunch & dinner daily. Map p 73.

★ **River Oyster Bar** BRICKELL *SEAFOOD* River Oyster Bar is a buzzy and unpretentious spot for some of the best oysters in town, shipped in daily from all over the world. Other delicious dishes include pan fried Alaskan halibut with roasted-garlic chive and pickled asparagus; monkfish paella with chorizo, roasted peppers, and pigeon peas; and outstanding braised short ribs with creamy mac and cheese. ***15 SE 10th St.*** ☎ ***305/ 374-9693. Oysters $1–$10; entrees $15–$28. AE, MC, V. Lunch & dinner Mon–Fri; dinner Sat–Sun. Map p 74.***

★ **Rosa Mexicano** BRICKELL *MEXICAN* Stunning decor with a 15-foot (4.5m) waterfall and a great bar scene are two assets, but Rosa's use of serious spices and tableside guacamole preparation, served in a lava-rock bowl with homemade tortillas (they make them right there in the middle of the dining room) make this one of Miami's most talked about. Among the dishes: a Veracruz mole with mulatto, ancho, and pasilla chilis; crispy pork shank, slow-roasted for 6 hours, dipped in the deep-fryer, and served with mushroom-chipotle cream sauce; and red bean–chorizo chili. ***900 S. Miami Ave.*** ☎ ***786/425-1001. www.rosamexicano.com. Entrees $13–$30. AE, DC, MC, V. Lunch & dinner Mon–Fri; dinner Sat–Sun. Map p 74.***

★★★ **Smith & Wollensky** SOUTH BEACH *STEAKHOUSE* Although it's a chain steakhouse, Miami Beach's Smith & Wollensky

Smith & Wollensky in Miami is known for its steaks and waterfront location.

has a waterfront view that separates it from the rest. Inside seating is typical steakhouse—dark woods and so on—but make sure to request a table by the window so you can watch the cruise ships pass by as they leave the port. Outdoor seating, weather permitting, is resplendent, with a bar that doubles as command central for the happy-hour set on Friday nights. The menu here is a lot more basic, with a few chicken and fish choices and beef served about a dozen ways; the classic is the sirloin, seared lightly and served naked. Service is erratic, from highly professional to rudely aloof. *1 Washington Ave. (in South Pointe Park). ☎ 305/673-2800. www.smithandwollensky.com. Reservations recommended. Main courses $20–$50. AE, DC, DISC, MC, V. Mon–Sat noon–2am; Sun 11:30am–2am. Map p 73.*

★ **Van Dyke Cafe** SOUTH BEACH *AMERICAN* Van Dyke is a local favorite at which people-watching is a premium (like News Cafe), but attitude is practically nonexistent (unlike News Cafe). The menu is simple—sandwiches, salads, eggs, and so on—and the warm, wood-floored interior, upstairs jazz bar, accessible parking, and intense chocolate soufflé make it a less taxing alternative than News Cafe. *846 Lincoln Rd. ☎ 305/534-3600. www.thevandykecafe.com. Main courses $9–$20. AE, DC, MC, V. Breakfast, lunch & dinner daily. Map p 73.*

★ **Versailles** LITTLE HAVANA *CUBAN* Versailles brings together Miami's Cuban power brokers, who meet daily over *café con leche* to discuss the future of the Cuban exiles' fate. A glorified diner, the place sparkles with glass, chandeliers, murals, and mirrors meant to evoke the French palace. There's nothing fancy here—nothing French, either—just straightforward food from the home country. *3555 SW 8th St. ☎ 305/444-0240. Entrees $5–$20. DC, DISC, MC, V. Breakfast, lunch & dinner daily. Map p 76.*

★★★ **Wish** SOUTH BEACH *ITALIAN* Located in the stylish Todd Oldham–designed The Hotel, this is one of the most beautiful, romantic outdoor restaurants in South Beach. Chef Marco Ferraro, who has worked under the toque of Jean-Georges Vongerichten, has taken the restaurant to a new level with a menu he describes as "fresh, seasonal, light, and vibrant." He's putting it mildly. The Maine lobster ravioli is exquisite, as is the oven-roasted Kurobuta pork chop served with parsley puree and luscious stuffed eggplant. *At The Hotel, 801 Collins Ave. ☎ 305/531-2222. Main courses $28–$46. AE, DC, MC, V. Lunch & dinner daily. Map p 73.* ●

Gorgeous garden dining can be had at Wish.

6 The Best Nightlife

Nightlife Best Bets

Best **Bar Food**
★★ Clarke's, *840 1st St. (p 92)*

Most **Kitsch**
★ Purdy Lounge, *1811 Purdy Ave. (p 94)*

Best **Happy Hour**
★ Tobacco Road, *626 S Miami Ave. (p 100)*

Best **Late-Night Noshing**
★★ Segafredo Espresso, *1040 Lincoln Rd. (p 96)*

Best **View**
★ Plunge, *at the Gansevoort South, 2399 Collins Ave. (p 94)*

Best **Irish Pub**
★ Playwright Irish Pub, *1265 Washington Ave. (p 94)*

Best **Place to Watch Soccer**
★★ Churchill's, *5501 NE 2nd Ave. (p 100)*

Best **Rock Club**
★★ Rok Bar, *1905 Collins Ave. (p 95)*

Best **Beer Bar**
★★ The Abbey, *1115 16th St. (p 92)*

Miami's warm weather is perfect for rooftop bars.

Best **Jazz Club**
★★★ Upstairs at the Van Dyke Cafe, *846 Lincoln Rd. (p 100)*

Best **Dive Bar**
★ Mac's Club Deuce, *222 14th St. (p 94)*

Best **Lobby Bar**
★★ Rose Bar, *1685 Collins Ave. (p 96)*

Best **Salsa Club**
★★★ Hoy Como Ayer, *2212 SW 8th St. (p 101)*

Best **Champagne Bar**
★ Cozy, *500 S. Pointe Dr. (p 92)*

Best **Salsa Club for Novices**
★ Bongo's Cuban Café, *601 Biscayne Blvd. (p 97)*

Best **Bowling and Lounge Combo**
★★★ Lucky Strike, *1691 Michigan Ave. (p 93)*

Best **Flamenco Club**
★★★ Casa Panza, *1620 SW 8th St. (p 100)*

Best **Subterranean Celeb Lounge**
★★★ The Florida Room, *1685 Collins Ave. (p 93)*

Best **Escape from the Hype**
★★ The Room, *100 Collins Ave. (p 95)*

Best **Techno Club**
★★★ Club Space, *34 NE 11th St. (p 97)*

Best **Dance Club Where Nobody Dances**
★★★ SET, *320 Lincoln Rd. (p 98)*

Best **New Scene**
★★★ LIV and Blade, *in the Fontainebleau, 4441 Collins Ave. (p 98)*

Best **Lounge**
★★★ Mokai, *235 23rd St. (p 94)*

Previous page: South Beach's nightlife is a big draw for visitors, locals, and celebrities.

South Beach Nightlife

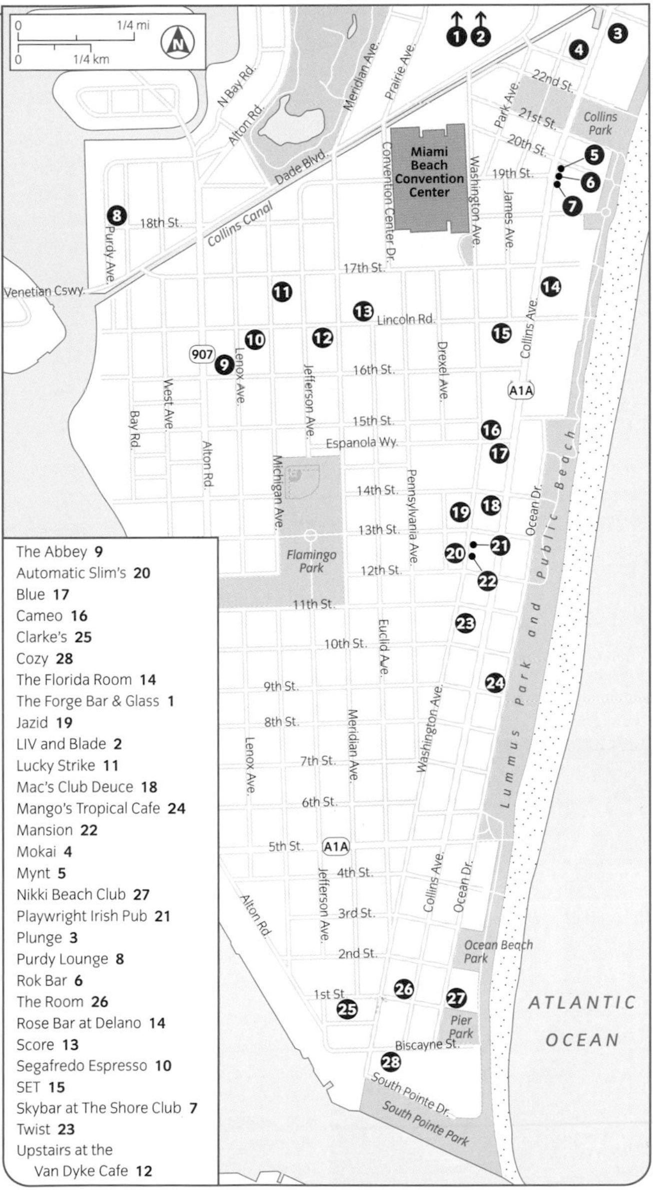
0
1/4 mi
0
1/4 km
N
Miami Beach Convention Center
Collins Park
Flamingo Park
Ocean Beach Park
Pier Park
South Pointe Park
Lummus Park and Public Beach
ATLANTIC OCEAN
N Bay Rd.
Alton Rd.
Meridian Ave.
Prairie Ave.
Dade Blvd.
Collins Canal
Convention Center Dr.
Washington Ave.
Park Ave.
James Ave.
22nd St.
21st St.
20th St.
19th St.
18th St.
17th St.
Lincoln Rd.
16th St.
15th St.
Espanola Wy.
14th St.
13th St.
12th St.
11th St.
10th St.
9th St.
8th St.
7th St.
6th St.
5th St.
4th St.
3rd St.
2nd St.
1st St.
Biscayne St.
South Pointe Dr.
Purdy Ave.
Venetian Cswy.
907
Lenox Ave.
West Ave.
Bay Rd.
Jefferson Ave.
Michigan Ave.
Drexel Ave.
Pennsylvania Ave.
Euclid Ave.
Collins Ave.
Ocean Dr.
A1A
The Abbey 9
Automatic Slim's 20
Blue 17
Cameo 16
Clarke's 25
Cozy 28
The Florida Room 14
The Forge Bar & Glass 1
Jazid 19
LIV and Blade 2
Lucky Strike 11
Mac's Club Deuce 18
Mango's Tropical Cafe 24
Mansion 22
Mokai 4
Mynt 5
Nikki Beach Club 27
Playwright Irish Pub 21
Plunge 3
Purdy Lounge 8
Rok Bar 6
The Room 26
Rose Bar at Delano 14
Score 13
Segafredo Espresso 10
SET 15
Skybar at The Shore Club 7
Twist 23
Upstairs at the Van Dyke Cafe 12

Miami **Nightlife A to Z**

Bars

★★ The Abbey SOUTH BEACH Dark, dank, and hard to find, this local microbrewery is a favorite for locals looking to escape the $20 candy-flavored martini scene. Best of all, there's never a cover and it's always open until 5am. *1115 16th St. ☎ 305/538-8110. Map p 91.*

★ Automatic Slim's SOUTH BEACH This is *the* bar where Ozzie and Harriet types become more like Ozzy and Sharon. As South Beach's most popular unpretentious bar, Automatic Slim's is indeed a slim space of bar, but it packs people in, thanks to an exhaustive list of cheap(er) drinks, lack of attitude, great rock music, and a decor that can only be described as white-trash chic. *1216 Washington Ave. ☎ 305/695-0795. Map p 91.*

★★ Badrutt's Place BRICKELL Owned by the same family that owns Switzerland's ritzy resort of the same name, this high-energy, high-style lounge and restaurant, complete with cozy velvet couches and an expansive outdoor terrace, is the place to be for champagne, foie gras, and a well-heeled crowd of Europeans, jet-setters, and scene shakers. *1250 S. Miami Ave. ☎ 305/415-0700. Map p 93.*

Lucky Strike makes for a twist on the usual night out.

★ Blue SOUTH BEACH The laid-back local scene here, set to a sultry soundtrack of deep soul and house music, has Miami's hipsters feeling the blues on a nightly basis from 10pm to 5am. This so-not-trendy-it's-trendy lounge is swathed in a pervasive color blue that will actually heighten your spirits as an eclectic haze of models, locals, and lounge lizards gather to commiserate over their dreaded trendy status. *222 Espanola Way. ☎ 305/534-1009. Map p 91.*

★★ Clarke's SOUTH BEACH This classy, brassy, and sassy Irish pub and restaurant in the chichi South of Fifth Street area of South Beach has become command central for everyone from Miami Heat basketball players to the Miami Beach police chief looking for cold beer and, surprisingly, a gourmet menu consisting of shepherd's pie, seared scallops, and the best burger in the 'hood. *840 1st St. ☎ 305/538-9885. www.clarkesmiamibeach.com. Map p 91.*

★ Cozy SOUTH BEACH A very French, very expensive piano bar in the South of Fifth neighborhood. Cozy lives up to its name in ambience with blood-red walls and chandeliers, but when it comes to the check, there's nothing cozy about it, with a cheese plate coming in at a whopping $50 and glasses of wine starting at $20. But if you're in the mood for a nightcap and some

Downtown Nightlife

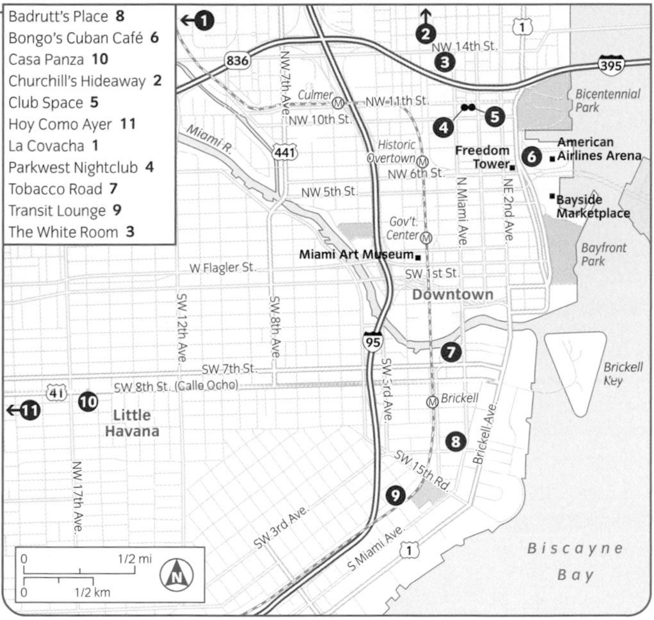

great live piano and surprise celebrity musicians (the Gypsy Kings drop in when in town), Cozy is worth the splurge. *500 S. Pointe Dr. ☎ 305/532-2699. Map p 91.*

★★★ **The Florida Room** SOUTH BEACH The Florida Room is a dimly chandelier-lit den where old-school Florida decor meets swanky cruise-ship lounge. Everyone from swanky sophisticates to the Golden Girls come here for a fancy night out. Designed by rocker Lenny Kravitz, the interior of this subterranean speakeasy is the antithesis of the sleek, stark hotel in which it resides. *In the Delano hotel, 1685 Collins Ave. ☎ 305/672-2000. Map p 91.*

★ **The Forge Bar and Glass** MIAMI BEACH The Forge hosts an unusual mix of the uptight and those who wear their clothes too tight. It's also where surgically altered ladies look for their cigar-chomping sugar daddies in a setting that's reminiscent of *Dynasty*. Call well in advance if you want to watch the parade of characters from a dinner table (p 80). The Forge owners also own **Glass,** a ritzier nightclub attached to the restaurant (they say it's a private club, but if you dine at the restaurant or are acquainted with someone in the know, you can get in). *432 41st St. ☎ 305/538-8533. Map p 91.*

★★★ **Lucky Strike** SOUTH BEACH Not just a bowling alley, but a flashy, splashy one, featuring a fantastic menu of above-average finger food, bars, big-screen TVs, and even celebrity bowlers. *1691 Michigan Ave. ☎ 305/532-0307. www.bowlluckystrike.com. Map p 91.*

Kick back with brews and pool at Mac's Club Deuce.

★ **Mac's Club Deuce** SOUTH BEACH Standing amid an oasis of trendiness, Mac's Club Deuce is the quintessential dive bar, with cheap drinks and a cast of characters ranging from your typical barfly to your atypical drag queen. It's got a well-stocked jukebox, friendly bartenders, and a pool table. Best of all, it's an insomniac's dream, open daily from 8am to 5am. *222 14th St. ☎ 305/673-9537. Map p 91.*

★★★ **Mokai** SOUTH BEACH This chic, cozy lounge is the brainchild of several South Beach nightlife impresarios who know how to attract the A-list. Reminiscent of an après-ski bar in Aspen, Mokai's stone walls, dim lighting, and plush leather couches are upscale reminders that elegant slumming doesn't come cheap. Drink prices are expectedly high, but it's the price you pay for hanging out with celebrities or the visiting DJs who spin everything from bar mitzvah kitsch to deep house. *235 23rd St. ☎ 305/531-4166. www.mokaimiami.com. Map p 91.*

★★★ **Mynt** SOUTH BEACH A massive 6,000-square-foot (557 sq. m) place, Mynt is nothing more than a huge living room in which models, celebrities, and assorted hangers-on bask in the green glow to the beat of very loud lounge and dance music. If you want to dance—or move, for that matter—this is not the place in which to do so. Unless you know the person at the door, be prepared to be ridiculed, emasculated, and socially shattered, as you may be forced to wait outside upward of an hour (it's not worth it). Wait next door at the Greek place for a celebrity sighting, since you'll have a better chance of seeing people from there instead of just waiting in the melee at the door. *1921 Collins Ave. ☎ 786/276-6132. Map p 91.*

★ **Playwright Irish Pub** SOUTH BEACH A great pre- or post-club spot, Playwright serves up pints of Guinness, soccer matches, and, from time to time, live music. *1265 Washington Ave. ☎ 305/534-0667. Map p 91.*

★ **Plunge** SOUTH BEACH Possibly the best thing about the Gansevoort South, Plunge is the hotel's rockin' rooftop pool lounge, where on any given day or night, scantily clad scene (and bikini) chasers can be found either in or out of the water, sipping colorful cocktails to the tune of DJ-spun music. *2399 Collins Ave. ☎ 305/604-1000. Map p 91.*

★ **Purdy Lounge** SOUTH BEACH With the exception of a wall of lava lamps, Purdy is not unlike your best friend's basement, featuring a pool table and a slew of board games; it even has a bingo and spelling-bee night. Because it's a no-nonsense bar with relatively cheap cocktails (by South Beach standards), Purdy gets away with not having a star DJ or fancy bass-heavy Bose sound system. A CD player somehow does the trick. With no cover and no attitude, a line is inevitable (it gets crowded inside), so be prepared to wait. Saturday night has become the preferred night for locals, while Friday night's happy hour draws a young professional crowd on the prowl. *1811 Purdy Ave.* ☎ *305/531-4622. Map p 91.*

★★ **Rok Bar** SOUTH BEACH Larger-than-life rocker Tommy Lee has assembled a motley Miami crew at this paradox of a bar that combines down-'n'-dirty rock 'n' roll with the swank comforts of a chic lounge. The place is claustrophobic, with limited seating, high-priced drinks, and an oxymoronic soundtrack of Lynyrd Skynyrd, Michael Jackson, and Kid Rock. *1905 Collins Ave.* ☎ *305/538-7171. Map p 91.*

★★ **The Room** SOUTH BEACH It's beer and wine only at this South of Fifth hideaway, where locals and NY expats (there are a few Rooms in NYC) come to get away from the insanity just a few blocks away. The beer selection is comprehensive, with brews from almost everywhere in the world (the wine is not so great). The tiny, industrial-style, candlelit spot doesn't have a DJ—just a CD player spinning indie tunes—or those pesky Paris Hilton sightings. *100 Collins Ave.* ☎ *305/531-6061. Map p 91.*

Celebrities are drawn to Mokai's lush lounges.

Cocktails come at a high price at the Rose Bar.

★★ **Rose Bar** SOUTH BEACH If every rose has its thorn, the thorn at this painfully chic hotel bar is the excruciatingly high price of cocktails. Otherwise, the crowd here is full of the so-called glitterati and other assorted poseurs who view life through (Italian-made) rose-colored glasses. ***In the Delano hotel, 1685 Collins Ave. ☎ 305/672-2000. Map p 91.***

★ **Score** SOUTH BEACH There's a reason this Lincoln Road hotbed of gay activity is called Score. In addition to the huge pickup scene, Score offers a multitude of bars, dance floors, lounge areas, and outdoor tables, in case you need to come up for air. Sunday afternoon tea dances are legendary. ***727 Lincoln Rd. ☎ 305/535-1111. www.scorebar.net. Map p 91.***

★★ **Segafredo Espresso** SOUTH BEACH Although Segafredo is technically a cafe, it has become an integral part of Miami's nightlife as command central for Euros who miss that very special brand of European cafe society. This is the place to hear great European lounge music, sip a few cocktails, snack on delicious sandwiches and pizza, and sit outside and people-watch. Although South Beach boasts the original, another Segafredo—with different owners, a larger food menu, and separate nightclub—is open in the Brickell Area at 1421 S. Miami Ave., and another is slated to open on Collins Avenue in the South of Fifth area sometime in 2009. ***1040 Lincoln Rd. ☎ 305/673-0047. Map p 91.***

★★ **Skybar at The Shore Club** SOUTH BEACH Skybar lives up to its name in terms of loftiness; something this place has perfected better than anyone else, whether at its original L.A. location or the sprawling South Beach location at the Shore Club. If you're not a hotel guest, not Beyoncé, or not on the "list," or if you're a guy with several other guys and no girls, forget about it. The Skybar is basically the entire backyard area of the Shore Club, consisting of several areas, including the Moroccan-themed garden area, the hip-hop-themed indoor Red Room, the Sand Bar by the beach, and the Rum Bar by the pool. Sunday afternoon pool parties are a magnet for celebs and locals alike. ***1901 Collins Ave. ☎ 305/695-3100. Map p 91.***

★★ **Transit Lounge** BRICKELL It's hard to locate, but once you find Transit Lounge, you'll be happy you did. Reminiscent of what locals describe as "a real big-city lounge,"

Transit is cavernous, featuring a huge bar, tons of cozy couches and tables, board games, a funky crowd, and, hallelujah, live music. *1729 SW 1st Ave.* ☎ *305/377-4628.* *Map p 93.*

★ **Twist** SOUTH BEACH One of the most popular and longest-running gay bars (and hideaways) on South Beach, this recently expanded bar (which is literally right across the street from the police station) has a casual yet lively atmosphere. *1057 Washington Ave.* ☎ *305/538-9478. www.twistsobe.com.* *Map p 91.*

Dance Clubs

★ **Bongo's Cuban Café** DOWNTOWN Gloria Estefan's latest hit in the restaurant business pays homage to the sights, sounds, and cuisine of pre-Castro Cuba, and on Friday after 11pm and Saturday after 11:30pm, it's transformed into the city's hottest 21-and-over salsa nightclub. Cover charges can be hefty, but consider it your ticket to an astounding show of some of the best salsa dancers in the city. Prepare yourself for standing room only. Salsa lessons are also available. *601 Biscayne Blvd.* ☎ *786/777-2100. $10–$20 cover.* *Map p 93.*

Cameo SOUTH BEACH Still haunted by the ghost of clubs past, the space formerly known as crobar has undergone much-needed renovations and reopened as Cameo, its original incarnation. Though not as see-and-be-seen as it used to be, it still boasts a supersonic sound system, star DJs, and plenty of VIP seating. Cameo also has a club-within-a-club upstairs known as **Vice.** *1445 Washington Ave.* ☎ *305/531-8225. $20–$25 cover.* *Map p 91.*

★★★ **Club Space** DOWNTOWN Clubland hits the mainland with this cavernous downtown warehouse of a club. With more than 30,000 square feet (2,787 sq. m) of dance space, you can spin around without having to worry about banging into someone. On Saturday and Sunday nights, the party usually extends to the next morning, sometimes as late as 10am. Known as the venue of choice for world-renowned DJs, Club Space sometimes charges ludicrous admission fees to cover its hefty price tags. ***Note:*** Club Space doesn't really get going until around 3am. Call for more information, as it doesn't have a concrete schedule. *34 NE 11th St.* ☎ *305/372-9378. www.clubspace.com. $10–$50 cover.* *Map p 93.*

Learn from some of salsa's best at Bongo's Cuban Café.

Blade is one of the newest—and hottest—of Miami's night spots.

★★★ LIV and Blade MIAMI BEACH The latest in Miami's celebrity-saturated nightlife, LIV (as in "celebrities live for LIV") and Blade are the recently revamped Fontainebleau's dance club and subterranean lounge/pool bar. Because they're new, they're at the top of the A-list. *4441 Collins Ave. ☎ 305/538-2000. www.fontainebleau.com. $10–$50 cover. Map p 91.*

★ Mansion SOUTH BEACH This massive multilevel lounge is entirely "VIP," meaning you'd best know someone to get in or else you'll be among the masses outside. Live DJs, models, and celebrities galore, plus high ceilings, wood floors, brick walls, and a decidedly nonsmoky interior, make this a *must* on the list of see-and-be-scenesters. *1235 Washington Ave. ☎ 305/531-5535. www.theopiumgroup.com. $10–$50 cover. Map p 91.*

Nikki Beach Club SOUTH BEACH What the Playboy Mansion is to L.A., the Nikki Beach Club is to South Beach. The allure is mostly for visiting tourists, who love to gawk at half-naked ladies and men venturing into the daylight on Sunday (around 4pm, which is ungodly in this town) to see, be seen, and, at times, be obscene. At night, it's very "Brady Bunch goes to Hawaii," with a sexy tiki hut/Polynesian style, albeit rated R. *101 Ocean Dr. ☎ 305/538-1111. www.nikkibeach.com. $10–$20 cover. Map p 91.*

★ Parkwest Nightclub DOWNTOWN A 6,000-square-foot (557 sq. m) dance and lounge palace, Parkwest features the usual top-of-the-line sound system and an unusual LED wall, the only one of its size in South Florida. With five bars—two of the most popular are **Stereo** and **Rehab,** the club's indie-rock-inspired dance lounge—VIP areas, and lounge seating throughout the space, Parkwest is for the hardcore clubgoer. *30 NE 11th St. ☎ 305/350-7444. www.stereomiami.com. $10–$50 cover. Map p 93.*

★★★ SET SOUTH BEACH The Opium Group's undisputed "it" child, SET is *the* place to be, at least at the time of this writing. A luxurious lounge with chandeliers and design mag–worthy decor is always full of trendsetters, celebs, and wannabes. Where you really want to be, however, is upstairs in the private VIP room. A classy place that doesn't designate the behavior of its patrons, SET is also known for a ruthless door policy. Ask your hotel concierge to get you in, or else you may find yourself standing on the wrong side of the velvet ropes. *320 Lincoln Rd. ☎ 305/531-2800. www.setmiami.com. $10–$50 cover. Map p 91.*

Stepping Out in Miami

- Nightlife on South Beach doesn't really get going until after 11pm. As a result, you may want to consider taking what is known as a disco nap so that you'll be fully charged until the wee hours.
- If you're unsure of what to wear out on South Beach, your safest bet is anything black.
- Do not try to tip the doormen manning the velvet ropes. That will only make you look desperate, and you'll find yourself standing outside for what will seem like an ungodly amount of time. Instead, try to land your name on the ever-present guest list by calling the club early in the day yourself or, better yet, having the concierge at your hotel do it for you. If you don't have connections and you find yourself without a concierge, then act assertive, not surly, at the velvet rope, and your patience will usually be rewarded with admittance. If all else fails—for men, especially—surround yourself with a few leggy model types, and you'll be noticed quicker.
- If you are a man going out with a group of men, unless you're going to a gay bar, you will most likely not get into any South Beach hot spot unless you are with women.
- Finally, have fun. It may look like serious business when you're on the outside, but once you're in, it's another story. Attacking Clubland with a sense of humor is the best approach to a successful, memorable evening out.

The White Room DOWNTOWN Yet another cavernous, warehousey cocktail hall featuring 6,000 square feet (557 sq. m) of outdoor space and 4,500 square feet (418 sq. m) of indoor space, where the long-running Britpop-themed Pop Life takes up residence every Saturday. ***1306***

The celebrity hangout SET can be hard to get into, but worth the wait.

Happy hour specials and a chill outdoor patio draw crowds to Tobacco Road.

N. Miami Ave. ☎ 305/995-5050. www.whiteroommiami.com. $5–$20 cover. Map p 93.

Live Music

★★ Churchill's Hideaway LITTLE HAITI British expatriate Dave Daniels couldn't live in Miami without a true English-style pub, so he opened Churchill's Hideaway, the city's premier space for live rock music. Filthy and located in a rather unsavory neighborhood, Churchill's is committed to promoting and extending the lifeline of the lagging local music scene. A fun, no-frills crowd hangs out here. Bring earplugs with you, as it is deafening once the music starts. Monday is open-mic night, while Wednesday is reserved for ladies' wrestling. *5501 NE 2nd Ave. ☎ 305/757-1807. www.churchillspub.com. Free–$10 cover. Map p 93.*

★ Jazid SOUTH BEACH Smoky, sultry, and illuminated by flickering candelabras, Jazid is the kind of place where you'd expect to hear Sade's "Smooth Operator" on constant rotation. Instead, you'll hear live jazz (sometimes acid jazz), soul, and funk. An eclectic mix of mellow folks convenes here for a much-needed respite from the surrounding Washington Avenue mayhem. *1342 Washington Ave. ☎ 305/673-9372. www.jazid.net. Free–$10 cover. Map p 91.*

★ Tobacco Road DOWNTOWN Al Capone used to hang out here when it was a speakeasy. Now locals flock here to see local bands perform, as well as national acts such as George Clinton and the P-Funk All-Stars, Koko Taylor, and the Radiators. Tobacco Road (the proud owner of Miami's very first liquor license) is small and gritty, and meant to be that way. *626 S. Miami Ave. ☎ 305/374-1198. www.tobacco-road.com. $5–$20 cover. Map p 93.*

★★★ Upstairs at the Van Dyke Cafe SOUTH BEACH The cafe's jazz bar, located on the second floor, resembles a classy speakeasy in which local jazz performers play to an intimate, enthusiastic crowd of mostly adults and sophisticated young things, who often huddle at the small tables until the wee hours. *846 Lincoln Rd. ☎ 305/534-3600. www.thevandykecafe.com. $5–$10 cover. Map p 91.*

Latin Clubs

★★★ Casa Panza LITTLE HAVANA This *casa* is one of Little Havana's liveliest and most popular nightspots.

Every Tuesday, Thursday, and Saturday night, Casa Panza becomes the House of Flamenco, with shows at 8 and 11pm. You can either enjoy a flamenco show or strap on your own dancing shoes. Enjoy a fantastic Spanish meal or a glass of sangria before the show. Open until 4am, Casa Panza is a hot spot for young Latin club kids and, occasionally, a few older folks who are so taken by the music and the scene that they've failed to realize it's well past their bedtime. *1620 SW 8th St.* ☎ *305/643-5343. www.casapanza.com. Map p 93.*

★★★ **Hoy Como Ayer** LITTLE HAVANA Formerly known as Cafe Nostalgia, Hoy Como Ayer was extremely popular with old-timers in its Cafe Nostalgia incarnation, and is now experiencing a resurgence among the younger generation. Its Thursday night party, Fuacata (slang for "Pow!"), is a magnet for Latin hipsters, featuring classic Cuban music mixed with modern DJ-spun sound effects. *2212 SW 8th St.* ☎ *305/541-2631. $10 cover. Map p 93.*

★★★ **La Covacha** WEST MIAMI This hut, located virtually in the middle of nowhere (West Miami), is the hottest Latin joint in the entire city. Sunday features the best in Latin rock, with local and international acts. But the shack is really jumping on weekend nights, when the place is open until 5am. Friday is *the* night here, so much so that the owners had to place a red velvet rope out front to maintain some semblance of order. Do not wear silk here, as you *will* sweat. *10730 NW 25th St. at NW 107th Ave.* ☎ *305/594-3717. www.lacovacha.com. $10–$20 cover. Map p 93.*

The Rhythm Is Gonna Get You

Before you hit the salsa clubs, brush up on your moves with lessons at the following:

Instructors from Latin Groove Dance Studios are on hand Thursday and Friday nights at **Bongo's Cuban Café** (p 97) to help you (for free) keep up with the pros who grace the dance floor here.

At **Ballet Flamenco La Rosa** (in the Performing Arts Network [PAN] building; 13126 W. Dixie Hwy.; ☎ 305/899-7730), you can learn to flamenco, salsa, or merengue. This is the only professional flamenco company in the area. Classes are $15.

Nobody teaches salsa like **Luz Pinto** (☎ 305/868-9418). She teaches 7 days a week, and you'll learn cool turns easily. She charges $50 for a private lesson for up to four people, and $10 per person for a group lesson. She also teaches group classes at PAN on Miami Beach. Although she teaches everything from ballroom to merengue, her specialty is Casino-style salsa, popularized in the 1950s in Cuba, Pinto's homeland.

Angel Arroyo has been teaching salsa to the clueless out of his home (16467 NE 27th Ave.; ☎ 305/949-7799) for the past 10 years. Just $10 will buy you an hour's time. He traditionally teaches Monday and Wednesday nights, but call ahead to check for any schedule and rate changes.

Winter Music Conference

Every March, Miami is besieged by the most unconventional conventioneers the city has ever seen. These fiercely dedicated souls descend upon the city in a very audible way, with dark circles under their eyes and bleeps, blips, and scratches that can wake the dead. No, we're not talking about a Star Trek convention, but, rather, the Winter Music Conference (WMC), the world's biggest and most important gathering of DJs, remixers, agents, artists, and pretty much anyone who makes a dime off of the booming electronic music industry hailing from more than 60 countries from all over the world. But unlike most conventions, this one is completely interactive and open to the paying public as South Beach and Miami's hottest clubs transform into showcases for the various audio wares. For 5 consecutive days and nights, DJs, artists, and software producers play for audiences comprised of A&R reps, talent scouts, and locals just along for the ride. Parties take place everywhere, from hotel pools to street corners. The WMC is worth checking out if you get ecstatic over names such as Hex Hector, Paul Oakenfold, Ultra Naté, Chris Cox, and Mark Ronson, among many, many others. For more information on WMC events, go to www.wmcon.com.

★★★ Mango's Tropical Cafe SOUTH BEACH One of the most popular spots on Ocean Drive, this outdoor enclave of Latin liveliness shakes with the intensity of a Richter-busting earthquake. Mango's is *Cabaret,* Latin style. Nightly live Brazilian and Latin music, not to mention scantily clad male and female dancers, draws huge gawking crowds in from the sidewalk. Incognito international musicians often lose their anonymity and jam with the house band on stage. Claustrophobics should avoid this spot. *900 Ocean Dr. ☎ 305/673-4422. www.mangostropicalcafe.com. $10–$20 cover. Map p 91.* ●

Party, Latin style, at Hoy Como Ayer.

7 The Best Arts & Entertainment

Arts & Entertainment Best Bets

Best Ballet
★★★ Miami City Ballet, *2200 Liberty Ave. (p 108)*

Best Modern Dance
★★★ Miami Contemporary Dance Co., *5101 Collins Ave. (p 108)*

Best Children's Theater
★★★ Actors' Playhouse at Miracle Theatre, *280 Miracle Mile (p 110)*

Best Theater for Fellini Fans
★★★ Miami Beach Cinematheque, *512 Espanola Way (p 109)*

Best Latin Theater
★★★ Manuel Artime Theater, *900 SW 1st St. (p 111)*

Best Choir
★★★ Seraphic Fire, *78 E. Washington St. (p 108)*

Best Opera
★★★ Florida Grand Opera, *Adrienne Arsht Center, 1300 Biscayne Blvd. (p 109)*

Best Avant Garde Theater Company
★★★ Miami Light Project, *3000 Biscayne Blvd. (p 111)*

Best Improv Comedy
★★ Laughing Gas, *4129 Laguna St. (p 108)*

Best Outdoor Concert Venue
Bayfront Park Amphitheater, *301 N. Biscayne Blvd. (p 109)*

Best Outdoor Sporting Event
★★★ Miami Beach Polo World Cup, *at The Setai, 2001 Collins Ave. (p 112)*

Best Venue for Popular Music
★★★ Fillmore Miami Beach, *1700 Washington Ave. (p 110)*

Best Sports Experience
★★★ University of Miami Hurricanes, *Dolphin Stadium, 2269 NW 199th St. (p 111)*

Ballet Flamenco La Rosa.

Previous page: Dolphin Stadium plays host to both the Miami Dolphins and the Miami Hurricanes.

South Beach Arts & Entertainment

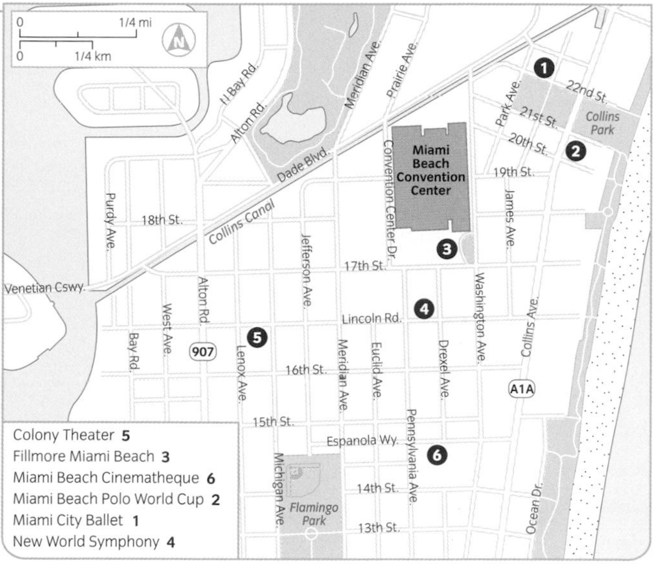

Coral Gables Arts & Entertainment

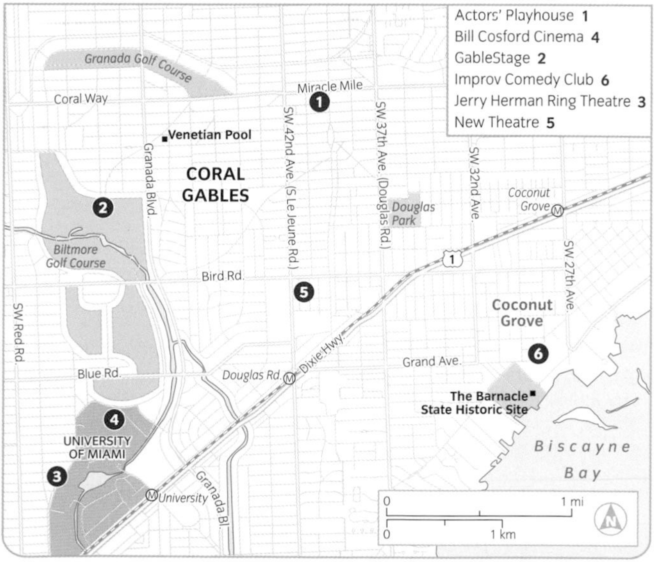

Miami Arts & Entertainment

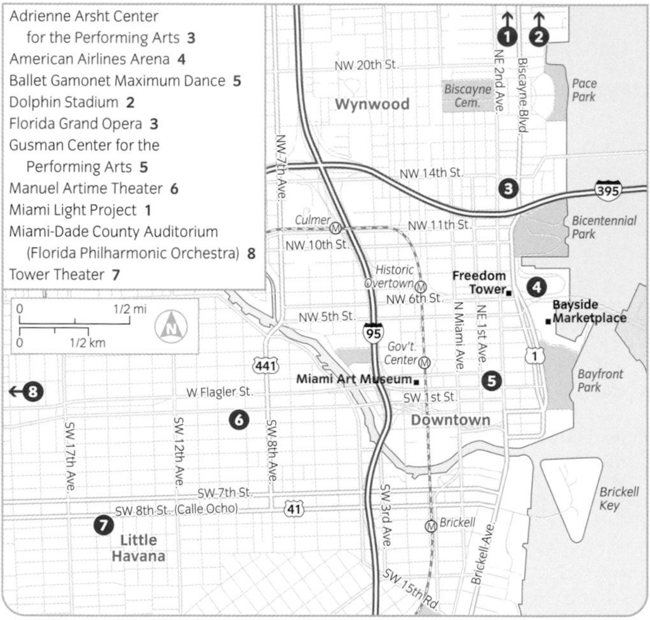

Classical Music Venues & Concerts

★ Adrienne Arsht Center for the Performing Arts DOWNTOWN The Adrienne Arsht Center for the Performing Arts opened in late 2006 after a whopping $446 million tab. In 2008, philanthropist Adrienne Arsht donated $30 million to the financially troubled center, which includes the 2,400-seat **Sanford and Dolores Ziff Ballet Opera House** and the 2,200-seat **Knight Concert Hall,** venues for the **Concert Association of Florida, Florida Grand Opera, Miami City Ballet, New World Symphony,** and an array of performances ranging from Broadway musicals to urban music. The **Studio Theater,** a flexible black-box space designed for up to 200 seats, hosts intimate performances of contemporary theater, dance, music, cabaret, and other entertainment. The **Peacock Education Center** acts as a catalyst for arts education and enrichment programs for children and adults. Finally, the **Plaza for the Arts** is a magnificent setting for outdoor entertainment, social celebrations, and informal community gatherings. Designed by world-renowned architect Cesar Pelli, the center is the focal point of a planned Arts, Media, and Entertainment District in mid-Miami. The complex is wrapped in limestone, slate, decorative stone, stainless steel, glass curtain walls, and tropical landscaping, and was completed in mid-2006. The biggest joke in town, however, is that after spending all that money, the planners forgot to

The Adrienne Arsht Center houses many cultural outlets.

include parking facilities. As a result, valet parking is available for $10 to $20, or you can park at the Marriott nearby; to make things easy, just take a cab. *1300 Biscayne Blvd.* ☎ *786/468-2000. www.arshtcenter.org. Map p 106.*

★ Florida Philharmonic Orchestra CORAL GABLES AND DOWNTOWN South Florida's premier symphony orchestra, under the direction of James Judd, presents a full season of classical and pops programs interspersed with several children's and contemporary popular music performances. The Philharmonic performs downtown in the Gusman Center for the Performing Arts and at the Miami-Dade County Auditorium. ☎ *800/226-1812. Tickets $15–$60. Map p 106.*

★★ Gusman Center for the Performing Arts DOWNTOWN In addition to hosting the Florida Philharmonic Orchestra and the Miami Film Festival, the elegant Gusman Center features pop concerts, plays, film screenings, and special events. The auditorium was built as the Olympia Theater in 1926, and its ornate palace interior is typical of that era, complete with fancy columns, a huge pipe organ, and twinkling "stars" on the ceiling. *174 E. Flagler St.* ☎ *773/372-0925. www.gusmancenter.org. Map p 106.*

★★★ New World Symphony SOUTH BEACH This organization, led by artistic director Michael Tilson Thomas, is a stepping stone for gifted young musicians seeking professional careers. The orchestra specializes in innovative, energetic performances, and often features

New World Symphony often performs at the Adrienne Arsht Center.

renowned guest soloists and conductors. The season lasts from October to May, during which time there are many free concerts. *541 Lincoln Rd.* ☎ *305/673-3331. www.nws.org. Tickets free–$60. Map p 105.*

★★★ **Seraphic Fire** MIAMI A fabulous choir specializing in Renaissance and baroque music, but they've also performed with Latin pop star Shakira. ☎ *305/476-0260. www.seraphicfire.org. Tickets $35.*

Comedy

★★★ **Improv Comedy Club** COCONUT GROVE Big-name comics attempt to kill at Miami's only bona fide comedy supper club. *3390 Mary St.* ☎ *305/441-8200. www.miamiimprov.com. Tickets $30–$50. Map p 105.*

★★ **Laughing Gas Improv** VARIOUS Miami's very own Second City, featuring hilarious 90-minute improv shows that rely on audience participation. ☎ *305/461-1161. www.laughinggasimprov.com. Tickets $10.*

Dance

★★★ **Ballet Flamenco La Rosa** MIAMI For a taste of local Latin flavor, see this lively troupe perform impressive flamenco and other styles of Latin dance on Miami stages. ☎ *305/899-7729. www.panmiami.org. Tickets $18–$20.*

★★★ **Miami City Ballet** SOUTH BEACH This artistically acclaimed and innovative company, directed by Edward Villella, features a repertoire of more than 60 ballets, many by George Balanchine, and has had more than 20 world premieres. The company's three-story center features eight rehearsal rooms, a ballet school, a boutique, and ticket offices. The City Ballet season runs from September to April. *2200 Liberty Ave.* ☎ *305/929-7010. www.miamicityballet.org. Tickets $19–$175. Map p 105.*

★★★ **Miami Contemporary Dance Co.** MIAMI The city's premier modern dance company helmed by artistic director Ray Sullivan, whose signature moves integrate traditional forms with

Miami Beach Cinematheque screens films in an intimate setting.

modern choreography. *5101 Collins Ave. ☎ 305/538-2988. www.miamicontemporarydance.net.*

★★★ **Momentum Dance Company** MIAMI Another excellent modern dance group, Momentum often features works by the likes of Isadora Duncan. Best of all, each show ends with a workshop for those who want to cut it up on the dance floor. *☎ 305/858-7002. www.momentumdance.com.*

Film

★★★ Bill Cosford Cinema

CORAL GABLES This well-endowed little theater has been revamped and boasts high-tech projectors, air-conditioning, and a new decor. It sponsors independent films as well as lectures by visiting filmmakers and movie stars. It also hosts the African American Film Festival, a Student Film Festival, and collaborations with the Fort Lauderdale Festival. *University of Miami. ☎ 305/284-4861. Tickets $6–$8. Map p 105.*

★★★ **Miami Beach Cinematheque** SOUTH BEACH This is the kind of place where people who call movies "films" like to hang out, with comfy couches and very arty foreign, domestic, and classic flicks. Directors, producers, and other film honchos have been known to make appearances here for various celluloid homages and theme nights. *508 Espanola Way. ☎ 305/673-4567. www.mbcinema.com. Tickets $8–$10. Map p 105.*

★★ **Tower Theater** LITTLE HAVANA This is a historic two-screen movie theater showing old-school and first-run movies in Spanish with English subtitles (sometimes) and vice versa. *1508 SW 8th St. ☎ 305/649-2960. http://www.mdc.edu/culture/tower.htm. Tickets free–$5. Map p 106.*

The Tower Theater shows Spanish-language films.

Opera

★★★ Florida Grand Opera

DOWNTOWN Around for more than 60 years, this company regularly features singers from top houses in both America and Europe. All productions are sung in their original language and staged with projected English supertitles. Tickets become scarce when Placido Domingo comes to town. The season runs roughly from November to April, with five performances each week. In 2007, the opera moved into more upscale headquarters in the Sanford and Dolores Ziff Ballet Opera House at the Arsht Center. *1300 Biscayne Blvd. ☎ 305/372-7611. www.fgo.org. Tickets $20–$135. Map p 106.*

Pop & Rock Venue

The Bayfront Park Amphitheater Located within Bayfront Park, the heart of downtown Miami, this is managed and operated by big name headliner wrangler Live Nation. It is currently undergoing renovations and is expected to reopen in June of 2009. *301 North Biscayne Blvd.* ☎ *305/358-7550. www.bayfrontparkmiami.com.*

★★★ Fillmore Miami Beach SOUTH BEACH In addition to its very modern Hard Rock–meets–Miami Beach decor, complete with requisite bars, chandeliers, and an homage to the original legendary Fillmore in San Francisco, Fillmore, which was taken over by Live Nation, brings major talent to the beach, from Kid Rock and Fall Out Boy to comediennes Sara Silverman and Lisa Lampanelli. Fillmore also hosts various awards shows, from the Food Network Awards to the Fox Sports Awards. *1700 Washington Ave. at 17th St.* ☎ *305/673-7300. Map p 105.*

Theater

★★★ kids Actors' Playhouse CORAL GABLES This is a grand 1948 Art Deco movie palace with a 600-seat main theater and a smaller theater/rehearsal hall that hosts a number of excellent musicals for children throughout the year. In addition to these two theaters, the Playhouse recently added a 300-seat children's balcony theater. *280 Miracle Mile.* ☎ *305/444-9293. www.actorsplayhouse.org. Tickets $27–$40. Map p 105.*

★★★ Colony Theater SOUTH BEACH An architectural showpiece of the Art Deco District, the Colony reopened in 2006 after a $4.3 million renovation that added wing and fly space, improved access for those with disabilities, and restored the lobby to its original Art Deco look. It's the home to various theater and comedy shows. *1040 Lincoln Rd.* ☎ *305/674-1040. www.colonytheater.com. Tickets vary. Map p 105.*

★★★ GableStage CORAL GABLES This theater stages at least one Shakespearean play, one classic, and one contemporary piece a year. The well-regarded theater usually

Manuel Artime Theater hosts various Latin performers throughout the year.

tries to secure the rights to a national or local premiere as well. *At the Biltmore Hotel, 1200 Anastasia Ave. ☎ 305/445-1119. www.gablestage.org. Tickets $15–$45. Map p 105.*

★ Jerry Herman Ring Theatre CORAL GABLES The University of Miami Department of Theater Arts uses this stage for advanced-student productions of comedies, dramas, and musicals. Faculty and guest actors are regularly featured, as are contemporary works by local playwrights. Performances are usually scheduled Tuesday through Saturday during the academic year. In the summer, don't miss "Summer Shorts," a selection of superb one-acts. *University of Miami. ☎ 305/284-3355. Tickets $16–$18. Map p 105.*

★★★ Manuel Artime Theater LITTLE HAVANA Latin opera stars, Brazilian bossa nova divas, and even Argentinean folk singers have been known to perform here. *900 SW 1st St. ☎ 305/575-5057. www.manuelartimetheater.com. Tickets vary. Map p 106.*

★★★ Miami Light Project WYNWOOD This avant garde theater group is known for the Here and Now Festival every March featuring cutting-edge works by local performers. MLP also has major clout with big names such as Laurie Anderson and Danny Hoch. *3000 Biscayne Blvd. ☎ 305/576-4350. www.miamilightproject.com. Tickets vary. Map p 106.*

★★ New Theatre CORAL GABLES This one prides itself on showing renowned works from America and Europe. As the name implies, you'll find mostly contemporary plays, with a few classics thrown in. *4120 Laguna St. ☎ 305/443-5909. www.new-theatre.org. Tickets $25–$40. Map p 105.*

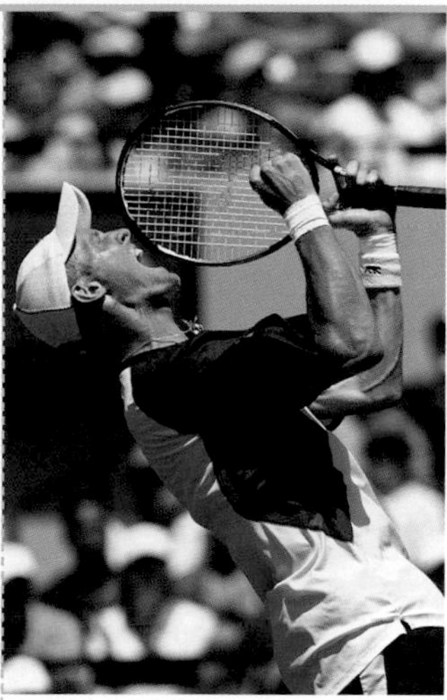

The Sony Ericsson Open takes place at Crandon Park Tennis Center.

Spectator Sports

American Airlines Arena DOWNTOWN Home of the Miami Heat basketball team as well as all the big musical acts who sweep into Miami, the Triple A, as it's known, is command central for sports and music fans. *601 Biscayne Blvd. ☎ 786/777-1000. www.aaarena.com. Map p 106.*

Crandon Park Tennis Center KEY BISCAYNE Home of the Sony Ericsson Open, this world-renowned tennis center features 17 hard courts, two European red clay, four American green clay, and two grass courts. *7300 Crandon Blvd. ☎ 305/365-2300. $3–$5 per person per hr. Tickets to tournaments vary.*

Dolphin Stadium NORTH MIAMI Home of the Miami Dolphins and the Miami Hurricanes, this out-of-the-way stadium sometimes hosts major concerts by the likes of Madonna, U2, and The Police. *2269 NW 199th St.*

☎ 305/623-6100. www.dolphinsstadium.com. Map p 106.

Homestead Miami Speedway HOMESTEAD NASCAR and Indy fans don't mind the long drive down south to reach the Speedway, which has hosted all sorts of races. Speedway also features special drive-along programs and race lessons. *1 Speedway Blvd. ☎ 305/230-5000. www.homesteadmiamispeedway.com. Tickets $25–$200.*

Drivers are shielded from the sun at Homestead Miami Speedway.

★★★ Miami Beach Polo World Cup SOUTH BEACH Forget Palm Beach—this tourney is the city's best, featuring hardcore sand-kicking polo matches, a parade of the ponies down the beach, and chic parties. General admission to matches throughout the weekend is free to the public, while VIP tickets are available for those seeking more than a view from the sidelines and for coveted events outside of the arena. *The Setai, 2001 Collins Ave. ☎ 866/468-7630. www.miamipolo.com. Tickets vary. Map p 105.*

Miami Beach Polo World Cup is held at The Setai.

8 The Best Hotels

Hotel Best Bets

Most **Luxurious**
★★★ The Setai $$$$ *2001 Collins Ave. (p 125)*

Best **Business Hotel**
★★★ Mandarin Oriental Miami $$$$ *500 Brickell Key Dr. (p 123)*

Best **Views**
★★★ The Ritz-Carlton Key Biscayne $$$$ *455 Grand Bay Dr. (p 124)*

Most **Historic**
★★★ The Biltmore $$$$ *1200 Anastasia Ave. (p 118)*

Hippest Hotel
★★★ Mondrian $$$$ *1100 West Ave. (p 123)*

Best **Off the Beaten Path Hotel**
★★ Miami River Inn $$ *118 SW S. River Dr. (p 123)*

Best **Art Deco Hotel**
★★★ The Raleigh $$$–$$$$ *1775 Collins Ave. (p 124)*

Best **Moderately Priced Hotel**
★★ The Catalina Hotel & Beach Club $–$$ *1732 Collins Ave. (p 118)*

Best **Family Hotel**
★★ Loews Hotel $$$–$$$$ *1601 Collins Ave. (p 122)*

The Pelican Hotel's rooms have quirky themes.

Best **Bathrooms**
★★★ Regent Bal Harbour $$$$ *10295 Collins Ave. (p 124)*

Best **Cheap Bed**
★ Hotel Shelley $ *844 Collins Ave. (p 122)*

Best **Swimming Pool**
★★★ The Standard $$$ *40 Island Ave. (p 126)*

Most **Romantic**
★★ Hotel St. Michel $$$ *162 Alcazar Ave. (p 122)*

Most **Comfortable**
★★★ The Tides $$$$ *1220 Ocean Dr. (p 127)*

Best **Lobby**
★★★ Delano $$$$ *1685 Collins Ave. (p 119)*

Best **Boutique Hotel**
★★★ The Sagamore $$$$ *1671 Collins Ave. (p 125)*

Best **Kitschy Hotel**
★★ The Pelican Hotel $$$ *826 Ocean Dr. (p 123)*

Best **for Celeb Stalkers**
★★ The Shore Club $$$–$$$$ *1901 Collins Ave. (p 126)*

Best **Spa Hotel**
★★★ Canyon Ranch Miami Beach $ *6900 Collins Ave. (p 118)*

Best **Vegas-esque Hotel**
★★★ Fontainebleau $$$$ *4441 Collins Ave. (p 120)*

Best **Golf Hotel**
★ Doral Golf Resort & Spa $$$ *4400 NW 87th Ave. (p 119)*

Best **Resort Not on the Beach**
★★★ Fairmont Turnberry Isle Resort & Club $$$$ *1999 W. Country Club Dr. (p 120)*

Previous page: Kelly Wearstler's design sense is evident at Viceroy Miami.

South Beach Hotels

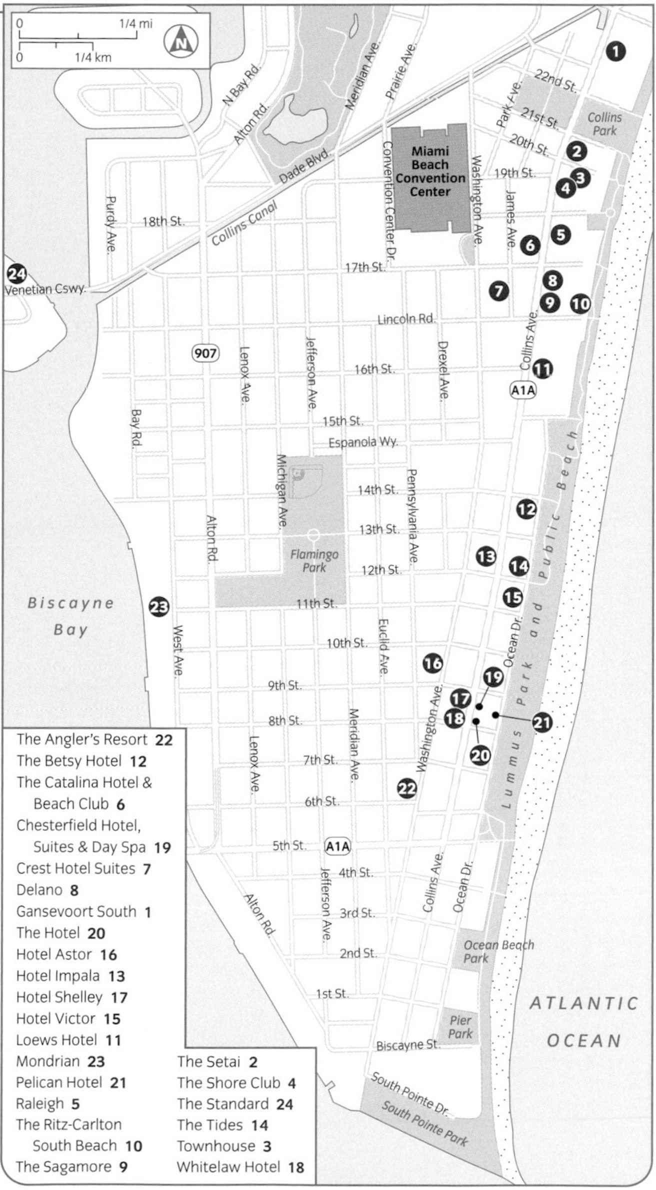

The Angler's Resort **22**
The Betsy Hotel **12**
The Catalina Hotel & Beach Club **6**
Chesterfield Hotel, Suites & Day Spa **19**
Crest Hotel Suites **7**
Delano **8**
Gansevoort South **1**
The Hotel **20**
Hotel Astor **16**
Hotel Impala **13**
Hotel Shelley **17**
Hotel Victor **15**
Loews Hotel **11**
Mondrian **23**
Pelican Hotel **21**
Raleigh **5**
The Ritz-Carlton South Beach **10**
The Sagamore **9**
The Setai **2**
The Shore Club **4**
The Standard **24**
The Tides **14**
Townhouse **3**
Whitelaw Hotel **18**

Miami & Coral Gables Hotels

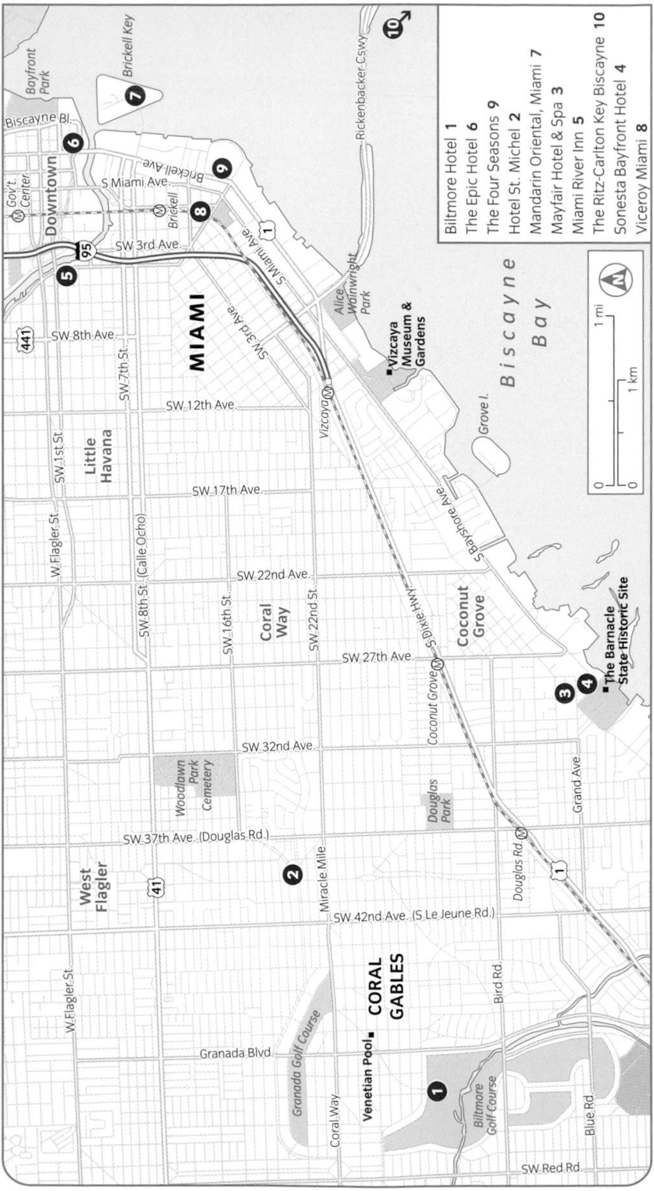

Miami **Hotels A to Z**

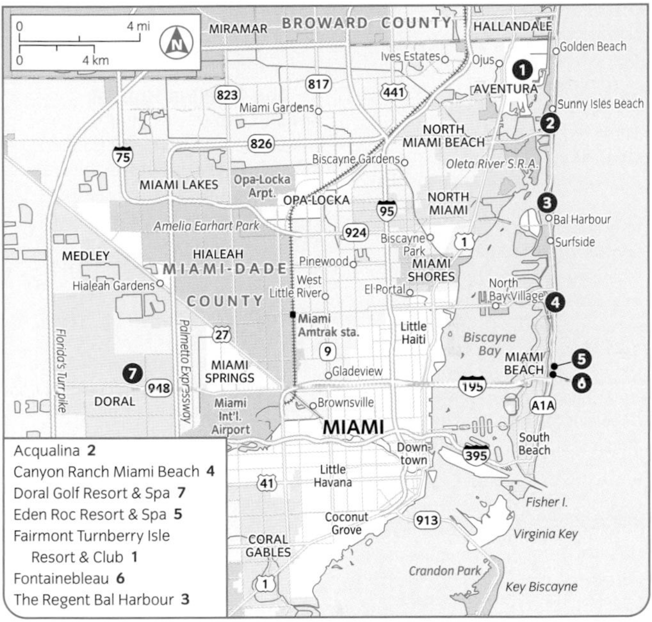

★ **Acqualina** SUNNY ISLES On 4½ beachfront acres (1.8 hectares) with more than 400 feet (120m) of Atlantic coastline, Acqualina is a Mediterranean-style resort towering over all the others with its baroque fountains, 97 impeccably appointed suites, and a branch of NYC's acclaimed Il Mulino restaurant. The ESPA is one of Miami's priciest and poshest spas, and while there are three pools just steps away from the beach, the outdoor area is uninspiring. The hotel's AcquaMarine Program has a splashy array of marine-biology activities for kids and adults. ***17875 Collins Ave. ☎ 305/918-8000. www.acqualina.com. 97 units. Doubles $475–$1,050. AE, DISC, MC, V. Map p 117.***

★ **The Angler's Resort** SOUTH BEACH Just 2 blocks from the beach, The Angler's is a swanky boutique hotel with the typical luxury comforts of Wi-Fi, flatscreen TVs, and iPods, plus a remote control that works all of these features—even the internal and external lights. An outdoor pool is surrounded by gardens. For those who'd rather do the beach than the pool, stop by the front desk to pick up a beach goodie bag complete with sunscreen, toys, water, snacks, and even the latest best-selling novel. ***660 Washington Ave. ☎ 305/534-9600. www.theanglersresort.com. 46 units. Doubles $225–$495. AE, DISC, MC, V. Map p 115.***

★ **The Betsy Hotel** MIAMI BEACH Listed on the National Register of Historic Places, The Betsy is the lone surviving example of "Florida Georgian" architecture on the famous byway, Ocean Drive. Behind its plantation-style shutters and columned facade, The Betsy Hotel offers a tropical colonial beachside haven. Each room and suite in the oceanfront hotel is a nod to the stately colonial rooms of yesteryear, blended with the modern aesthetic of South Beach. The Betsy boasts the South Florida installment of New York's BLT Steak restaurant by A-list chef Laurent Tourondel; a roof deck solarium with Zen garden for sunning, spa services, drinks, and light fare; a well-heeled lobby bar scene; and a private basement lounge where guests enter by-invitation-only. While the beach is a few steps away, the hotel also offers a serene outdoor pool scene. *1440 Ocean Dr. ☎ 866/531-8950 or 305/531-3934. www.thebetsyhotel.com. 63 units. Doubles $309–$879. DC, DISC, MC, V. Map p 115.*

★★★ **Biltmore Hotel** CORAL GABLES Built in 1926, this is the oldest Coral Gables hotel and a National Historic Landmark—one of only two in Florida. Rising above the Spanish-style estate is a majestic 300-foot (90m) copper-clad tower, modeled after the Giralda bell tower in Seville. Large Moorish-style rooms are decorated with tasteful decor, writing desks, and some high-tech amenities. The landmark 23,000-square-foot (2,137 sq. m) winding pool has a private cabana, alfresco bar, and restaurant. *1200 Anastasia Ave. ☎ 800/727-1926 or 305/445-1926. www.biltmorehotel.com. 276 units. Doubles $229–$895. AE, DISC, MC, V. Map p 116.*

★★★ **Canyon Ranch Miami Beach** MIAMI BEACH Here the main draw is a 75,000-square-foot (6,968-sq.-m) health club that includes a climbing wall. The resort has a full-time medical staff including a Chinese medicine specialist, nutritionist, and physical therapist. Because the resort operates as a condo as well, every suite has fine furnishings, top electronics, and a designer kitchen. All have balconies. *6900 Collins Ave. ☎ 800/742-9000 or 305/514-7000. www.canyonranch.com. 150 units. Doubles $650–$1,500. AE, DC, DISC, MC, V. Map p 117.*

★★ **The Catalina Hotel & Beach Club** SOUTH BEACH Stylish but not at all stuffy, the Catalina is perhaps the only hotel in the area that can pull off using red shag carpeting—though it tends to get a bit mangy. The hotel has a happening bar and lounge scene with a decidedly European jet-set vibe and a splashy beach club where you can get poolside manicures and pedicures. Free passes to nightclubs and free transportation to and from Miami International are among the many perks here. *1732 Collins Ave. ☎ 305/674-1160. www.catalinahotel.com. 136 units. Doubles $125–$300. AE, DISC, MC, V. Map p 115.*

★★ **Chesterfield Hotel, Suites & Day Spa** SOUTH BEACH This is a great hotel with little attitude, and has won the loyalty of fashion industrialists and romantics alike. The central location (1 block from the ocean) is a plus, especially since the hotel lacks a pool. Most of the rooms are immaculate and reminiscent of a loft apartment; large bathrooms with big, deep tubs are especially enticing. *841 Collins Ave. ☎ 305/673-3767. www.thechesterfieldhotel.com. 90 units. Doubles $125–$245. AE, DISC, MC, V. Map p 115.*

★ **Crest Hotel Suites** SOUTH BEACH The Crest Hotel has a quietly fashionable, contemporary, relaxed atmosphere with friendly service, Art Deco architecture, and rooms resembling cosmopolitan apartments. All suites have a living room/dining room area, kitchenette, and executive work space. An indoor/outdoor cafe with terrace and poolside dining attracts a younger crowd. *1670 James Ave. ☎ 800/531-3880 or 305/531-0321.*

www.crestgrouphotels.com. 64 units. Doubles $115–$175. AE, DISC, MC, V. Map p 115.

★★★ **Delano** SOUTH BEACH South Beach's original see-and-be-seen hotel has a stunning pool area, Rose Bar, Agua Spa, Lenny Kravitz–designed speakeasy The Florida Room, and Blue Door restaurant, but is now kinder and gentler. Rooms were recently revamped with splashes of color and reworked bathrooms. *1685 Collins Ave. ☎ 800/555-5001 or 305/672-2000. www.delano-hotel.com. 194 units. Doubles $425–$825. AE, DC, DISC, MC, V. Map p 115.*

★ kids **Doral Golf Resort & Spa** WEST MIAMI This sprawling 650-acre (263-hectare) resort is all about golf, hosting world-class tournaments, and home to the excruciating Blue Monster and Great White courses, the latter the Southeast's first desertscape course. Enhancements to the golf courses, spa suites, and driving range have brought the resort up to speed. There's a phenomenal kids program and the Blue Lagoon water park featuring two 80,000-gallon pools and a 125-foot (38m) water slide. *4400 NW 87th Ave. ☎ 800/71-DORAL or 305/592-2000. www.doralresort.com. 693 units. Doubles $119–$400. AE, DC, DISC, MC, V. Map p 117.*

The Delano's rooms were recently revamped.

★★ **Eden Roc Resort and Spa** MIAMI BEACH This flamboyant hotel received a $190-million face-lift in 2008 that doubled its size to 631 rooms, complete with a new oceanfront tower, bungalow suites, five pools, two restaurants, and a spa. The focal point of what they're touting as the "Bold New Eden Roc" is an oasis of pools, water features, and gardens, threaded with walkways and intimate seating areas. *4525 Collins Ave. ☎ 800/327-8337 or 305/531-0000. www.edenrocresort.com. 349 units. Doubles $99–$425. AE, DISC, MC, V. Map p 117.*

★★★ **Epic** DOWNTOWN Although it's yet another condo/hotel, the new in 2009 Epic, a Kimpton Hotel, doesn't make you feel like you're intruding on someone's privacy. In fact, it feels as if you are a resident in a posh, plush highrise with stunning views of the Miami skyline and Biscayne Bay. The dramatic lobby—separate from the resident lobby—features vaulted ceilings, glass walls, and shimmering pools, not to mention a buzzing two-story lounge and a yet-to-be-announced restaurant from a star chef. The guestrooms and suites are full of open space and light, offering breathtaking views, exceptional Aqua di Parma amenities, and a huge bathroom with open cut-out into the bedroom area. Luxury services include an onsite spa as well as in-room spa treatments, multiple swimming pools, and an excellent seafood restaurant and lounge, Area 31, on the 16th floor. The hotel is extremely pet friendly, offering beds, bones, and bottled water for your furry friend. Another perk: A daily wine reception in the lobby features free

Fairmont Turnberry Isle Resort & Club has one of the area's best golf courses.

pours along with some tasty snacks. *270 Biscayne Blvd. Way. ☎ 305/424-5226. www.epichotel.com. 411 units. Doubles $369–$519. AE, DC, DISC, MC, V, JTB. Map p 116.*

★★★ **Fairmont Turnberry Isle Resort & Club** AVENTURA This gorgeous 300-acre (121-hectare) retreat has every possible facility for active guests, particularly golfers. The main attractions are two Raymond Floyd championship courses, available only to members and guests of the hotel, and Bourbon Steak, a restaurant by star chef Michael Mina. The Willow Stream Spa offers an unabridged menu of treatments. A location in the well-manicured residential and shopping area of Aventura appeals to those who want peace, quiet, and a great mall. A complimentary shuttle bus takes guests to and from the Ocean Club and Aventura Mall. *19999 W. Country Club Dr. ☎ 866/612-7739 or 786/279-6770. www.fairmont.com. 392 units. Doubles $199–$699. AE, DC, DISC, MC, V. Map p 117.*

★★★ **Fontainebleau** MIAMI BEACH Reopened in 2008 as a modern Vegas-style hotel, entertainment, and dining complex, the Fontainbleau features all the trappings of a luxury hotel—flatscreen TVs, plush bedding, and a 40,000-square-foot (3,716-sq.-m) spa with mineral-rich water therapies. Celebrity chefs and their restaurants—Alfred Portale's Gotham Steak, Scott Conant's hot NYC Italian outpost Scarpetta, and London's highly rated Chinese restaurant Hakkasan—are among the 11 restaurants and lounges. *4441 Collins Ave. ☎ 800/548-8886 or 305/538-2000. www.fontainebleau.com. 334 units. Doubles $229–$699. AE, DC, DISC, MC, V. Map p 117.*

★★★ **The Four Seasons** BRICKELL The 70-story Four Seasons resembles an office building and is smack in the middle of the business district. The rooms and suites are plush and service is paramount. Most rooms overlook Biscayne Bay, and while all rooms are cushy, the bland decor leaves a lot to be desired. The best rooms are the corner suites with views facing both south and east over the water. There are three gorgeous pools spread out on more than 2 acres (1 hectare). *1435 Brickell Ave. ☎ 305/358-3535. www.fourseasons.com. 260 units. Doubles $350–$575. AE, DC, DISC, MC, V. Map p 116.*

★ **Gansevoort South** SOUTH BEACH One of NYC's hippest

hotels opened on South Beach in 2008. This hotel features the flagship David Barton Gym and Spa, expansive oceanview rooftop pool and bar, trendy meatery STK, oceanfront pool, and a shark tank with 27 types of fish and sharks. Rooms scream with hot pink, magenta, and yellow furniture, set against charcoal-gray suede walls dotted with pictures of '40s pinup girls. Most rooms have balconies overlooking the ocean. *2377 Collins Ave. ☎ 305/604-1000. www.gansevoortsouth.com. 334 units. Doubles $300–$495. AE, DC, DISC, MC, V. Map p 115.*

★ **The Hotel** SOUTH BEACH Kitschy fashion designer Todd Oldham whimsically restored this 1939 gem (formerly the Tiffany Hotel), lacing it with lush, cool colors, hand-cut mirrors, and glass mosaics, and adding artisan detailing, terrazzo floors, and porthole windows. The small, soundproof rooms are very comfortable and incredibly stylish, though the bathrooms are a bit cramped. *801 Collins Ave. ☎ 877/843-4683 or 305/531-2222. www.thehotelofsouthbeach.com. 53 units. Doubles $205–$525. AE, DC, DISC, MC, V. Map p 115.*

★ **Hotel Astor** SOUTH BEACH This venerable Deco hotel has been spruced up with highly stylized rooms with handcrafted furniture, whangee-wood floors, sisal carpets, and blond oak and whangee-wood cabinetry. Other new additions to the hotel include a nightlife butler who will guide you through South Beach's crazy club scene, a new restaurant, and a spa lap pool. *956 Washington Ave. ☎ 800/270-4981 or 305/531-8081. www.hotelastor.com. 40 units. Doubles $125–$220. AE, DC, DISC, MC, V. Map p 115.*

★ **Hotel Impala** SOUTH BEACH This charming Mediterranean hideaway is one of the area's best and most beautiful, with Greco-Roman frescoes and friezes and an intimate garden. Rooms have super-cushy sleigh beds, sisal floors, wrought-iron fixtures, imported Belgian cotton linens, wood furniture, and fabulous-looking, but also incredibly small, bathrooms done up in stainless steel and coral rock. *1228 Collins Ave. ☎ 800/646-7252 or 305/673-2021. www.hotelimpalamiamibeach.com.*

Get a taste of old-world Europe at the Hotel St. Michel.

Miami River Inn is the city's only bed-and-breakfast.

17 units. Doubles $145–$225. AE, DC, DISC, MC, V. Map p 115.

★ **Hotel Shelley** SOUTH BEACH The architecturally sound boutique hotel in the heart of the Art Deco district has reinvented itself with a $1.5 million renovation. Complete with Mascioni 300-thread-count linens, goose-down pillows and comforters, LCD plasma TVs, and custom-built cabinetry, the guest rooms allow you to chill out after a long day at the beach or rock out before a big night of partying. *844 Collins Ave. ☎ 305/531-3341. www.hotelshelley.com. 49 units. Doubles $75–$225. AE, DC, DISC, MC, V. Map p 115.*

★★ **Hotel St. Michel** CORAL GABLES This European-style hotel is one of the city's most romantic options. The accommodations and hospitality are straight out of old-world Europe, complete with dark wood-paneled walls, cozy beds, beautiful antiques, and a quiet elegance. Everything here is charming—from the brass elevator to the paddle fans. One-of-a-kind furnishings make each room special. *162 Alcazar Ave. ☎ 800/848-HOTEL or 305/444-1666. www.hotelstmichel.com. 28 units. Doubles $135–$299. AE, DC, DISC, MC, V. Map p 116.*

★★ **Hotel Victor** SOUTH BEACH Hotel Victor is a hyperluxe, boutique, see-and-be-seen hotel. Deluxe rooms all have ocean views, white marble, ebony-lacquered furniture, a full—not mini—bar, flatscreen plasma TVs, and massive white-marbled bathrooms with infinity-edge bathtubs and rain-head showers. *1144 Ocean Dr. ☎ 305/428-1234. www.hotelvictorsouthbeach.com. 88 units. Suites $289–$1,045. AE, DC, DISC, MC, V. Map p 115.*

★★ **Loews Hotel** kids SOUTH BEACH This behemoth is considered an eyesore by many, an architectural triumph by others. Rooms are a bit boxy and bland, but are clean and have new carpets and bedspreads. If you can steer your way past all the conventioneers in the lobby, escape to the equally massive pool (with a gorgeous, landscaped entrance that's more Maui than Miami). In addition to the Loews Loves Kids program, the hotel hosts fun activities for adults, such as Dive in Movies at the pool, salsa lessons, and bingo. *1601 Collins Ave. ☎ 800/23-LOEWS or 305/604-1601. www.loewshotels.com. 790 units. Doubles $289–$679. AE, DC, DISC, MC, V. Map p 115.*

★★★ **Mandarin Oriental, Miami** BRICKELL Catering to business travelers, big-time celebrities, and the leisure traveler who doesn't mind spending big bucks, the swank Mandarin Oriental features a waterfront location, residential-style rooms with Asian touches (all with balconies), and upscale dining. ***500 Brickell Key Dr. ☎ 305/913-8383. www.mandarinoriental.com. 326 units. Suites $435–$900. AE, DC, DISC, MC, V. Map p 116.***

★★ **Mayfair Hotel & Spa** COCONUT GROVE Complimentary Wi-Fi, terry robes, 300-thread-count sheets, and plasma TVs are in every room of this newly renovated gem. The Cabana One Rooftop Pool & Lounge features a floating cabana roof and planks of teakwood, private cabanas, and a serpentine bench built into the parapet winding around a fire feature. The famed New York steakhouse, Angelo & Maxie's, is here, as is the Jurlique Spa. ***3000 Florida Ave. ☎ 800/433-4555 or 305/441-0000. www.mayfairhotelandspa.com. 179 units. Suites $149–$679. AE, DC, DISC, MC, V. Map p 116.***

★★ **Miami River Inn** DOWNTOWN The Miami River Inn, listed on the National Register of Historic Places, is a quaint, country-style hideaway (Miami's *only* bed-and-breakfast), consisting of four cottages smack in the middle of downtown Miami. Every room has hardwood floors and is furnished with antiques. In one room, you might find a hand-painted bathtub, a Singer sewing machine, and an armoire from the turn of the 20th century, restored to perfection. ***118 SW S. River Dr. ☎ 800/468-3589 or 305/325-0045. www.miamiriverinn.com. 38 units. Doubles $89–$299. AE, DC, DISC, MC, V. Map p 116.***

★★★ **Mondrian** SOUTH BEACH The Mondrian is painfully trendy, but it's also refreshingly different. It's located on the western, residential bay side of South Beach, and panoramic views of the bay and skyline are stunning. The hotel, inspired by Sleeping Beauty's castle, has whimsical adult playground-style environments, and also features an Agua spa and Asia de Cuba restaurant. ***1100 West Ave. ☎ 305/672-2662. www.mondriansouthbeach.com. 335 units. Doubles $495–$645. AE, DC, DISC, MC, V. Map p 115.***

★★ **Pelican Hotel** SOUTH BEACH Owned by the same creative folks behind the Diesel Jeans company, the fashionable Pelican is South Beach's only self-professed "toy-hotel," in which each of its 30 rooms and suites is decorated as outrageously as some of the area's more colorful drag queens; room no. 309, for instance, is the "Psychedelic(ate) Girl" room. ***826 Ocean Dr. ☎ 800/7-PELICAN or 305/673-3373. www.pelicanhotel.com.***

The Mondrian's design was inspired by Sleeping Beauty's castle.

The Raleigh's outdoor area is perfect for warm Miami evenings.

30 units. Doubles $165–$450. AE, DISC, MC, V. Map p 115.

★★★ **Raleigh** SOUTH BEACH This is old-school Miami Beach with a modern twist. The entire outdoor area is a stunning oasis. Rooms have been redone with period furnishings, iPod docking stations, gourmet minibars, and terrazzo floors (those overlooking the pool and ocean are the most peaceful). *1775 Collins Ave. ☎ 800/848-1775 or 305/534-6300. www.raleighhotel.com. 104 units. Doubles $225–$925. AE, DC, DISC, MC, V. Map p 115.*

Bathrooms at The Regent Bal Harbour come with stunning views.

★★★ **The Regent Bal Harbour** BAL HARBOUR The ultimate in luxury, Regent suites are resplendent in mahogany floors, with leather walls, panoramic views of the ocean, and bathrooms with floor-to-ceiling windows and a free-standing tub overlooking the ocean. Elevators take you directly into your suite. A Guerlain spa, butler service, spectacular pool and beach area, and world-class dining will cost you a pretty penny, but if you're looking to be doted on hand and foot without lifting a finger, this is the place. ***Note:*** At press time, this property was up for sale, with its new owner yet to be determined. Contact the hotel for details prior to booking. *10295 Collins Ave. ☎ 800/545-4000 or 305/455-5400. www.regentbalharbour.com. 124 units. Doubles $295–$2,000. AE, DC, DISC, MC, V. Map p 117.*

★★★ **kids** **The Ritz-Carlton Key Biscayne** KEY BISCAYNE Decorated in British colonial style, the oceanfront Ritz-Carlton is straight out of Bermuda, with its impressive flower-laden landscaping. The Ritz Kids programs provide children ages 5 to 12 with fantastic activities, and the 1,200-foot (360m) beachfront offers everything from pure relaxation to fishing, boating, or windsurfing. *455 Grand Bay Dr. ☎ 800/241-3333 or 305/365-4500. www.ritzcarlton.com. 402 units. Doubles $269–$629. AE, DC, DISC, MC, V. Map p 116.*

★★★ **The Ritz-Carlton South Beach** SOUTH BEACH The Ritz-Carlton provides comfort to those who prefer 100% cotton Frette sheets and goose-down pillows to high-style minimalism. The best rooms, by far, are the poolside and oceanview lanai rooms. There's also a tanning butler who will spritz you with SPF and water whenever you want. *1 Lincoln Rd. ☎ 800/241-3333 or 786/276-4000. www.ritzcarlton.com. 375 units. Doubles $359–$609. AE, DC, DISC, MC, V. Map p 115.*

★★★ **The Sagamore** SOUTH BEACH Although the lobby and its requisite restaurant, bar, and lounge areas have become command central for the international chic elite and celebrities, the Sagamore's all-suite, apartment-like rooms are havens from the hype, with all the cushy comforts of home and then some. Cabanas with plasma TVs dot the sprawling outdoor lawn, along with a pool and beachfront. *1671 Collins Ave. ☎ 877/SAGAMORE or 305/535-8088. www.sagamorehotel.com. 93 units. Doubles $245–$4,500. AE, DC, DISC, MC, V. Map p 115.*

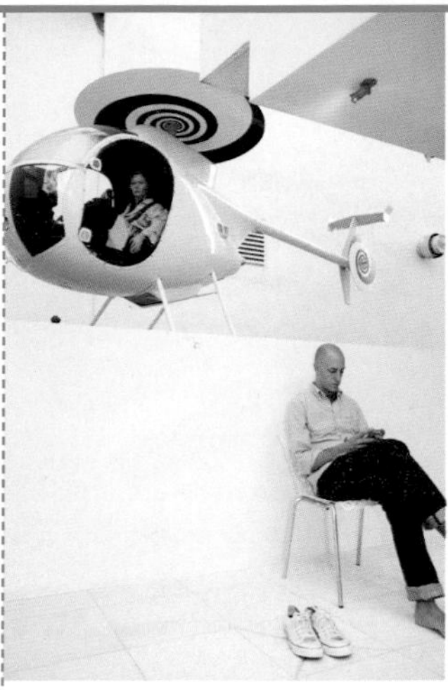

Quirky art dominates the lobby at The Sagamore.

★★★ **The Setai** SOUTH BEACH If you want to splurge, this is where to do it. All of the suites—some are actually condos—are gorgeous apartments with floor-to-ceiling

Lush greenery surrounds The Ritz-Carlton Key Biscayne.

The Setai's penthouse suite offers a great view of the city and the water.

windows, full kitchens, and Jacuzzi bathtubs bigger than a small swimming pool. All are adorned in sleek Asian decor with over-the-top comforts including Lavazza espresso makers, Aqua di Parma bathroom amenities, and washer/dryers. The garden area with reflecting pools is lovely, but not as cool as the pool area with a bar serving $30 burgers. ***2001 Collins Ave.*** ☎ ***305/520-6000. www.setai.com. 135 units. Doubles $950. AE, DC, DISC, MC, V. Map p 115.***

★★ **The Shore Club** SOUTH BEACH An outpost of L.A.'s celebrity-laden Skybar reigns supreme, with a Marrakech-meets-Miami motif that stretches throughout the hotel's sprawling pool, patio, and garden areas. There's also a branch of Robert De Niro's pricey pasta spot, Ago. Rooms—80% of which have an ocean view—are loaded with state-of-the-art amenities and have a bit more personality than those at the Delano. ***1901 Collins Ave.*** ☎ ***877/640-9500 or 305/695-3100. www.shoreclub.com. 309 units. Doubles $409–$715. AE, DC, DISC, MC, V. Map p 115.***

★ **Sonesta Bayfront Hotel** COCONUT GROVE With a great location offering panoramic views of Biscayne Bay, the marina, and the Miami skyline, the Sonesta is more than just a chain hotel—it's a condo, too. It's meticulously maintained and features 225 contemporary styled guest rooms, all with flatscreen TVs and balconies, many with ocean views. The fantastic 8th-floor pool and hot tub overlooks the water. The restaurant, Panorama, serves delicious Peruvian cuisine. ***2889 McFarlane Rd.*** ☎ ***800/SONESTA or 305/529-2828. www.sonesta.com. 225 units. Doubles $249–$569. AE, DC, DISC, MC, V. Map p 116.***

★★★ **The Standard** SOUTH BEACH This revamped motel is full of all the modern trappings of a swank spa resort, with a bayfront view and a serene location on the Venetian Causeway—walking distance to all the South Beach craziness. Whitewashed guest rooms are serviced by roaming carts offering herbal teas and aromatherapy footbaths. There's a cedar sauna, a Turkish hammam, tongue-in-cheek treatments such as the cellulite-fighting Standard Spanking, and a chlorine-free plunge pool with a 12-foot-tall (3.6m) waterfall and DJ-spun music piped underwater. ***40 Island Ave.*** ☎ ***305/673-1717. www.standardhotel.com. 105 units. Doubles $165–$1,250. AE, DC, DISC, MC, V. Map p 115.***

When Is the Off Season?

South Florida's tourist season is well defined, beginning in mid-November and lasting until Easter. Hotel prices escalate until about March, after which they begin to decline. During the off season, hotel rates are typically 30% to 50% lower than their winter highs. Rates also depend on your hotel's proximity to the beach and how much ocean you can see from your window. Small motels a block or two from the water can be up to 40% cheaper than similar properties right on the sand. Remember, too, that state and city taxes can add as much as 12.5% to your bill in some parts of Miami. Some hotels, especially those in South Beach, also tack on additional service charges, and don't forget that parking is a pricey endeavor.

★★★ **The Tides** SOUTH BEACH This 10-story Art Deco masterpiece is reminiscent of a gleaming ocean liner with porthole windows. Rooms have been newly washed in warm earth tones, have a breathtaking panoramic view of the ocean, and are at least twice the size of a typical South Beach hotel room. ***1220 Ocean Dr. ☎ 800/439-4095 or 305/604-5070. www.tidessouthbeach.com. 45 units. Doubles $395–$595. AE, DC, DISC, MC, V. Map p 115.***

★ **Townhouse** SOUTH BEACH The charm of this hotel is in its simple yet chic design with quirky details: exercise equipment stands alone in the hallways, free laundry machines in the lobby, and a water bed–lined rooftop. Rooms boast L-shaped couches for extra guests (for whom you aren't charged). Though the rooms are all pretty much the same, consider the ones with the partial ocean view. ***150 20th St. ☎ 877/534-3800 or 305/534-3800. www.townhousehotel.com. 70 units.***

The Standard's pool is the best in Miami.

Doubles $115–$450. AE, DC, DISC, MC, V. Map p 115.

★★ **Viceroy Miami** DOWNTOWN Opened in early 2009, the Viceroy showcases Kelly Wearstler's Asian sensibilities, whether in the rooftop Club 50 or the signature restaurant, which opens up to the infinity pool (the longest in the state). Rooms, a soft sea-foam green, are accented by Asian art, and bathrooms offer tons of counter space and double sinks. All have balconies, and those ending in 16 have the best (river) views. The spa, a Philippe Starck creation, is beautiful. *485 Brickell Ave. ☎ 866/720-1991 or 305/503-4400. www.viceroymiami.com. 162 units. Doubles $300–$500. AE, DC, DISC, MC, V. Map p 116.*

★ **Whitelaw Hotel** SOUTH BEACH Only half a block from Ocean Drive, this hotel, like its clientele, is full of distinct personalities, pairing such disparate elements as luxurious Belgian sheets with shag carpeting to create an innovative setting. All-white rooms manage to be homey and plush. *808 Collins Ave. ☎ 305/398-7000. www.whitelawhotel.com. 49 units. Doubles $95–$195. AE, DC, DISC, MC, V. Map p 115.* ●

Decisions, Decisions

The city's long-lasting status on the destination A-list has given rise to an ever-increasing number of upscale hotels, and no place in Miami has seen a greater increase in construction than Miami Beach. While the increasing demand for rooms on South Beach means increasing costs, you can still find a decent room at a fair price.

- Unless you plan your vacation entirely in and around your hotel, most of the cheaper Deco hotels are adequate and a wise choice for those who plan to use the room only to sleep.
- Many of the old hotels from the 1930s, 1940s, and 1950s have been totally renovated. Always ask what specific changes were made during a renovation, and be sure to ask if a hotel will be undergoing construction while you're there.
- Find out how near your room will be to the center of the nightlife crowd; trying to sleep directly on Ocean Drive or Collins and Washington avenues, especially during the weekend, is next to impossible.
- Along South Beach's Collins Avenue, there are dozens of hotels and motels—in all price categories.
- For a less expensive stay that's only a 10-minute cab ride from South Beach, Miami Beach proper (the area north of 23rd St. and Collins Ave. all the way up to 163rd St. and Collins Ave.) offers a slew of reasonable stays, right on the beach.
- For a less frenetic, more relaxed, and more tropical experience, opt for a ritzy resort on Key Biscayne, across the water from the spectacular Miami skyline.
- Shoppers will enjoy North Miami Beach's proximity to the Aventura Mall, while Coral Gables has an old-world European flair.

9 The Best Day Trips & Excursions

Fort Lauderdale

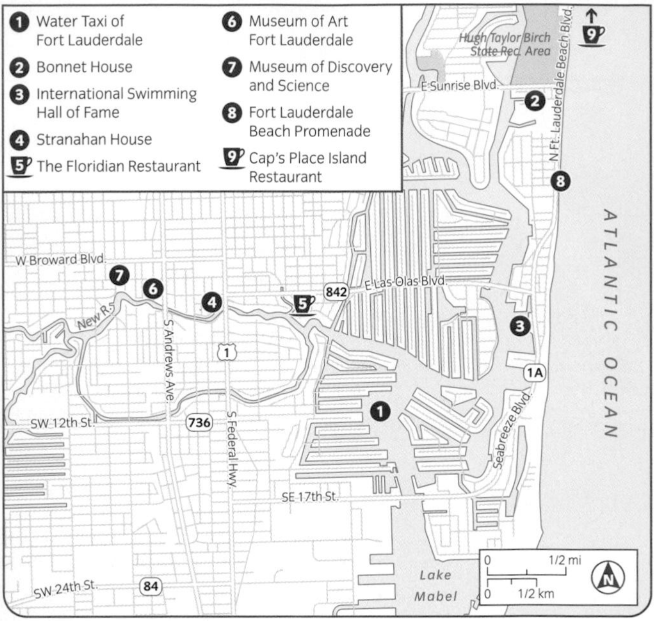

Fort Lauderdale, with its well-known strip of beaches, restaurants, bars, and souvenir shops, has undergone a transformation. Once famous (or infamous) for the annual mayhem it hosted during spring break, this area is now attracting a more affluent, better-behaved yachting crowd. In addition to beautiful wide beaches, Fort Lauderdale, known as the Venice of America, has more than 300 miles (480km) of navigable waterways and innumerable canals, in which thousands of residents anchor their boats and visitors sail in rented boats or a moderately priced water taxi.

START: Hop on the Water Taxi to navigate Fort Lauderdale by boat.

1 Water Taxi of Fort Lauderdale. A trusty fleet of older port boats serves the dual purpose of transporting and entertaining visitors. Because of its popularity, the water-taxi fleet has welcomed several sleek, 70-passenger "water buses," featuring indoor and outdoor seating with an atrium-like roof. Taxis operate on demand and also along a fairly regular route, carrying up to 48 passengers to 20 stops. ☎ *954/467-6677. www.watertaxi.com. Starting daily at 8am, boats run until midnight 7 days a week, depending on the weather. Check the website for exact pickup times. All-day pass with unlimited stops $13;*

Previous page: The Everglades are home to a variety of flora and fauna.

Fort Lauderdale's Water Taxi is a good way to get around and see the area.

to South Beach $24. Tickets available onboard; no credit cards.

2 ★ Bonnet House. This historic 35-acre (14-hectare) plantation home and estate, accessible by guided tour only, will provide you with a fantastic glimpse of Old Florida. Built in 1921, the sprawling two-story waterfront home (surrounded by formal tropical gardens) is really the backdrop of a love story, which the very chatty volunteer guides will share with you if you ask. The worthwhile tour introduces you to quirky people, whimsical artwork, lush grounds, and interesting design. 🕘 *1–2 hr. 900 N. Birch Rd.* ☎ *954/563-5393. www.bonnethouse.org. Admission $20 adults, $18 seniors, $16 students 16 & under, free for kids 6 & under.*

3 ★★ International Swimming Hall of Fame. Any aspiring Michael Phelps (who may or may not donate one of his million gold medals to the museum) or those who appreciate the sport will love this splashy homage to the best

Bonnet House plantation home sits on 35 acres.

International Swimming Hall of Fame.

backstrokers, frontstrokers, and divers in the world. *1 hr. 1 Hall of Fame Dr. ☎ 954/462-6536. www.ishof.org. Guided tours $8 adults, $6 seniors & $4 children 12 & over.*

4 ★★ Stranahan House. This is Fort Lauderdale's oldest standing structure and a prime example of classic "Florida Frontier" architecture. Built in 1901 by the "father of Fort Lauderdale," Frank Stranahan, this house once served as a trading post for Seminole trappers who came here to sell pelts. It's been a post office, town hall, and general store, and now serves as a small, worthwhile museum of South Florida pioneer life, with turn-of-the-19th-century furnishings and historical photos of the area. *1 hr. for a guided tour. 335 SE 6th Ave. ☎ 954/524-4736. www.stranahanhouse.org. Admission $12 adults, $11 seniors, $7 students & kids. Wed–Sat 10am–3pm; Sun 1–3pm. Tours are on the hour; last tour at 3pm. Accessible by water taxi.*

5 ★ The Floridian Restaurant, known as "The Flo," has been filling South Florida's diner void for more than 63 years, serving breakfast, lunch, and dinner 24/7. It's especially busy on weekend mornings when locals and tourists come in for huge omelets, fresh oatmeal, sausage, and biscuits. *1410 E. Las Olas Blvd. ☎ 954/463-4041. $.*

6 ★ Museum of Art Fort Lauderdale. A fantastic modern-art facility, the Museum of Art Fort Lauderdale has permanent collections, including those from William Glackens; the CoBrA Movement in Copenhagen, Brussels, and Amsterdam with more than 200 paintings; 50 sculptures; 1,200 works on paper from 1948 to 1951, including the largest repository of Asger Jorn graphics outside the Silkeborg Kunstmuseum in Denmark; stunning Picasso ceramics; and contemporary works from more than 90 Cuban artists in exile around the world. *1–2 hr. 1 E. Las Olas Blvd. ☎ 954/525-5500. www.moafl.org. Admission $10 adults, $7 seniors, students & kids 6–17; children 5 & under free. Oct–May daily 11am–5pm, Thurs until 8pm; June–Sept Mon & Wed–Sun 11am–5pm, closed Tues.*

The Stranahan House has had many past lives, including one as a post office.

Fort Lauderdale's "Strip."

7 kids Museum of Discovery and Science. This museum's high-tech, interactive approach to education proves that science can equal fun. Adults won't feel as if they're in a kiddie museum, either. Kids ages 7 and under enjoy navigating their way through the excellent explorations in the Discovery Center. Florida Ecoscapes is particularly interesting, with a living coral reef, bees, bats, frogs, turtles, and alligators. *1–2 hr. 401 SW 2nd St. ☎ 954/467-6637. www.mods.org. Admission to both museum & an IMAX movie $15 adults, $14 seniors & $12 for kids 2–12. Mon–Sat 10am–5pm; Sun noon–6pm.*

8 Ft. Lauderdale Beach Promenade (aka "The Strip"). After a $26 million renovation, the famous strip looks fantastic. It's especially peaceful in the mornings, when there's just a smattering of joggers and walkers; but even at its most crowded on weekends, the expansive promenade provides room for everyone. On the sand just across the road, most days you'll find hardcore volleyball players who always welcome anyone with a good spike, and an inviting ocean for swimmers of any level. The unusually clear waters are under the careful watch of some of Florida's best-looking lifeguards. *A1A between Las Olas & Sunrise blvds. ☎ 954/828-4597.*

Just 15 minutes north of Fort Lauderdale, **9 Cap's Place Island Restaurant** is one of the area's best-kept secrets. Although it's no longer a rum-running restaurant and casino, its illustrious past (FDR and Winston Churchill dined here together) landed it a spot on the National Register of Historic Places. To get here, you have to take a ferryboat, provided by the restaurant. The short ride across the Intracoastal definitely adds to the Cap's Place experience. The food—traditional seafood dishes such as Florida or Maine lobster, clams casino, and oysters Rockefeller—is good, not great. *2765 NE 29th Court. ☎ 954/941-0418. www.capsplace.com. $$–$$$.*

Palm Beach

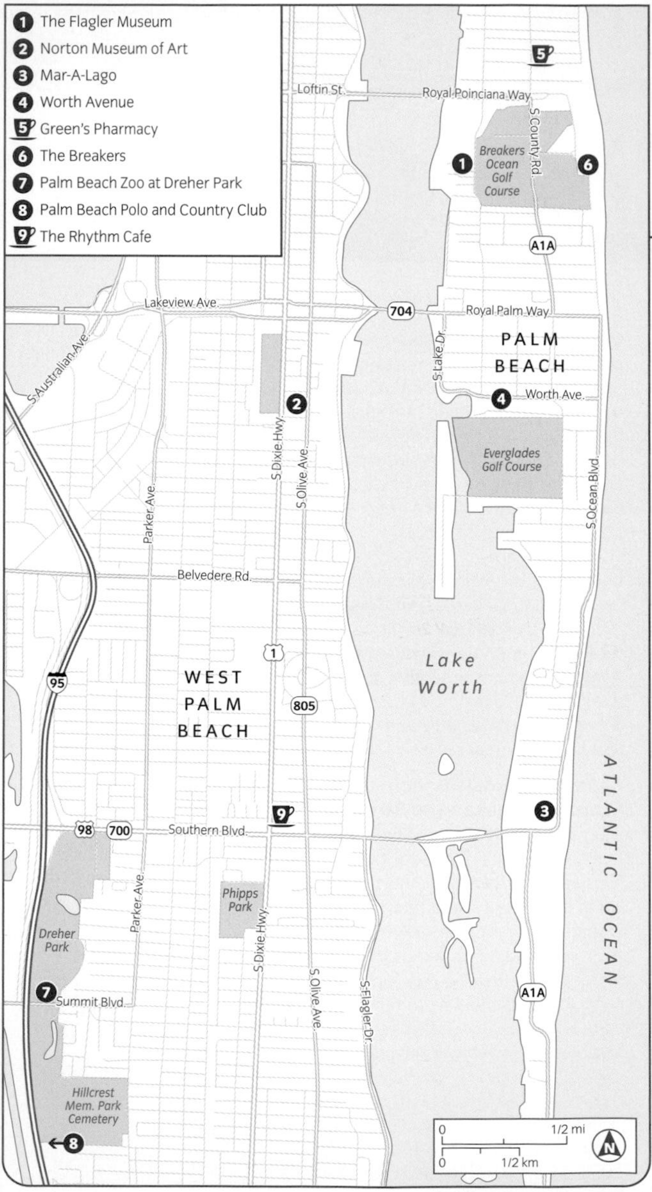
1 The Flagler Museum
2 Norton Museum of Art
3 Mar-A-Lago
4 Worth Avenue
5 Green's Pharmacy
6 The Breakers
7 Palm Beach Zoo at Dreher Park
8 Palm Beach Polo and Country Club
9 The Rhythm Cafe
Loftin St.
Royal Poinciana Way
S County Rd.
Breakers Ocean Golf Course
A1A
Lakeview Ave.
704
Royal Palm Way
PALM BEACH
S Lake Dr.
Worth Ave.
S Australian Ave.
S Dixie Hwy.
S Olive Ave.
Everglades Golf Course
S Ocean Blvd.
Parker Ave.
Belvedere Rd.
1
WEST PALM BEACH
805
95
Lake Worth
ATLANTIC OCEAN
98
700
Southern Blvd.
Phipps Park
Dreher Park
Summit Blvd.
S Flagler Dr.
Hillcrest Mem. Park Cemetery
0
1/2 mi
1/2 km
N

Palm Beach County encompasses cities from Boca Raton in the south to Jupiter and Tequesta in the north. But it is Palm Beach, the small island town across the Intracoastal Waterway, that has been the traditional winter home of America's aristocracy—the Kennedys, the Rockefellers, the Pulitzers, the Trumps. It's something to be seen, despite the fact that some consider it over the top and, frankly, obscene. But this is not only a city of upscale resorts and chic boutiques; Palm Beach holds some surprises, from a world-class art museum to one of the top bird-watching areas in the state. **START: The Flagler Museum.**

The Beaux Arts–style Flagler Museum.

❶ **The Flagler Museum.** The Gilded Age is preserved in this luxurious mansion, commissioned by Standard Oil tycoon Henry Flagler as a wedding present to his third wife. Whitehall is a classic Beaux Arts–style mansion containing 55 rooms, including a Louis XIV music room, a Louis XV ballroom, and 14 guest suites outfitted with original antique European furnishings. Out back you can climb aboard Rail Car No. 91, Mr. Flagler's private restored railroad car. Group tours are available, but for the most part this is a self-guided museum (a free audio tour is available). ⌚ *1½–2 hr. 1 Whitehall Way.* ☎ *561/655-2833. www.flaglermuseum.us. Admission $15 adults, $8 ages 13–18, $3 children 6–12. Tues–Sat 10am–5pm; Sun noon–5pm.*

❷ ★ **Norton Museum of Art.** The Norton is world-famous for its prestigious permanent collection and top temporary exhibitions. The museum's major collections are divided geographically. The American galleries contain major works by Hopper, O'Keeffe, and Pollock, while Impressionist and post-Impressionist paintings by Cézanne, Degas, Gauguin, Matisse, Monet, Picasso, Pissarro, and Renoir can be found in the French collection. ⌚ *1–2 hr.*

Bohemian buys and more can be found along Worth Avenue.

1451 S. Olive Ave. ☎ 561/659-4689. www.norton.org. Admission $8 adults, $3 ages 13–21. Mon–Sat 10am–5pm; Sun 1–5pm. Closed Mon May–Oct & all major holidays.

3 ★ Mar-A-Lago. No trip to Palm Beach is complete without at least a glimpse of Mar-A-Lago, the stately residence of Donald Trump. In 1985, Trump purchased the estate of cereal heiress Marjorie Merriweather Post to the great consternation of locals, who feared that he would turn the place into a casino. Instead, Trump, who sometimes resides in a portion of the palace, opened the house to the public—for a price, of course—as a tony country club (membership fee: $100,000). *5 min. 1100 S. Ocean Blvd. There are currently no tours open to the public, but you can see it as you cross the bridge from West Palm Beach into Palm Beach.*

4 ★★ Window Shop on Worth Avenue. No matter what your budget is, be sure to take a stroll down Worth Avenue, the "Rodeo Drive of the South" and a window-shopper's dream. Between South Ocean Boulevard and Cocoanut Row, there are more than 200 boutiques, posh shops (Gucci, Chanel, Armani, Hermès, Louis Vuitton), art galleries, and upscale restaurants. If you want to fit in, dress as if you are going to an elegant luncheon, not the mall down the street. *1–2 hr. www.worth-avenue.com.*

5 ★ Green's Pharmacy offers one of the best meal deals in Palm Beach. Both breakfast and lunch are served, either at a Formica bar or at tables on a black-and-white checkerboard floor. Breakfast specials include eggs and omelets served with home fries and bacon, sausage, or corned-beef hash. The grill serves burgers and sandwiches, as well as ice-cream sodas and milkshakes. *151 N. County Rd. ☎ 561/832-0304. $.*

6 ★★★ The Breakers. This 140-acre (57-hectare) beachfront hotel is quintessential Palm Beach, where old money mixes with new money, and the Old World gives way, albeit reluctantly, to a bit of modernity. The seven-story building is a marvel, with a frescoed lobby and long, palatial hallways. Just walk into the lobby and you can smell the money. *15 min. 1 S. County Rd. 888/BREAKERS or 561/655-6611. www.thebreakers.com.*

7 kids Palm Beach Zoo at Dreher Park. Unlike big-city zoos, this intimate 23-acre (9-hectare) attraction is more like a stroll in the park than an all-day excursion. It features about 500 animals representing more than 100 different species. The monkey exhibit and petting zoo are favorites with kids. *1–2 hr. 1301 Summit Blvd. 561/547-WILD. www.palmbeachzoo.org. Admission $13 adults, $10 seniors, $9 children 3–12. Daily 9am–5pm. Closed Thanksgiving.*

8 Polo, Palm Beach Style. The posh **Palm Beach Polo and Country Club** and the **International Polo Club** are two of the world's premier polo grounds and host some of the sport's top-rated players. Even if you're not a sports fan, you must attend a match at one of these fields, which are on the mainland in a rural area called Wellington. Matches are open to the public and are surprisingly affordable. Dress is casual; a navy or tweed blazer over jeans or khakis is the standard for men, while neat-looking jeans or a pantsuit is the norm for women. On warmer days, shorts and, of course, polo shirts, are fine, too. *1–4 hr. 11809 Polo Club Rd. & 3667 120th Ave. South Wellington, 10 miles (16km) west of the Forest Hill Boulevard Exit I-95. 561/793-1440 or 561/204-5687. www.internationalpoloclub.com. Admission $15–$45; box seats (members only) $75–$100. Matches held throughout the week. Schedules vary, but the big names usually compete Jan–Apr Sun at 3:30pm.*

The Breakers' frescoed lobby.

Over the bridge in West Palm Beach, **9 The Rhythm Cafe** is where those in the know come to eat some of West Palm Beach's most laid-back gourmet food. On the handwritten, photocopied menu (which changes daily), you'll always find a fish specialty, accompanied by a hefty dose of greens and garnishes. Reliably outstanding is the pork tenderloin with mango chutney. Salads and soups are a great bargain, since portions are relatively large. The kitschy decor of this tiny cafe comes complete with vinyl tablecloths and a changing display of paintings by local amateurs. *3800 S. Dixie Hwy. 561/833-3406. www.rhythmcafe.com. $–$$.*

The Florida Everglades

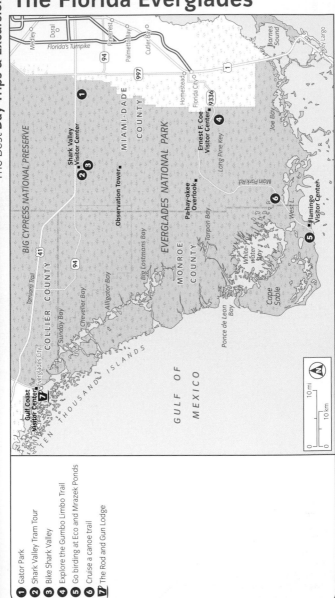

1. Gator Park
2. Shark Valley Tram Tour
3. Bike Shark Valley
4. Explore the Gumbo Limbo Trail
5. Go birding at Eco and Mrazek Ponds
6. Cruise a canoe trail
7. The Rod and Gun Lodge

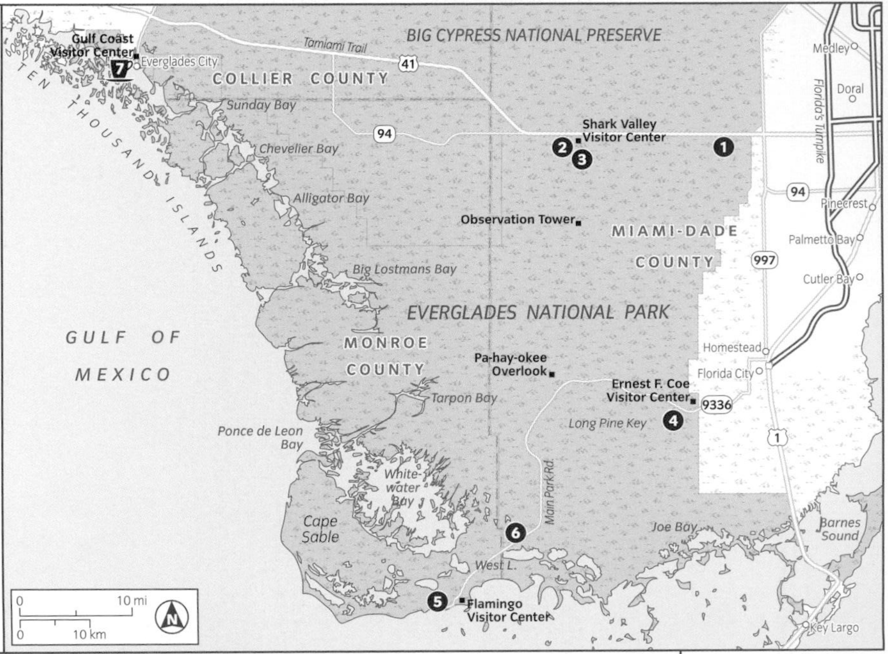

The Everglades were declared "an irreplaceable primitive area" by President Harry S. Truman, who said, "Here is land, tranquil in its quiet beauty, serving not as the source of water, but as the last receiver of it. To its natural abundance we owe the spectacular plant and animal life that distinguishes this place from all others in our country." There's no better reality show than the one that exists in the Everglades. Up-close-and-personal views of alligators, crocodiles, and bona fide wildlife make for an interesting and photo-friendly experience. **START: Gator Park, located 12 miles (19km) west of the Florida Turnpike.**

Gator Park offers airboat tours and gator shows.

1 kids **Gator Park.** This is one of the most informative and entertaining airboat-tour operators around, not to mention the only one to give out free earplugs. Some of the guides deserve a medal for getting into the water and poking a massive alligator, even though they're not really supposed to. After the boat ride, there's a free interactive wildlife show that features alligator wrestling and several other frightening acts involving scorpions. *1 hr. 24050 SW 8th St. ☎ 305/559-2255. www.gatorpark.com. Admission $21 adults, $11 children 6–11. Includes airboat tour & show. Airboats leave every 20 minutes. Daily 9am–7pm.*

2 ★★★ Shark Valley Tram Tour. At the Everglades' Shark Valley entrance, open-air tram buses take visitors on 2-hour naturalist-led tours that delve 7½ miles (11km) into the wilderness and are the best quick introduction you can get to the Everglades. At the trail's midsection, passengers can disembark and climb a 65-foot (20m) observation tower with good views of the 'glades (though the tower on the Pa-hay-okee Trail is better). Visitors will see plenty of wildlife and endless acres of saw grass. *2 hr. Shark Valley Entrance, 36000 SW 8th St. ☎ 305/221-8455. www.sharkvalleytramtours.com. Tours run Dec–Apr daily on the hour 9am–4pm; May–Nov 9:30 & 11am and 1 & 3pm. Reservations recommended Dec–Mar. $15 adults, $14 seniors & $9.25 children 12 & under.*

3 ★★★ Bike Shark Valley. This is South Florida's most scenic bike trail. You'll share the flat, paved road with other bikers, trams, and a menagerie of wildlife (gators lounging in the sun, deer munching on grass). There are no shortcuts, so if you get tired or are unable to complete the entire 15-mile (24km) trip, turn around and return on the same road. *2–3 hr. Shark Valley*

Entrance, 36000 SW 8th St. ☎ 305/ 221-8455. www.sharkvalleytram tours.com/biking.html. Bike rentals $6.50 per hr.; rentals can be picked up anytime between 8:30am–3pm & must be returned by 4pm.

4 ★★★ Explore the Gumbo Limbo Trail. If you want to see a greater array of plant and animal life, venture into the park through the main entrance, pick up a trail map, and dedicate at least a day to exploring from there. Stop first along the Anhinga and Gumbo Limbo trails, which start right next to each other, 3 miles (5km) from the park's main entrance. These trails provide a thorough introduction to the Everglades' flora and fauna and are highly recommended for first-time visitors. Each is a ½-mile (1km) round-trip. **Gumbo Limbo Trail** (the best walking trail in the Everglades) meanders through a gorgeous, shaded, jungle-like hammock of gumbo-limbo trees, royal palms, ferns, orchids, air plants, and a general blanket of vegetation, though it doesn't put you in close contact with much wildlife. **Anhinga Trail** is one of the most popular trails in the park because of its abundance of wildlife: There's more water and wildlife in this area than in most parts of the Everglades, especially during dry season. Alligators, lizards, turtles, river otters, herons, egrets, and other animals abound, making this one of the best trails for seeing wildlife. Arrive early to spot the widest selection of exotic birds, such as the trail's namesake, the Anhinga. *🕘 2 hr. Royal Palm Visitor Center, located 4 miles (6.5km) west of the Main Park Entrance west of Homestead & Florida City. ☎ 305/242-7700. www.nps.gov/ever/plan yourvisit/gumbo-limbo-trail.htm. Park entry $10 per car.*

5 Go birding at Eco and Mrazek Ponds. More than 350 species of birds make their home in the Everglades. Tropical birds from the Caribbean and temperate species from North America can be found here, along with exotics that have flown in from more distant regions. Eco and Mrazek ponds, located near Flamingo, are two of the best places for birding, especially in early morning or late afternoon in the dry winter months. Pick up a free birding checklist from one of the visitor centers. *🕘 1–2 hr. Flamingo Visitor Center, 38 miles*

The observation tower at Shark Valley.

You'll come across many plants and animals along the Gumbo Limbo Trail.

(61km) southwest from the main entrance at the southern end of the park. ☎ 941/695-2945. Entrance $10 per car.

❻ **Cruise a canoe trail.** Everglades National Park's longest "trails" are designed for boat and canoe travel, and many are marked as clearly as walking trails. The **Noble Hammock Canoe Trail,** a 2-mile (3km) loop, takes 1 to 2 hours and is recommended for beginners. The **Hell's Bay Canoe Trail,** a 3- to 6-mile (5–10km) course for hardier

Wildlife Exploration: From Gators to Manatees to Turtles

One of the most scenic areas on this stretch of the coast is **Jonathan Dickinson State Park ★**, 20 miles north of West Palm Beach at 16450 S. Federal Hwy. (U.S. 1), Hobe Sound (☎ 772/546-2771). Dozens of species of Florida's unique wildlife, including alligators and manatees, live on the park's more than 11,300 acres, and bird-watchers will catch glimpses of rare and endangered species such as the bald eagle, the Florida scrub-jay, and the Florida sandhill crane. You can rent canoes from the concessions stand to explore the Loxahatchee River on your own. Admission is $4 per car of up to eight adults; $3 for one person. Day hikers, bikers, and walkers pay $1 each. The park is open from 8am until sundown.

Close to Jonathan Dickinson State Park is **Hobe Sound Wildlife Refuge,** on North Beach Road off S.R. 708, at the north end of Jupiter Island (☎ 772/546-6141). This is one of the best places to spot sea turtles that nest on the shore in the summer months, especially in June and July. Admission is $4 per car, and the preserve is open daily from sunrise to sunset. Exact times are posted at each entrance and change seasonally.

Navigating the Everglades

General inquiries and specific questions should be directed to **Everglades National Park Headquarters,** 40001 S.R. 9336, Homestead, FL 33034 (☎ 305/242-7700). Ask for a copy of *Parks and Preserves,* a free newspaper filled with up-to-date information about goings-on in the Everglades. Headquarters is staffed by helpful phone operators daily from 8:30am to 4:30pm. You can also try www.nps.gov.

Note that all hours listed are for the high season, generally November through May. During the slow summer months, many offices and outfitters keep abbreviated hours. Always call ahead to confirm hours of operation.

The **Ernest F. Coe Visitor Center,** located at the Park Headquarters entrance, west of Homestead and Florida City, is the best place to gather information for your trip. In addition to details on tours and boat rentals, and free brochures outlining trails, wildlife, and activities, you will find state-of-the-art educational displays, films, and interactive exhibits.

The **Royal Palm Visitor Center** is a smaller information center and the departure point for the popular Anhinga and Gumbo Limbo trails. The center is open daily from 8am to 4pm.

Knowledgeable rangers, who provide brochures and personal insight into the park's activities, also staff the **Flamingo Visitor Center,** 38 miles (61km) from the main entrance, at the park's southern access, with natural-history exhibits and information on visitor services, and the **Shark Valley Visitor Center,** at the park's northern entrance. Both are open daily from 8:30am to 5pm.

paddlers, takes 2 to 6 hours, depending on how far you choose to go. Fans of this trail like to say, "It's hell to get in and hell to get out." ⏱ *1–4 hr. Canoe rentals available at the Ivey House B&B, 107 Camelia St.* ☎ *877/577-0679. www.evergladesadventures.com. $50 for 24 hrs., $35 per full day (any 8-hr. period), or $25 per half-day (1–5pm only). Kayaks and tandem kayaks also available. The rental agent will shuttle your party to the trail head of your choice and pick you up afterward. Rental facilities open daily 8am–5pm.*

Experience the Everglades' most historic hotel and seafood restaurant, **7 The Rod and Gun Lodge,** where Hoover vacationed after his 1928 election victory, and Truman flew in to sign Everglades National Park into existence in 1947. *Riverside & Broadway, Everglades City.* ☎ *239/695-2101. www.evergladesrodandgun.com. $.* ●

10 The Best of the Keys

Best of the Keys in One Day

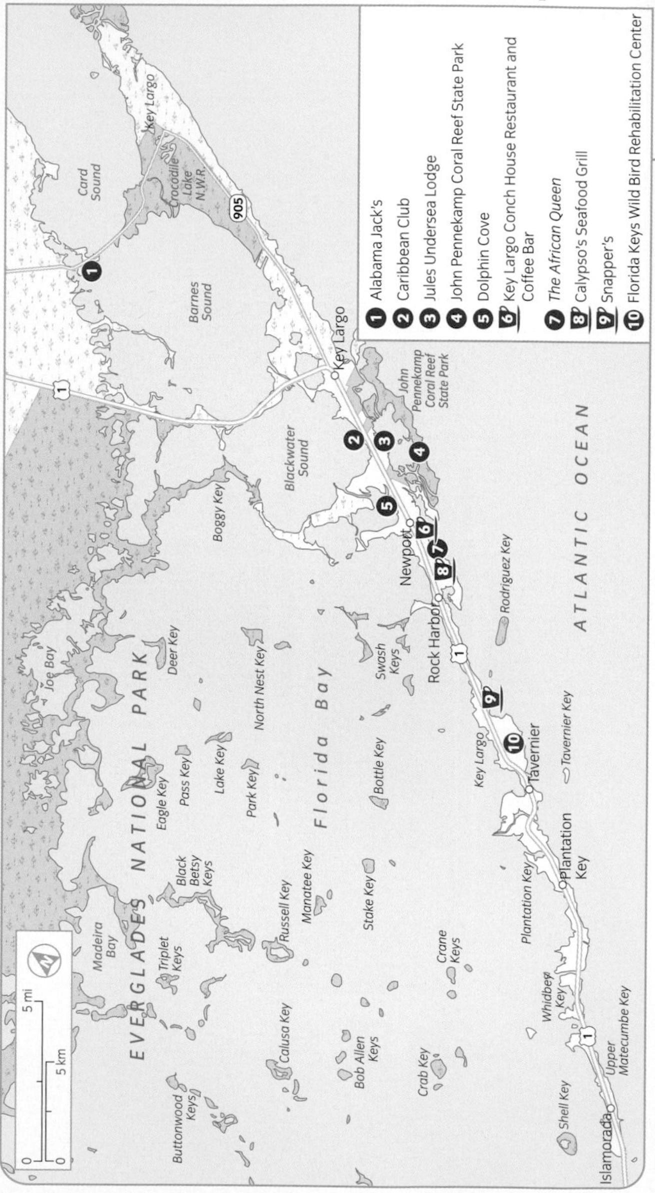

Previous page: Sunsets in the Keys are as colorful as the local characters.

With one day to spend in the Keys, focus on the drive from Miami to Key Largo, a slow descent into an unusual but breathtaking American ecosystem: On either side of you, for miles ahead, lie nothing but emerald waters. (On weekends, however, you will also see plenty of traffic.) More than 400 islands make up this 150-mile-long (242km) necklace, strung out across the Atlantic Ocean like loose strands of cultured pearls. **START: Alabama Jack's.**

Get good views and grub at Alabama Jack's.

1 ★★★ Get in the Keys mood at Alabama Jack's. On its own, there's not much to the waterfront shack that is Alabama Jack's. The bar serves beer and wine only, and the restaurant specializes in delicious, albeit greasy, bar fare. But this quintessential Old Floridian dive, located in a historic fishing village called Card Sound between Homestead and Key Largo, is a colorful must on the drive south, especially on Sunday, when bikers mix with barflies, anglers, line dancers, and Southern belles. Live country music resurrects the legendary Johnny Cash and Co. Pull up a barstool, order a cold one, and take in the sights—the views of the mangroves are spectacular. *1 hr. 5800 Card Sound Rd.* ☎ *305/248-8741. To get here, pick up Card Sound Rd. (the old Rte. 1) a few miles after you pass Homestead, heading toward Key Largo. Alabama Jack's is on the right side.*

2 Caribbean Club. Although most of the Humphrey Bogart classic *Key Largo* was filmed in California, several scenes were shot in this first of the Florida Keys, primarily at this former men's fishing club turned dive bar, which still attracts salty locals on a daily—and nightly—basis. 🕘 *10–30 min. MM 104.* ☎ *305/451-4466.*

3 ★★★ Under the Keys at Jules Undersea Lodge. Staying here is certainly an experience of a lifetime—if you're brave enough to take the plunge. Originally built as a research lab, this small underwater compartment, which rests on pillars on the ocean floor, now operates as a two-room hotel. As expensive as it is unusual, Jules is most popular with diving honeymooners. To get inside, guests swim 21 feet (6m) under the structure and pop up into the unit through a 4×6-foot (1×2m) "moon pool" that gurgles soothingly all night. The 30-foot-deep (9m) underwater suite consists of two separate bedrooms that share a common living area. Room service will deliver your meals, daily newspapers, and even a late-night pizza in waterproof containers, at no extra charge. If you don't have time or a desire to spend the night, you can hang out and explore the lodge for 3 hours for $125 to $165 per person. 🕘 *3 hr. 51 Shoreland Dr.* ☎ *305/451-2353. www.jul.com.*

4 ★★★ kids Viewing the Keys from a glass-bottom boat. The 188-square-mile (487-sq.-km) John Pennekamp Coral Reef State Park is the nation's first undersea preserve: It's a sanctuary for part of the only living coral reef in the continental United States. Because the water is extremely shallow, the 40 species of coral and more than 650 species of fish here are accessible to divers, snorkelers, and glass-bottom boat passengers. Watch for the lobsters and other sea life residing in the fairly shallow ridge walls beneath the coastal waters. 🕘 *2½ hr. MM 102.5.* ☎ *305/451-6300. www.pennekamppark.com. Admission to park $5 per vehicle plus 50¢ per passenger. Glass-bottom boat tours $24 adults, $17 children 11 & under.*

The colorful creatures at Pennekamp Coral Reef State Park can be seen from a glass-bottom boat.

Tours depart daily 9:15am and 12:15 & 3pm.

5 ★★★ Swim with the Dolphins. Dolphin Cove, a marine education and dolphin facility set on a natural lagoon, offers opportunities to splash around with the friendly critters or watch them ham it up for audiences in a variety of shows. 🕘 *1–2 hr. MM 101.9.* ☎ *305/451-4060. www.dolphinscove.com. Dolphin swim $165–$185. Daily 8am–5pm.*

At **6 Key Largo Conch House Restaurant and Coffee Bar** (☎ 305/453-4844; www.keylargocoffeehouse.com), you can sip a coffee on the veranda of a Victorian house set amidst lush foliage. Don't forget to order a slice of Key lime pie, either.

7 Channel your best Bogey and Bacall. Local entrepreneurs bought Bogey's boat, ***The African Queen,*** the one he occupied with costar Katharine Hepburn in the flick of the same name. You can see the boat at the Key Largo Holiday Inn. *Key Largo Holiday Inn, MM 100.* ☎ *305/451-4655.*

8 Calypso's Seafood Grill is a rustic, off-the-beaten-path waterfront spot serving cold beer, sangria, and some of the best She-Crab soup in town. *1 Seagate Blvd. near MM 99.5.* ☎ *305/451-0600. $.* Or, stop by waterfront fave **9 Snapper's,** where the blackened mahi-mahi is out of this world and lively happy hours are out of a Jimmy Buffett video. *139 Seaside Ave. at MM 94.5.* ☎ *305/852-5956. $.*

10 ★★★ kids Take in the view from the Florida Keys Wild Bird Rehab Center. Wander through lush canopies of mangroves on wooden walkways to see some of the Keys' most famous residents—the large variety of native birds, including broad-wing hawks, great blue and white herons, roseate spoonbills, cattle egrets, and pelicans. This not-for-profit center operates as a hospital for the many birds that have been injured by accident or disease. Also here: the World Parrot Mission, focusing on caring for parrots and educating the public about the birds. Visit at feeding time, usually about 3:30pm. ⌚ *1 hr. MM 93.6.* ☎ *305/852-4486. www.fkwbc.org. Free. Daily 8am–6:30pm.*

Tip: Don't Be Fooled

Avoid the many "tourist information centers" that dot the main highway. Most are private companies hired to lure visitors to specific lodgings or outfitters. (Anything that says free Disney tickets or something like that is probably a scam or timeshare racket.) You're better off sticking with the official, not-for-profit centers (the legit ones usually don't advertise on the turnpike), which are extremely well located and staffed.

See native birds and those being rehabilitated at the Florida Keys Wild Bird Rehab Center.

Best of the Keys in Two Days

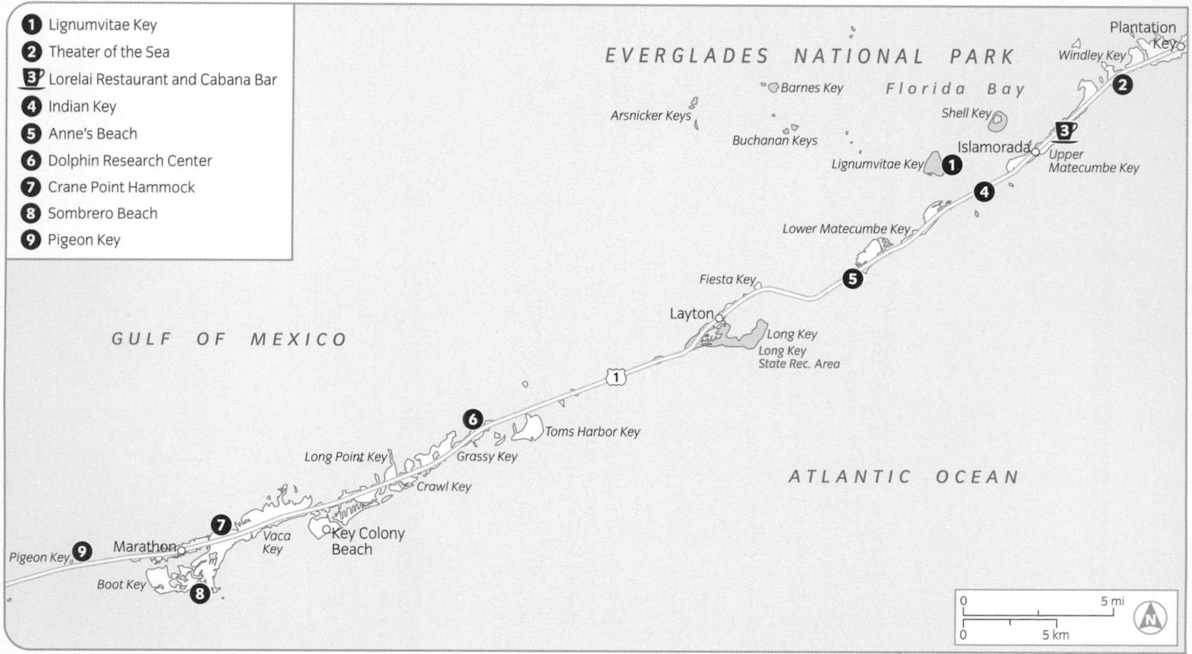
1 Lignumvitae Key
2 Theater of the Sea
3 Lorelai Restaurant and Cabana Bar
4 Indian Key
5 Anne's Beach
6 Dolphin Research Center
7 Crane Point Hammock
8 Sombrero Beach
9 Pigeon Key
EVERGLADES NATIONAL PARK
Florida Bay
Plantation Key
Windley Key
Barnes Key
Arsnicker Keys
Buchanan Keys
Shell Key
Islamorada
Upper Matecumbe Key
Lignumvitae Key
Lower Matecumbe Key
Fiesta Key
Layton
Long Key
Long Key State Rec. Area
GULF OF MEXICO
1
Toms Harbor Key
Long Point Key
Grassy Key
Crawl Key
ATLANTIC OCEAN
Vaca Key
Key Colony Beach
Marathon
Pigeon Key
Boot Key
0
5 mi
0
5 km
N

On your second day in the Keys, explore Islamorada and the Middle Keys. Islamorada, the unofficial capital of the Upper Keys, has the area's best atmosphere, food, fishing, entertainment, and lodging. It's an unofficial "party capital" for mainlanders seeking a quick tropical excursion. Islamorada is composed of four islands, and here nature lovers can enjoy walking trails, historic exploration, and big-purse fishing tournaments. For a more tranquil, less party-hearty Keys experience, all other keys besides Key West and Islamorada are better choices. **Marathon,** smack in the middle of the Florida Keys, is known as the heart of the Keys and is one of the most populated. It is part fishing village, part tourist center, and part nature preserve. **START: Anne's Beach.**

1 ★ Lignumvitae Key. This key supports a virgin tropical forest, the kind that once thrived on most of the Upper Keys. Over the years, human settlers imported "exotic" plants and animals to the Keys, irrevocably changing the botanical makeup of many backcountry islands and threatening much of the indigenous wildlife. Over the past 25 years, however, the Florida Department of Natural Resources has successfully removed most of the exotic vegetation from this key, leaving the 280-acre (113-hectare) site much as it existed in the 18th century. The island also holds the Matheson House, a historic structure built in 1919. You can go inside, but it's interesting only if you appreciate the coral rock of which the house is made. More interesting are the Botanical Gardens, which surround the house and are a state preserve. *2–4 hrs. MM 88.5. ☎ 305/664-2450. Take Robbie's Ferry Service, MM 77.5. ☎ 305/664-9814. www.robbies.com. A visit to Lignumvitae Key costs $20 adults, $12 kids 12 & under; includes the $1 park admission.*

2 kids ★ Theater of the Sea. The park's dolphin and sea lion shows are entertaining and informative, especially for children. While we suggest you swim with the dolphins at the Dolphin Research Center (p 150), the Theater of the Sea also permits you to swim with sea lions. (Children 4 and under cannot participate.) There are twice-daily 4-hour adventure and snorkel cruises ($69 adults, $45 children 3–12), during which you can learn about the history and ecology of the marine environment. *1–3 hr. MM 84.5, Islamorada. ☎ 305/664-2431. www.theaterofthesea.com. Admission $26 adults, $19 children 3–12. Dolphin swim $175; sea lion swim $135. Reservations required.*

Kids will love the shows at the Theater of the Sea.

Daily 10am–5pm (ticket office closes at 4pm).

3 Lorelai Restaurant and Cabana Bar, a big old fish house and bar, offers excellent views of the bay, and is a great place for a snack, a meal, or a beer. Lorelai's legendary sunset happy hours feature live music and lots of local color. *MM 82. ☎ 305/664-4656. $.*

4 Indian Key. A much smaller island on the Atlantic side of Islamorada, this was occupied by Native Americans for thousands of years before European settlers arrived. The 10-acre (4-hectare) historic site was also the original seat of Dade County before the Civil War. You can see the ruins of the previous settlement and tour the lush grounds on well-marked trails. *2–4 hrs. MM 79. ☎ 305/664-4815. Take Robbie's Ferry Service, MM 77.5. ☎ 305/664-9814. www.robbies.com. Combined visit with Lignumvitae Key costs $25.*

5 Anne's Beach. This is more a picnic spot than full-fledged beach, but diehard tanners still congregate on this lovely but tiny strip of coarse sand. *1–2 hrs. MM 73.5, on Lower Matecumbe Key, at the southwest end of Islamorada. Daily sunrise–sunset.*

6 ★★★ kids More fun with Dolphins. The Dolphin Research Center is one of the most respected. Knowledgeable trainers at the center will tell you that the dolphins need stimulation and enjoy human contact. They certainly seem to. The "family" of 15 dolphins swims in a 90,000-square-foot (8,361 sq. m) natural saltwater pool carved out of the shoreline. If you can't get into the daily swim program, you can still watch the frequent shows, sign up for a class in hand signals, or feed the dolphins from docks. *2–4 hr. MM 59, Marathon. ☎ 305/289-1121. www.dolphins.org. Admission $20 adults, $17 seniors, $14 children 4–12. Dolphin swims $130–$180. Daily 9am–4pm. Educational walking tours daily 10 & 11am and 12:30, 2 & 3:30pm.*

7 ★ kids Crane Point Hammock. This privately owned, 64-acre (26-hectare) nature area is considered one of the most important historic sites in the Keys. It contains what is probably the last virgin thatch-palm hammock in North America, as well as a rainforest exhibit and an archaeological site with prehistoric Indian and Bahamian artifacts. The impressive nature museum has simple, informative displays of the Keys' wildlife, including a walk-through replica of a coral-reef cave. Kids can climb through a scaled-down pirate ship and touch a variety of indigenous creatures. *1 hr. MM 50, Marathon. ☎ 305/743-9100. www.cranepoint.net.*

The nature museum at Crane Point Hammock has simple, yet impressive, exhibits.

The Seven-Mile Bridge at Pigeon Key.

$8 adults, $7 seniors 66 & over, $5 students, free for children 5 & under. Mon–Sat 9am–5pm; Sun noon–5pm.

❽ **Sombrero Beach.** This wide swath of uncluttered beachfront has more than 90 feet (27m) of sand and is dotted with palms, Australian pines, and royal Poincianas, as well as grills, clean restrooms, and Tiki huts. It's also a popular nesting spot for turtles that lay their eggs at night. *1–2 hrs. In Marathon, at the end of Sombrero Beach Rd. near MM 50. Daily sunrise–sunset.*

❾ ★★ kids **Picnicking on Pigeon Key.** This 5-acre (2-hectare) island once held the camp for the crew that built the railway in the early 20th century. From here, the vista includes the vestiges of Henry Flagler's Seven Mile Bridge, as well as many old wooden cottages and a tranquil stretch of lush foliage and sea. If you miss the shuttle tour from the Pigeon Key visitor center or would rather walk to the site, the bridge is about 2½ miles (4km). Either way, you may want to bring a picnic to enjoy after a brief self-guided walking tour of the Key and a visit to the museum, which features artifacts and photographs of the old bridge. *1–3 hr. MM 45, Marathon. ☎ 305/743-5999. www.pigeonkey.net. Admission $11 adults, $8.50 children 12 & under. Prices include shuttle transportation from the visitor center. Daily 10am–3pm; shuttle tours run hourly 10am–4pm.*

Bridge Mix

The Seven-Mile Bridge is the longest fragmented (unconnected pieces) bridge in the world. Completed in 1985, it was constructed parallel to the original bridge, part of Henry Flagler's Florida East Coast Railroad, which served as the original link to the Lower Keys. Some people may recognize the remnants of the old bridge from the Arnold Schwarzenegger movie *True Lies.* Others fearfully contemplate a wrong turn leading them to the old bridge instead of the new one. Not to worry: The old bridge is closed to cars and has been transformed into the world's longest fishing pier.

Best of the Keys in Three Days

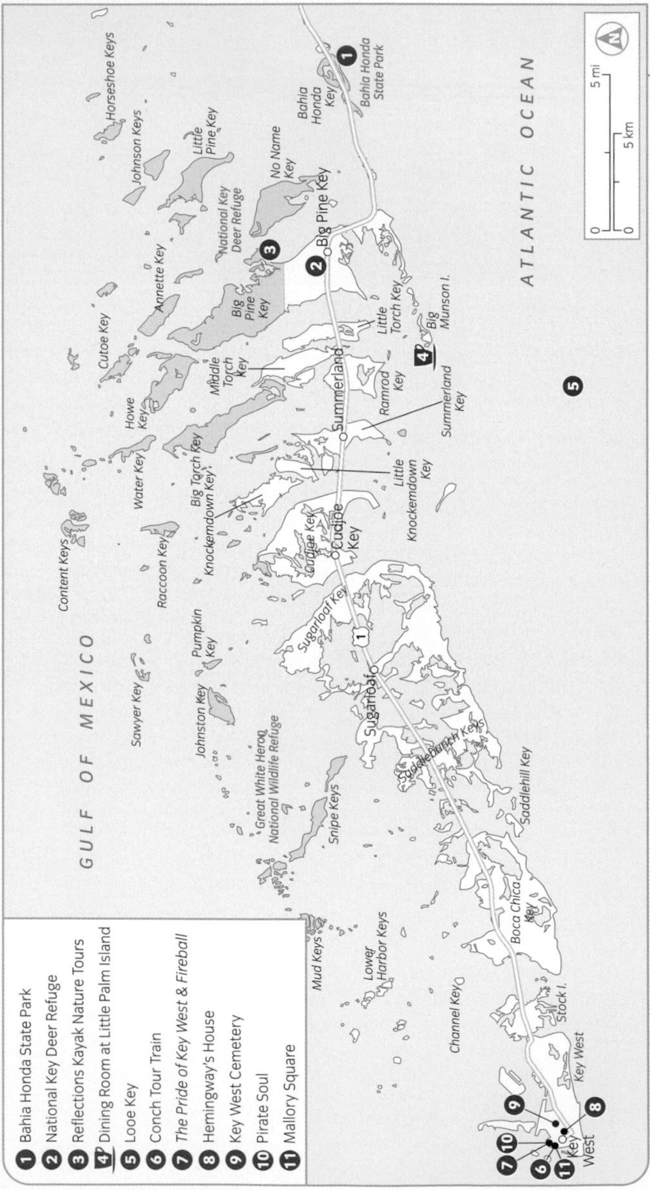

On your third day in the Keys, keep driving south, to the Southernmost Point, The Conch Republic, aka Key West. Be sure to stop at one of the state's best and most beautiful parks on the way. **START: Bahia Honda State Park, Big Pine Key.**

Bahia Honda State Park offers nature lovers everything from camping to trails.

1 ★★★ Bahia Honda State Park. Bahia (pronounced Bah-ya) Honda is a great place for hiking, bird-watching, swimming, snorkeling, and fishing. The 524-acre (212-hectare) park encompasses a wide variety of ecosystems, including coastal mangroves, beach dunes, and tropical hammocks. There are miles of trails packed with unusual plants and animals, plus a small white-sand beach. Shaded seaside picnic areas are fitted with tables and grills. Although the beach is never wider than 5 feet (1.5m), even at low tide, this is the Lower Keys' best beach area. Snorkeling trips go from the Bahia Honda concessions to Looe Key National Marine Sanctuary (4 miles/6.5km offshore). They depart twice daily March through September and cost $30 for adults, $25 for children 6 to 14, and $8 for equipment rental. *1–4 hr. at MM 37.5, Big Pine Key. ☎ 305/872-2353. www.bahiahondapark.com. Entry to the park $5 per vehicle (plus 50¢ per person), $1.50 per pedestrian or bicyclist, free for children 5 & under. If you're alone in a car, you'll pay only $2.50. Daily 8am–sunset.*

2 ★★★ kids National Key Deer Refuge. The most famous residents of the Lower Keys are the tiny Key deer. Of the estimated 300 existing in the world, two-thirds live here. Start out at the Blue Hole, a former rock quarry now filled with the fresh water that's vital to the deer's survival. The ½-mile (.8km) Watson Hammock Trail, about ⅓ mile (.5km) past the Blue Hole, is the refuge's only marked footpath. The deer are more active in cool hours, so try coming out to the path in the early morning or late evening. There is an observation deck from which you can watch and photograph

Two-thirds of the world's Key deer population are at the National Key Deer Refuge.

the protected species. Don't be surprised to see a lazy alligator warming itself in the sun, particularly in outlying areas around the Blue Hole. If you do see a gator, keep your distance. Also, whatever you do, do not feed the deer—it will threaten their survival. 🕘 *2 hr. Key Deer Refuge Ranger Station, the rangers' office at the Winn-Dixie Shopping Plaza, near MM 30.5 off U.S. 1.* ☎ *305/872-2239. The refuge is open Mon–Fri 8am–5pm. To reach the Blue Hole, turn right at Big Pine Key's only traffic light onto Key Deer Blvd. (take the left fork immediately after the turn) and continue 1½ miles (2.4km) to the observation-site parking lot, on your left. Children must be at least 3 years old and provide proof of age with birth certificate, or 38 in. (97cm) tall to enter. Daily at least 11am–4:30pm, but often longer.*

3 ★ Reflections Kayak Nature Tours. The Overseas Highway (U.S. 1) touches on only a few dozen of the many hundreds of islands that make up the Keys. To really see the Lower Keys, rent a kayak or canoe—perfect for these shallow waters. Reflections Kayak Nature Tours offers fully outfitted backcountry wildlife tours, either on your own or with an expert. 🕘 *3–4 hr. 1791 Bogie Dr., MM 30, Big Pine Key.* ☎ *305/872-4668. www.floridakeyskayaktours.com. 3-hr. kayak tour $50 per person; extended 4-hr. backcountry tour for 2–6 people costs $125 per person and uses a mother ship to ferry kayaks and paddlers to the remote reaches of the refuge. Reservations required.*

4 If you're in the mood to splurge on a swanky private island, try the **Dining Room at Little Palm Island.** You need to take the hotel's ferry to this private island, where you can indulge at the exquisite oceanside restaurant even if you're not staying over. *MM 285, Little Torch Key.* ☎ *305/872-2551. $$$*

5 Snorkeling at Looe Key. Snorkelers and divers should not miss the Keys' most dramatic reefs at the Looe Key National Marine Sanctuary. Here you'll see more

Snorkelers at Looe Key.

The Pride of Key West.

than 150 varieties of hard and soft coral—some centuries old—as well as every type of tropical fish, including gold and blue parrotfish, moray eels, barracudas, French angels, and tarpon. Looe Key Dive Center offers a mind-blowing 5-hour tour aboard a 45-foot (14m) catamaran with two shallow 1-hour dives for snorkelers and scuba divers. On Wednesday and Saturday, you can do a fascinating dive to the *Adolphus Busch, Sr.*, a shipwreck off Looe Key in 100 feet (30m) of water, for $80. ⏲ *2–4 hrs. U.S. 1 at MM 27.5, Ramrod Key.* ☎ *305/872-2215. www.diveflakeys.com. Snorkelers $40, divers $80. Equipment available for rental for $10.*

6 ★★★ Tour by train. Key West's whole story is packed on the Conch Tour Train, which covers the island and all its rich, raunchy history. In operation since 1958, the cars are open-air, which can make the ride uncomfortable in bad weather. The engine of the "train" is a propane-powered jeep disguised as a locomotive. ⏲ *90 min. Tours depart from both Mallory Sq. and the Welcome Center, near where U.S. 1 becomes N. Roosevelt Blvd., on the less-developed side of the island.* ☎ *305/294-5161. www.conchtour train.com. The cost is $29 adults, $14 children 4–12. Tickets are cheaper on the website. Daily departures every half-hour 9am–4:30pm.*

7 ★★★ kids Key West by Sea. Seeing Key West by boat is one of the best ways to explore the island and its surroundings. The catamaran *The Pride of Key West* and the glass-bottom boat *Fireball* depart on daytime coral-reef tours and evening sunset cruises. ⏲ *2–3 hrs. 0 Duval St.* ☎ *305/296-6293. www.keywestattractions.org/pride-of-key-west.php. Reef trips $35 per person, sunset cruises $37 per person; kids ages 5–12 sail on all cruises for $15.*

8 ★★★ Hemingway's House. Ernest Hemingway's particularly handsome stone Spanish colonial house, built in 1851, was one of the first on the island to be fitted with indoor plumbing and a built-in fireplace. It also has the first swimming pool built on Key West (look for the penny that Hemingway pressed into the cement near the pool). The author owned the home from 1931 until his death in 1961, and lived here with about 50 cats, whose descendants, including the famed six-toed felines, still roam the premises. It was during those years that the Nobel Prize–winning author wrote some of his most famous works. ⏲ *1 hr. 907 Whitehead St.*

Six-toed cats roam the grounds of The Hemingway House.

(btw. Truman Ave. & Olivia St.). ☎ 305/294-1136. www.hemingwayhome.com. Admission $11 adults, $6 children. Daily 9am–5pm.

9 ★★★ Key West Cemetery. This cemetery is the epitome of quirky Key West. Many tombs are stacked several high, condominium style, since the rocky soil made digging 6 feet under nearly impossible for early settlers. Epitaphs reflect residents' lighthearted attitudes toward life and death. "I told you I was sick," is one of the more famous, as is the tongue-in-cheek widow's inscription "At least I know where he's sleeping tonight." *30 min. Entrance at the corner of Margaret & Angela sts. Free admission. Daily dawn–dusk.*

10 kids ★★★ Pirate Soul. This museum is dedicated to everything about the legendary seafaring rogues, featuring more than 500 artifacts from the golden age of piracy, as well as animatronics and interactive exhibits. Among the highlights are the only authentic pirate treasure chest in America, originally belonging to Captain Thomas Tew, and Blackbeard's original blunderbuss. *524 Front St. ☎ 305/292-1113. www.piratesoul.com. Admission $15 adults, $9 children 6–12. Tickets are cheaper on the website. Daily 9am–7pm.*

11 Sunset Celebration. Every evening, locals and visitors gather at the docks behind Mallory Square (at the westernmost end of Whitehead St.) to celebrate the day gone by among portrait artists, acrobats, food vendors, animal acts, and other performers. **Westin's Sunset Deck** (☎ 305/294-4000) is a luxurious second-floor bar on Front Street, right next door to Mallory Square.

Also near the Mallory madness is the bar at the **Ocean Key Resort,** at the very tip of Duval Street (☎ 800/328-9815 or 305/296-7701), a long open-air pier serving drinks and decent bar food. For the best

Comical headstones are the star of the Key West Cemetery.

potent cocktails and great bar food, try **Pier House Resort and Caribbean Spa's Havana Docks,** 1 Duval St. (☎ 305/296-4600). There's usually live music and a lively gathering of visitors. The bar is right on the water and makes a prime sunset-viewing spot. In season, the crowd can be overwhelming, especially when the cruise ships are in port. Also, hold on to your bags and wallets, as the tight crowds make Mallory Square at sunset prime pick-pocketing territory.

If you'd rather sail into the sunset, try **Sunset Culinaire Tours,** onboard *RB's Lady*. It includes a tour of Key West harbor and a gourmet dinner (5555 College Rd.; ☎ 305/296-0982; www.sunsetculinaire.com; boarding time 5pm; $75 per person).

A Performer at Mallory Square.

The 10 "Keymandments"

The Keys have always attracted independent spirits, from Ernest Hemingway and Tennessee Williams to Jimmy Buffett, Zane Grey, and local hero Mel Fisher. Writers, artists, and freethinkers have long drifted down here to escape.

Although you'll generally find a very laid-back and tolerant code of behavior in the Keys, some rules do exist. Be sure to respect the 10 "Keymandments" while you're here, or suffer the consequences.

- Don't anchor on a reef. (Reefs are alive.)
- Don't feed the animals. (They'll want to follow you home.)
- Don't trash our place.
- Don't touch the coral. (After all, you don't even know them. Some pose a mild risk of injury to you as well.)
- Don't speed (especially on Big Pine Key, where deer reside and tar-and-feathering is still practiced).
- Don't catch more fish than you can eat. (Better yet, let them go. Some of them support schools.)
- Don't collect conch. (This species is protected.)
- Don't disturb the birds' nests. (They find it very annoying.)
- Don't damage the sea grass (and don't even think about making a skirt out of it).
- Don't drink and drive on land or sea. (There's nothing funny about it.)

Best of **Key West in One Day**

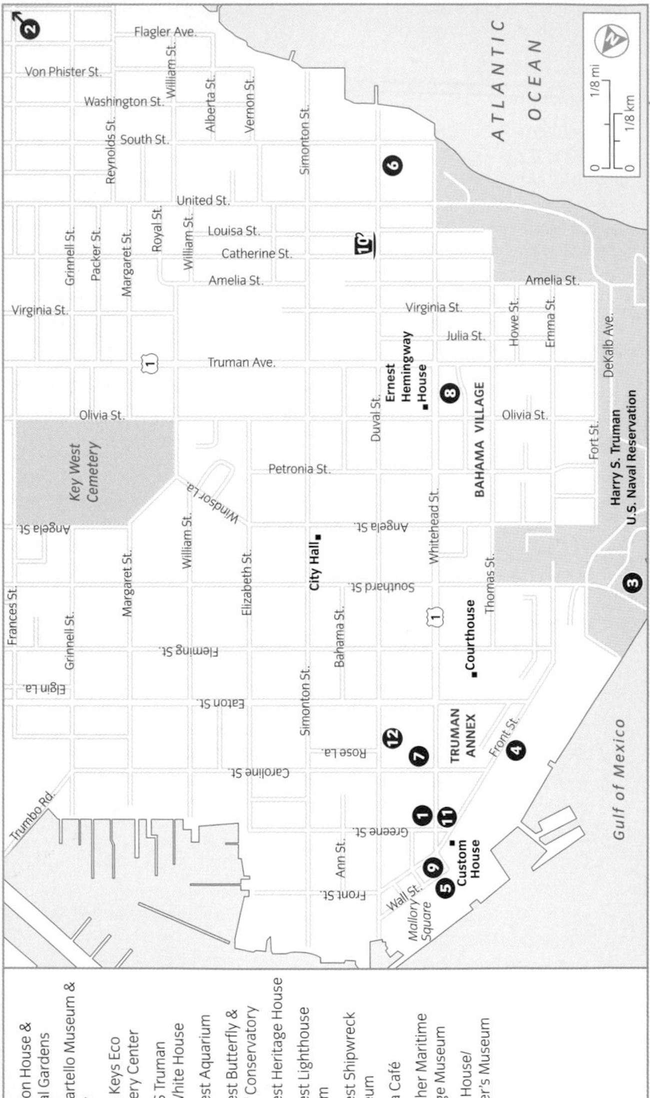

1. Audubon House & Tropical Gardens
2. East Martello Museum & Gallery
3. Florida Keys Eco Discovery Center
4. Harry S Truman Little White House
5. Key West Aquarium
6. Key West Butterfly & Nature Conservatory
7. Key West Heritage House
8. Key West Lighthouse Museum
9. Key West Shipwreck Historeum

10. Banana Café

11. Mel Fisher Maritime Heritage Museum
12. Oldest House/ Wrecker's Museum

Singer Jimmy Buffett may have immortalized Key West as a boozy, bluesy island, which it is, but before Buffett, Key West already had a reputation as a haven for rum runners, pirates, presidents, artists, and intellectuals. And let's not forget the animals—the partying kind and otherwise. **START: Audubon House & Tropical Gardens.**

1 ★★ Audubon House & Tropical Gardens. This well-preserved 19th-century home stands as a prime example of early Key West architecture. Named after renowned painter and bird expert John James Audubon, the graceful two-story structure is a peaceful retreat from the bustle of Old Town. Included in the price of admission is a self-guided, half-hour audio tour that spotlights rare Audubon prints, gorgeous antiques, historical photos, and lush tropical gardens. *1 hr. 205 Whitehead St. (btw. Greene & Caroline sts.). ☎ 305/294-2116. www.audubonhouse.com. Admission $11 adults, $6.50 children 12–17, $5 children 6–12. Daily 9:30am–5pm (last entry 4:30pm).*

2 East Martello Museum and Gallery. East Martello Museum is in a Civil War–era brick fort that itself is worth a visit. The museum contains a bizarre variety of exhibits that do a thorough job of interpreting the city's intriguing past. Historic artifacts include model ships, a deep-sea diver's wooden air pump, and a horse-drawn hearse. *30 min. 3501 S. Roosevelt Blvd. ☎ 305/296-3913. www.kwahs.com/martello.htm. Admission $6 adults, $5 seniors, $3 children 8–12. Daily 9:30am–4:30pm (last entry 4pm).*

3 ★★★ kids Florida Keys Eco Discovery Center. The Center features 6,000 square feet (557 sq. m) of interactive exhibits depicting Florida Keys underwater and upland habitats—with emphasis on the ecosystem of North America's only living contiguous barrier coral reef, which parallels the Keys. Kids dig the interactive yellow submarine, while adults get into the cinematic depiction of an underwater abyss. *30 min. 35 E. Quay Rd. ☎ 305/809-4750. Free admission. Open Tues–Sat 9am–4pm.*

4 ★ Harry S. Truman Little White House. President Truman used to refer to the White House as

The buck stops at Truman's Little White House.

the "Great White Jail." On temporary leave from the Big House, Truman discovered the serenity of Key West and made his escape to what became known as the Little White House, which is open to the public for touring. The house is fully restored; the exhibits document Truman's time in the Keys. 🕘 *30 min–1hr. if you take tour. 111 Front St.* ☎ *305/294-9911. www.trumanlittlewhitehouse.com. Admission $12 adults, $6 children 11 & under. Daily 9am–4:30pm.*

❺ ★★ kids **Key West Aquarium.** The oldest attraction on the island, this is a modest but fascinating place. A long hallway of eye-level displays showcases dozens of varieties of fish and crustaceans. Kids can touch sea cucumbers and sea anemones in a shallow tank. If possible, catch one of the free guided tours—you can witness the dramatic feeding frenzy of the sharks, tarpon, barracudas, stingrays, and turtles. 🕘 *1½ hr. 1 Whitehead St. (at Mallory Sq.).* ☎ *305/296-2051. www.keywestaquarium.com. Admission $12 adults, $5 children 4–12. Daily 10am–6pm; tours at 11am and 1, 3 & 4pm.*

❻ ★★ kids **Key West Butterfly & Nature Conservatory.** This 13,000-square-foot (1,208 sq. m) pavilion includes a 5,000-square-foot (465 sq. m) glass-enclosed butterfly aviary, a gallery, a learning center, and a gift shop. Inside, more than 1,500 butterflies and 3,500 plants, including rare orchids, and fish and turtles coexist in a controlled climate. You'll walk freely among the butterflies, so if you have even the slightest fear of the creatures, consider twice before entering. 🕘 *1 hr. 1316 Duval St.* ☎ *305/296-2988. www.keywestbutterfly.com. Admission $10 adults, $8.50 seniors, $7.50 children 4–12. Daily 9am–5pm.*

❼ **Key West Heritage House Museum.** For a glimpse into one of the oldest houses in Key West, check out the Heritage House Museum, the former 1834 home of Jessie Porter, a Key West preservationist who hosted the likes of Robert Frost, Tennessee Williams, and Ernest Hemingway. Furnished with 19th-century antiques, the house is a fascinating look at 19th- and early-20th-century Key West. Guided tours are informative and entertaining. 🕘 *30 min. 410 Caroline St.* ☎ *305/296-3573. www.heritagehousemuseum.org. Guided tour $7, self-guided tour $5. Mon–Sat 10am–4pm.*

The Key West Butterfly & Nature Conservatory.

8 Key West Lighthouse Museum. When the Key West Lighthouse opened in 1848, it signaled the end of a profitable era for the pirate salvagers who looted reef-stricken ships. The story of this and other area lighthouses is illustrated in a small museum that was formerly the keeper's quarters. It's worth mustering the energy to climb the 88 claustrophobic steps to the top, where you'll be rewarded with magnificent panoramic views of Key West and the ocean. ⌚ *30 min–1hr. 938 Whitehead St.* ☎ *305/295-6616. www.kwahs.com. Admission $10 adults, $9 seniors & locals, $5 children 7–12. Daily 9:30am–4:30pm.*

See pirate booty and more at the Mel Fisher Maritime Heritage Museum.

9 kids Key West Shipwreck Historeum. This museum is the place to be for everything you ever wanted to know about shipwrecks and more. See movies, artifacts, and a real-life wrecker, who will be more than happy to indulge your curiosity about the wrecking industry that preoccupied the early pioneers of Key West. ⌚ *1hr. 1 Whitehead St. (at Mallory Sq.).* ☎ *305/292-8990. www.shipwreckhistoreum.com. Admission $12 adults, $5 children 4–12. Website sells tickets for $1 cheaper. Shows daily every 30 min. 9:45am–4:45pm.*

Salvage some strength to devour the most delicious crepes on the island at **10 ★★★ Banana Café,** sporting a French-country look with fresh ingredients and almost always a line out the door. *1211 Duval St.* ☎ *305/294-7227. $–$$.*

11 ★★ kids Mel Fisher Maritime Heritage Museum. If you're into diving, pirates, and sunken treasures, check out this small museum, full of doubloons, pieces of eight (pirate currency), and solid-gold bars. A 1700 English merchant slave ship, the only tangible evidence of the transatlantic slave trade, is on view on the museum's second floor. An exhibition telling the story of more than 1,400 African slaves captured in Cuban waters and brought to Key West for sanctuary is the museum's latest, most fascinating exhibit. ⌚ *1–2 hr. 200 Greene St.* ☎ *305/294-2633. www.melfisher.org. Admission $12 adults, $11 students & seniors, $6 children 6–12. Daily 9:30am–5pm. Take U.S. 1 to Whitehead St. and turn left on Greene.*

12 ★ Oldest House/Wrecker's Museum. Dating from 1829, this New England Bahama House has survived pirates, hurricanes, fires, warfare, and economic ups and downs. The one-and-a-half-story home was designed by a ship's carpenter and incorporates many features from maritime architecture, including portholes and a ship's hatch designed for ventilation before the advent of air-conditioning. Especially interesting is the detached kitchen building outfitted with a brick "beehive" oven and vintage cooking utensils. ⌚ *30 min. 322 Duval St.* ☎ *305/294-9501. Admission free. Daily 10am–4pm.*

Best of the **Outdoors**

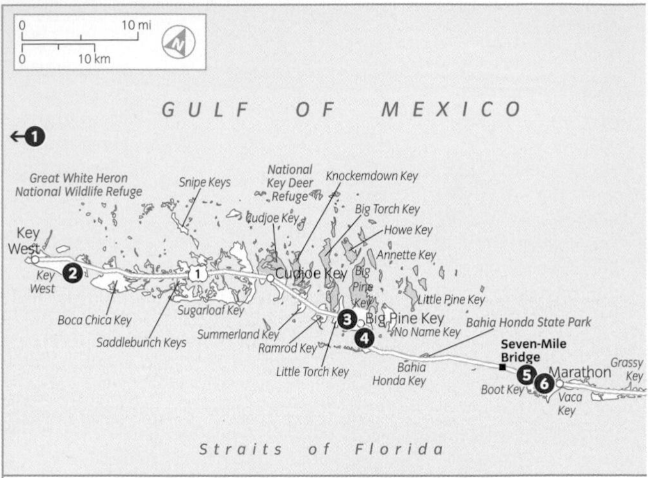

Blue Planet Kayak Tours **2**
Bud 'n' Mary's Fishing Marina **8**
Captain Pip's **5**
Dry Tortugas **1**
Florida Bay Outfitters **10**
Florida Keys Dive Center **9**
Florida Keys Kayak & Sail **7**
Hall's Dive Center & Career Institute **6**
Reflections Kayak Nature Tours **4**
Robbie's Pier **7**
Strike Zone Charters **3**

The Upper and Middle Keys are a popular year-round refuge for South Floridians, who take advantage of the islands' proximity to the mainland. This is the fishing and diving capital of America, and the swarms of outfitters and billboards never let you forget it. The Lower Keys (including Big Pine, Sugarloaf, and Summerland) are devoid of rowdy spring-break crowds, boast few t-shirt and trinket shops, and have almost no late-night bars. What they do offer are the very best opportunities to enjoy the vast natural resources that make the area so rich. Stay overnight in the Lower Keys, rent a boat, and explore the reefs.

Blue Planet Kayak Tours. Nature lovers can slip through the silent backcountry waters off Key West and the Lower Keys in a kayak, discovering the flora and fauna that make up the unique Keys ecosystem. All excursions are led by an environmental scientist. The starlight tours last between 2½ and 3 hours. No previous kayaking experience is necessary. ☎ *305/294-8087. www.blue-planet-kayak.com. Guided kayak tour $50 per person.*

Bud 'n' Mary's Fishing Marina. One of the largest marinas between Miami and Key West, Bud 'n' Mary's is packed with sailors offering backcountry fishing charters. This is the place to go if you want to stalk tarpon, bonefish, and snapper. If the seas are not too rough, deep-sea and coral

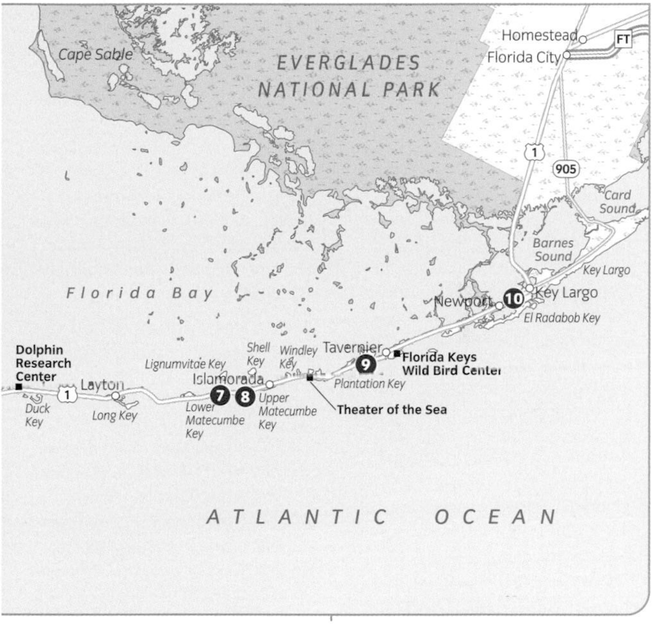

fishing trips can also be arranged. *U.S. 1 at MM 79.8, Islamorada. ☎ 800/742-7945 or 305/664-2461. www.budnmarys.com. Charters $400–$550 half-day, $500–$650 full day; splits begin at $125 per person.*

Bud 'n' Mary's is one of the largest marinas between Miami and Key West.

Captain Pip's. There are slews of boat-rental places in the Upper Keys, but at Captain Pip's, you can rent a boat and a room for an affordable price. Rooms are comfortable and charming, with ceiling fans, tile floors, and pine paneling, and the best part is that every room comes with an 18- to 21-foot (5.5–6m) boat for use during your stay. *U.S. 1 at MM 47.5, Marathon. ☎ 800/707-1692 or 305/743-4403. www.captainpips.com. Boat only $145–$300 per day; overnight accommodations (including boat rental) 2-night minimum $250–$450 in season, $225–$415 off season, weekly $1,185–$2,595.*

Dry Tortugas. This chain of seven islands, about 70 miles (113km) west of Key West, was named after the area's many sea turtles (you can see four endangered species here), which still flock here during the warm summer months. The islands are perfect for bird-watching (more than 200 winged varieties pass through here annually) and snorkeling. Fort Jefferson, a huge, six-sided, 19th-century fortress, is on Garden Key, the most visited island. Loggerhead Key, Middle Key, and East Key are open only during the day and are for hiking. Bush Key is a nesting area for birds only (peak season mid-Mar to mid-May), though it's open from October to January for special excursions. Hospital and Long keys are closed to the public. The islands are accessible by boat tours with Yankee Fleet (☎ 800/634-0939 or 305/294-7009; www.yankeefleet.com/keywest.cfm) and Sunny Days Catamarans (☎ 800/236-7937 or 305/292-6100; www.sunnydayskeywest.com). ☎ *305/242-7700. www.fortjefferson.com.*

Florida Bay Outfitters. Rent canoes and sea kayaks for use in and around John Pennekamp Coral Reef State Park. *U.S. 1 at MM 104, Key Largo.* ☎ *305/451-3018; www.kayakfloridakeys.com. $40–$75 half-day; $50–$90 full day.*

Florida Keys Dive Center. This center takes snorkelers and divers to the reefs of John Pennekamp Coral Reef State Park and environs every day. PADI (Professional Association of Diving Instructors) training courses are available for the uninitiated. *U.S. 1 at MM 90.5, Tavernier.* ☎ *305/852-4599. www.floridakeysdivectr.com. $35 per person to snorkel (plus $10 rental fee for mask, snorkel, and fins); $50 per person to dive (plus an extra $24 if you need to rent all the gear). Tours daily 8am & 12:30pm.*

Florida Keys Kayak & Sail. Offers backcountry tours, botanical-preserve tours of Lignumvitae Key, historic-site tours of Indian Key, and sunset tours through the mangrove tunnels and saltwater flats. *At Robbie's Pier, U.S. 1 at MM 75.5, Islamorada.* ☎ *305/664-4878. www.floridakeyskayakandski.com. Tours $39–$49; single kayak rentals $15 per hour–$45 per day, double kayak $20 per hour–$60 per day.*

Hall's Dive Center and Career Institute. Snorkelers and divers can dive at Looe Key, Sombrero Reef, Delta Shoal, Content Key, or Coffins Patch. You'll spend 1 hour at each of two sites per tour. *U.S. 1 at*

Sea life at John Pennekamp Coral Reef State Park.

MM 48.5, Marathon. ☎ 305/743-5929. www.hallsdiving.com. $50 per person to snorkel (gear included), $60 per person to dive (tanks $9 each). Tours daily 9am & 1pm.

Reflections Kayak Nature Tours. Offers guided kayak excursions through the Lower Keys. *Old Wooden Bridge Fishing Camp, 1791 Bogie Dr., MM 30, Big Pine Key. ☎ 305/872-4668. www.floridakeyskayaktours.com. $50 per person for a 3-hr. tour, $40 per person for a 2-hr. full-moon tour; 3-hr. custom tours start at $125 for 1 person & $195 for 2 people. Reservations required.*

Robbie's Pier. This is one of the best and definitely one of the cheapest attractions in the Upper Keys. Here the fierce steely tarpons, a prized catch for backcountry anglers, have been gathering for the past 20 years. These prehistoric-looking giants grow up to 200 pounds, and many are displayed as trophies on local restaurant walls. To see them alive, head to Robbie's Pier, where at times hundreds of these behemoths circle the shallow waters waiting for you to feed them. Robbie's Pier also offers ranger-led boat tours and guided kayak tours to Indian Key, where you can go snorkeling. You can also rent boats at Robbie's and explore on your own ($135–$235), rent a fishing boat, or go on a day or night deep-sea and reef-fishing trip aboard a 65-foot (20m) party boat ($35). Big-game fishing charters are also available, and "splits" are arranged for solo fishers ($120–$900). *U.S. 1 at MM 77.5, Islamorada. ☎ 305/664-9814. www.robbies.com. Admission $1. Bucket of fish $2. Daily 8am–5pm. Look for the Hungry Tarpon restaurant sign on the right after the Indian Key channel.*

Check out the tarpons at Robbie's Pier.

Strike Zone Charters. Strike Zone offers the best fishing trips, including daily trips to Looe Key National Marine Sanctuary on a glass-bottom boat ($25–$40). Strike Zone's 5-hour Eco Island excursion ($53) offers a vivid history of the Keys from the glass-bottom boat. The tour stops for snorkeling and light tackle fishing and eventually docks at an island for their famous island fish cookout. *U.S. 1 at MM 29.5, Big Pine Key. ☎ 305/872-9863.*

Tip

Since the real beauty of the Keys lies mostly beyond the highways, there is no better way to see this area than by boat, and if you're traveling with a group, houseboats can be economical. To rent a houseboat, contact Houseboat Vacations. *85944 Overseas Hwy., Islamorada. ☎ 305/664-4009. www.thefloridakeys.com/houseboats. $847–$1,012 for 3 nights. Boats accommodate up to 8 people.*

Dining Best Bets

Best Steakhouse
★★★ Michael's $$$ *532 Margaret St. (p 174)*

Best Conch Fusion Cuisine
★★ Hot Tin Roof $$$$ *0 Duval St. (p 171)*

Best Key West Dining Experience
★★★ Blue Heaven $$ *340 W. Armitage Ave. (p 169)*

Best Views
★★ Louie's Backyard $$$$ *700 Waddell Ave. (p 173)*

Best Seafood
★★★ Seven Fish $$–$$$ *632 Olivia St. (p 176)*

Best Breakfast
★★★ Banana Café $$ *1211 Duval St. (p 169)*

Best Value
★ Mangia, Mangia $ *900 Southard St. (p 173)*

Best Old Key West Ambience
★ Pepe's $ *806 Caroline St. (p 175)*

Banana Café is popular for its breakfast.

Best New York Import
★★ Sarabeth's $ *530 Simonton St. (p 175)*

Most Romantic
★★★ Pierre's $$$$ *U.S. 1 at MM 81.6 (bay side) (p 175)*

Best For Kids
★ Turtle Kraals Wildlife Grill $$ *213 Margaret St. (p 176)*

Best Burger
★ Island Dogs Bar $ *505 Front St. (p 171)*

Best Pre- or Post-dinner Drink Spot
★ La Trattoria's Virgilio $ *524 Duval St. (p 173)*

Best Gourmet Keys Cuisine
★★★ Butterfly Cafe $$$ *2600 Overseas Hwy. (p 170)*

Best Sushi
★★★ Kaiyó *81701 Old Hwy. (p 171)*

Best Place to Spot a Manatee
★★ Islamorada Fish Company $$ *MM 81.5 (p 171)*

Best Old Meets New Keys Cuisine
★★★ Green Turtle Inn $$$ *81219 Overseas Hwy. (p 171)*

Best Spot for a Snack and a Sunset
★★★ Lorelai Restaurant & Cabana Bar $ *MM 82 (p 150)*

Best Lunch
★ Island Grill $ *MM 88.5 (p 171)*

Best Blackened Mahi-Mahi
★ Snapper's $ *139 Seaside Ave. (p 176)*

Best Local Experience
★★ Mangrove Mama's $ *MM 20 (p 173)*

Key West Restaurants

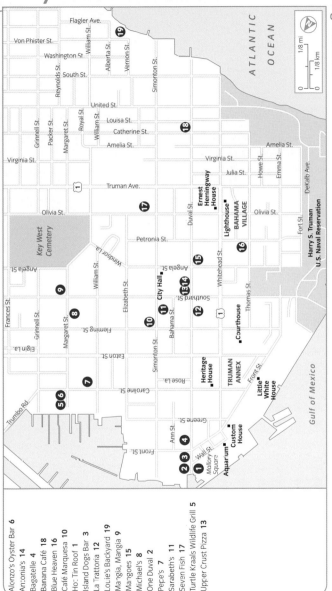

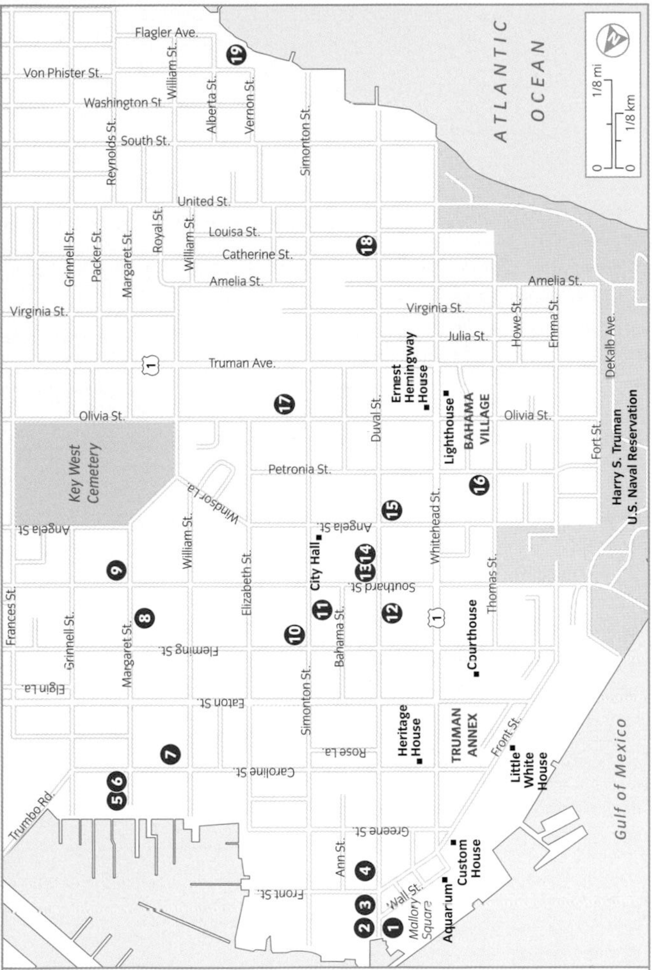

Alonzo's Oyster Bar 6
Antonia's 14
Bagatelle 4
Banana Café 18
Blue Heaven 16
Café Marquesa 10
Hot Tin Roof 1
Island Dogs Bar 3
La Trattoria 12
Louie's Backyard 19
Mangia, Mangia 9
Mangoes 15
Michael's 8
One Duval 2
Pepe's 7
Sarabeth's 11
Seven Fish 17
Turtle Kraals Wildlife Grill 5
Upper Crust Pizza 13

Keys Restaurants A to Z

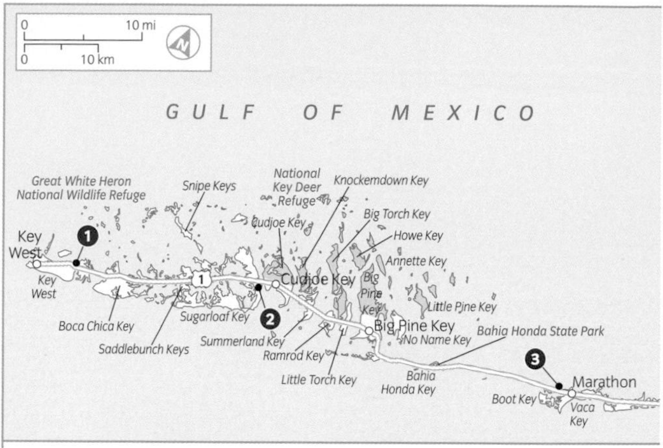

Butterfly Cafe **3**
Calypso's Seafood Grill **11**
Green Turtle Inn **4**
Islamorada Fish Company **5**
Island Grill **9**
Kaiyó **7**
Key Largo Conch House Restaurant and Coffee Bar **12**
Mangrove Mama's **2**
Marker 88 **8**
Pierre's **6**
Snapper's **10**
Tavern n Town **1**

★ **Alonzo's Oyster Bar** KEY WEST *SEAFOOD* Alonzo's serves good seafood in a casual setting. It's on the ground floor of the A&B Lobster House, at the end of Front Street in the marina; if you want to dress up, go upstairs for the "fine dining." To start your meal, try the steamed beer shrimp—tantalizingly fresh jumbo shrimp in a sauce of garlic, Old Bay seasoning, beer, and cayenne pepper. ***231 Margaret St. ☎ 305/294-5880. www.alonzosoysterbar.com. Main courses $11–$17. MC, V. Daily 11am–11pm.***

★★ **Antonia's** KEY WEST *ITALIAN* From the perfectly seasoned homemade focaccia to an exemplary crème brûlée, this elegant standout is amazingly consistent. The menu includes a small selection of classics: linguine with shrimp; delicious, pillowy gnocchi; zuppa di pesce (fish soup); and veal Marsala. ***615 Duval St. ☎ 305/294-6565. Fax 305/294-3888. www.antoniaskeywest.com. Reservations suggested. Main courses $20–$30; pastas $15–$30. AE, DC, MC, V. Daily 6–11pm.***

★★★ **Bagatelle** KEY WEST *SEAFOOD* Reserve a seat at the elegant second-floor veranda overlooking Duval Street's mayhem. Start your meal with the zingy conch ceviche or the sashimi-like seared sesame tuna rolled in black peppercorns. The best chicken and beef dishes are given a tropical treatment: grilled with papaya, ginger, and soy. The Jamaican curry chicken is a favorite. ***115 Duval St. ☎ 305/296-6609. www.bagatellekeywest.com. Reservations recommended. Main courses $15–$25; lunch***

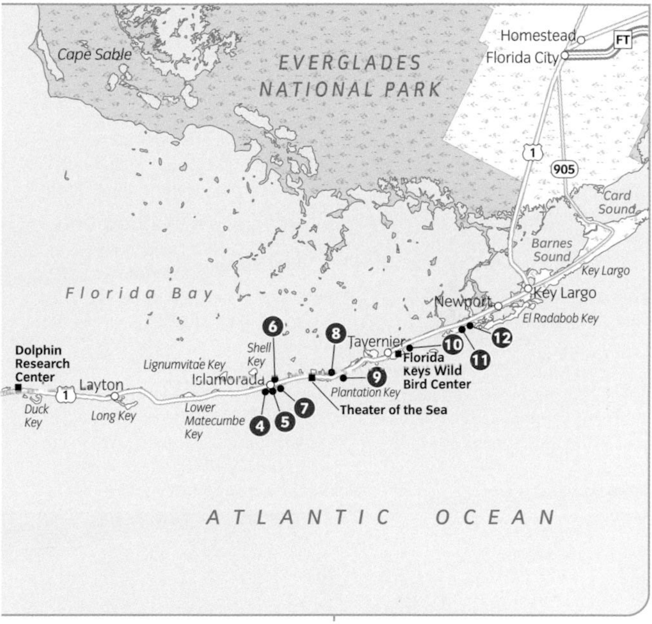

$5–$15. AE, DISC, MC, V. Sun–Thurs 11:30am–10pm; Fri–Sat 11:30am–11pm.

★★★ **Banana Café** KEY WEST *FRENCH* Banana benefits from a French country-cafe look and feel. The upscale local eatery, discovered by savvy visitors on the less-congested end of Duval Street, has retained its loyal clientele with affordable prices and delightful, light preparations. The crepes are legendary on the island for breakfast or lunch; the fresh ingredients and French-themed menu bring daytime diners back for the casual, classy, tropical-influenced dinner menu. ***1211 Duval St. ☎ 305/294-7227. Main courses $5–$25; breakfast & lunch $2–$10. AE, DC, MC, V. Daily 8am–11pm.***

★★★ **Blue Heaven** KEY WEST *AMERICAN* This hippie-run restaurant has become the place to be in Key West—and with good reason. Be prepared to wait in line. The food here is some of the best in town—especially at breakfast, which features homemade granola, tropical-fruit pancakes, and seafood Benedict. Dinners are just as good and run the gamut from fresh-caught fish and Jamaican jerk chicken to curried soups and vegetarian stews. Some people are put off by the dirt floors and roaming cats and birds, but frankly, it adds to the charm. The building used to be a bordello, where Hemingway was said to hang out watching cockfights. ***305 Petronia St. ☎ 305/296-8666. Main courses $10–$30; lunch $6–$14; breakfast $5–$11. DISC, MC, V. Daily 8–11:30am, noon–3pm & 6–10:30pm; Sun brunch 8am–1pm. Closed mid-Sept to early Oct.***

★★★ Butterfly Cafe MARATHON *SEAFOOD* The newest gourmet hot spot in the Lower Keys has water views and a stellar menu of fresh local seafood. Among the dishes not to miss: Cuban-spiced grilled double-cut pork chops with mango-lime *mojo* and spiced macadamia basmati rice. ***2600 Overseas Hwy., in the Tranquility Bay Resort. ☎ 305/289-0888. www.tranquilitybay.com. Main courses $18–$37. AE, MC, V. Daily 7–10am & 11:30am–10pm. Sun brunch 10:30am–2:30pm.***

★★★ Café Marquesa KEY WEST *CONTEMPORARY AMERICAN* If you're looking for fabulous dining (and service) in Key West, this is the place. The intimate, 50-seat restaurant is something to look at, but it's really the food that you'll want to admire. Specialties include macadamia-crusted yellowtail snapper; prosciutto-wrapped black Angus filet; and roast duck breast with red curry–coconut sauce. If you're looking to splurge, this is the place. ***In the Marquesa Hotel, 600 Fleming St. ☎ 305/292-1919. Reservations highly recommended. Main courses $25–$38. AE, DC, MC, V. Summer daily 7–11pm; winter daily 6–11pm.***

★★ Calypso's Seafood Grill KEY LARGO *SEAFOOD* With a motto proudly declaring "Yes, we know the music is loud and the food is spicy. That's the way we like it!" you know you're in a typical Keys eatery. Thankfully the food is anything but, with inventive seafood dishes in a casual and rustic waterside setting. ***1 Seagate Blvd. (near***

Café Marquesa serves contemporary American cuisine in a beautiful setting.

MM 99.5). ☎ *305/451-0600. Main courses $10–$20. MC, V. Wed–Mon 11:30am–10pm; Fri–Sat 11:30am–11pm. From the south, turn right at the blinking yellow lights near MM 99.5 to Ocean Bay Dr. and then turn right. Look for the blue vinyl-sided building on the left.*

★★★ **Green Turtle Inn** ISLAMORADA *SEAFOOD* A must for anyone looking for a fabulous dining experience. Among the classic menu items—the famous turtle chowder with pepper sherry, and luscious conch chowder. Pan-seared scallops with goat-cheese whipped potatoes, sherry-vinegar brown butter, white truffle oil, and sizzled leeks make for an excellent main course. *81219 Overseas Hwy., at MM 81.2.* ☎ *305/664-2006. www.greenturtlekeys.com. Main courses $20–$38. AE, MC, V. Daily 7–10am & 11:30am–10pm.*

★★ **Hot Tin Roof** KEY WEST *FUSION* Hot Tin Roof, Ocean Key Resort's chichi restaurant, transforms South American, Asian, French, and Keys cuisine into an experience unlike any other. *In the Ocean Key Resort, 0 Duval St.* ☎ *305/296-7701. Reservations highly recommended. Main courses $20–$40. AE, DC, MC, V. Daily 7:30–11am & 5–10pm.*

★★ kids **Islamorada Fish Company** ISLAMORADA *SEAFOOD* It looks like an average diner but has fantastic seafood, pastas, and breakfasts. Locals gather here for politics and gossip as well as delicious grits, oatmeal, omelets, and pastries. Keep your eyes open while dining outside—you may see baby manatees floating around. *U.S. 1 at MM 81.5 (up the st. from Cheeca Lodge).* ☎ *800/258-2559 or 305/664-9271. www.islamoradafishco.com. Reservations not accepted. Main courses $10–$37. DISC, MC, V. Sun–Thurs 11am–9pm; Fri–Sat 11am–10pm.*

Green Turtle Inn's most popular dishes include turtle chowder.

★★ **Island Dogs Bar** KEY WEST *AMERICAN* A great casual option for delicious burgers, chicken fingers, and chicken wings to the tune of live music or the big game on the big screens. *505 Front St.* ☎ *305/295-0501. Main courses $5–$10. AE, DISC, MC, V. Daily 11am–2am.*

★ **Island Grill** ISLAMORADA *SEAFOOD* Located just under the bridge and on the bay, Island Grill is a local favorite, with an expansive outdoor deck and bar and cozy waterfront dining room serving fresh fare, including their famous tuna nachos, guava barbecued shrimp, and graham cracker–dusted calamari. An entree of whole yellowtail snapper with Thai sweet chili sauce is out of this world. Bring your own catch, and they'll cook it for you, served family-style with veggies and rice for only $12. Live entertainment almost every night brings in a great, colorful Keys crowd. *MM 88.5 (oceanside at Snake Creek Bridge).* ☎ *305/664-8400. www.keysislandgrill.com. Main courses $8–$25. Sun–Thurs 11am–10pm; Fri–Sat 11am–11pm.*

★★★ **Kaiyó** ISLAMORADA *JAPANESE* Kaiyó fuses Florida's fine ingredients with some of the

Get good food in a casual setting at Island Dogs Bar.

freshest raw fish this side of Tokyo. *81701 Old Hwy., U.S. 1 at MM 82.* ☎ *305/664-5556. www.kaiyokeys.com. Reservations recommended. Main courses $12–$36; sushi $7.50–$16. AE, DC, MC, V. Mon–Sat noon–10pm.*

★★ Key Largo Conch House Restaurant and Coffee Bar KEY LARGO *AMERICAN* A funky, cozy, and off-the-beaten-path hot spot for breakfast, lunch, and dinner, Key Largo Conch House is a house set amidst lush foliage, complete with a resident dog and parrot, a wraparound veranda for outdoor dining, and a warm and inviting indoor dining room. *U.S. 1 at MM 100.* ☎ *305/453-4844. www.keylargocoffeehouse.com. Reservations recommended. Main courses $8–$21. AE, DC, DISC, MC, V. Daily 7am–10pm.*

Key Largo Conch House Restaurant and Coffee Bar.

★ **La Trattoria** KEY WEST *ITALIAN* Have a true Italian feast in a relaxed atmosphere. Each dish here is prepared and presented according to old Italian tradition. Before you leave, visit Virgilio's, the restaurant's resplendent cocktail lounge with live jazz until 2am. ***524 Duval St. ☎ 305/296-1075. www.latrattoria.us. Main courses $16–$40; pasta $14–$26. AE, DC, DISC, MC, V. Daily 5:30–11pm.***

★★ **Louie's Backyard** KEY WEST *CARIBBEAN* Famed chef Norman Van Aiken of Norman's in Miami brought his talents farther south and started what has become one of the finest dining spots in the Keys. As a result, this is one of the hardest places to score a reservation: call way in advance or hope that your hotel concierge has some pull. Try the sweet-and-sour sweetbreads with sticky rice, or the grilled chili-rubbed Berkshire pork chop. After dinner, sit at the dockside bar and watch the waves crash, almost touching your feet, while enjoying a cocktail. ***700 Waddell Ave. ☎ 305/294-1061. www.louiesbackyard.com. Reservations highly recommended. Main courses $25–$35; lunch $10–$20. AE, DC, MC, V. Daily 11:30am–3pm & 6–10:30pm.***

★ **Mangia, Mangia** KEY WEST *ITALIAN* Off the beaten track, this great Chicago-style pasta place has some of the best Italian food in the Keys. The family-run restaurant serves superb homemade pastas of every description, including one of the tastiest marinara sauces around. ***900 Southard St. (at Margaret St.). ☎ 305/294-2469. Reservations not accepted. Main courses $9–$15. AE, MC, V. Daily 5:30–10pm.***

★★★ **Mangoes** KEY WEST *FLORIBBEAN* This restaurant's large brick patio, shaded by overgrown banyan trees, is so alluring to passersby

La Trattoria houses a cocktail lounge, Virgilio's, with live jazz.

that it's packed almost every night of the week. Many people don't realize how pricey the meals can be here because, upon first glance, it looks like a casual cafe. Crispy curried chicken and local snapper with passion-fruit sauce are typical among the entrees, but the garlic and lime pinks—a half-pound of Key West pink shrimp seasoned and grilled with a roasted garlic and Key lime glaze—is the menu's best offering by far. ***700 Duval St. (at Angela St.). ☎ 305/292-4606. Main courses $15–$30; pizzas $10–$15; lunch $7–$18. AE, DC, DISC, MC, V. Daily 11am–midnight; pizza until 1am.***

★★ **Mangrove Mama's** SUGARLOAF KEY *SEAFOOD* This is a true Lower Keys institution and a dive in the best sense of the word (the restaurant is a shack that used to have a gas pump as well as a grill). Guests share the property with stray cats and some miniature horses out back. It's run down, but in a charming Keys sort of way—they serve beer in a jelly glass. A handful of simple tables, inside and out, are shaded by banana trees and palm fronds. Fish is the menu's mainstay, although soups, salads, sandwiches, and omelets are also good. ***U.S. 1***

Louie's Backyard has a sweeping view of the water.

at MM 20. ☎ 305/745-3030. Main courses $10–$20; lunch $6–$10; brunch $5–$15. MC, V. Daily 11am–3pm & 5:30–10pm.

★★★ **Marker 88** ISLAMORADA *SEAFOOD* An institution in the Upper Keys, Marker 88 has been pleasing locals and visitors since it opened in the 1970s. New chefs and owners have infused a new life into the place and the menu, which still utilizes fresh fruits, local ingredients, and fish caught in the Keys' waters. *U.S. 1 at MM 88 (bay side). ☎ 305/852-9315. www.marker88.info. Reservations suggested. Main courses $20–$39. AE, DC, DISC, MC, V. Tues–Sun 5–11pm. Closed Sept.*

Steaks are done Key West–style at Michael's.

★★★ **Michael's** KEY WEST *STEAK* Tucked in a residential neighborhood, Michael's is a meaty oasis in a big sea of fish, with steaks flown in daily from Chicago. Unlike most steakhouses, Michael's exudes a relaxed, tropical ambience with a fabulous indoor/outdoor setting that's romantic but not stuffy. *532 Margaret St. ☎ 305/295-1300. www.michaelskeywest.com. Reservations recommended. Main courses $15–$40. AE, DC, DISC, MC, V. Daily 5–11pm.*

★★★ **One Duval** KEY WEST *CARIBBEAN* One Duval blends the ingredients of the Caribbean and Florida with an innovative twist. For starters, the crabmeat stuffed in phyllo is outstanding, and the goat-cheese soufflé

Acquaint Yourself

Fans of stone crabs can get further acquainted with the seasonal crustaceans on 3-hour tours offered by **Keys Fisheries,** aboard 40- to 50-foot vessels that leave from Marathon. The tour includes views of fishermen as they collect crabs from traps and process their claws. The $450 cost includes up to six passengers and up to 6 pounds of fresh claws iced for travel or prepared at a dockside restaurant. Stone-crab season is October 15 to May 15. Call ☎ 305/743-4353, or check www.keysfisheries.com for more information.

is incredibly hedonistic. For main courses, try the macadamia nut–crusted mahi-mahi or the lobster thermidor stuffed with crabmeat. ***In the Pier House Resort, 1 Duval St. ☎ 305/296-4600. Reservations highly recommended. Main courses $25–$36. AE, DC, MC, V. Daily 6–10:30pm.***

★ **Pepe's** KEY WEST *AMERICAN* This dive has been serving good, basic food for nearly a century. Steaks and Apalachicola Bay oysters are the big draws for regulars, who appreciate the rustic barroom setting and historical photos on the walls. Look for original scenes of Key West in 1909, when Pepe's first opened. If the weather is nice, choose a seat on the patio under a stunning mahogany tree. Burgers, fish sandwiches, and standard chili satisfy hearty eaters. Buttery sautéed mushrooms and rich mashed potatoes are the best comfort foods in Key West. ***806 Caroline St. ☎ 305/294-7192. No reservations. Main course $7–$16. Daily 7:30am–10:30pm.***

★★★ **Pierre's** ISLAMORADA *FRENCH* The food challenges the

The plantation setting at Pierre's.

stunning waterfront West Indies plantation-style setting, with amazing flavors and gorgeous presentation. The tempura lobster tail with hearts of palm hash, soy glaze, and wasabi crème fraîche, and the Florida Keys hogfish meunière with roasted creamer potatoes, pattypan squash, and baby zucchini are outstanding. ***U.S. 1 at MM 81.6 (bay side). ☎ 305/664-3225. www.pierres-restaurant.com. Main courses $35–$42. AE, MC, V. Sun–Thurs 6–10pm; Fri–Sat 6–11pm. Lounge open at 5pm daily. Restaurant closed on Tues during the summer.***

★★ **Sarabeth's** KEY WEST *AMERICAN* An offshoot of the popular New York City breakfast hot spot, Sarabeth's brings a much-needed shot of cosmopolitan comfort food to Key West in the form of delicious breakfasts with Sarabeth's signature homemade jams and jellies. Choose from buttermilk to lemon-ricotta pancakes or almond-crusted cinnamon French toast. For lunch, the traditional Caesar salad, burger, or Key West pink shrimp roll with avocado are all excellent choices. Dinner is simple, but savory, with top-notch dishes from chicken potpie and meatloaf to a divine green-chili-pepper macaroni with three cheeses. ***530 Simonton St. ☎ 305/293-8181. Main courses $13–$20; breakfast $5.50–$10; lunch $5.75–$14. MC, V. Mon 8am–3pm; Wed–Sun 8am–3pm & 6–10pm.***

★★★ **Seven Fish** SEAFOOD One of the most popular restaurants with locals, Seven Fish is a chic seafood spot serving some of the best fish dishes on the island. Crab and shiitake-mushroom pasta and gnocchi with blue cheese and sautéed fish are among the dishes to choose from. ***632 Olivia St. ☎ 305/296-2777. www.7fish.com. Reservations recommended. Main courses $15–$26. AE, MC, V. Wed–Mon 6–10pm.***

★ **Snapper's** KEY LARGO *SEAFOOD* A local waterfront favorite, Snapper's serves fresh seafood caught by local fishermen—or by you. The blackened mahi-mahi is exceptional and a bargain, complete

Locals go to Seven Fish for fabulous seafood.

Flavors of the Keys

It's not a coincidence that Key Lime pie is the official dessert of Florida; it's named after the small limes found throughout the Keys. The American Pie Council has continuously recognized **Key Lime Pie Co.** (MM 22.8, Cudjoe Key; ☎ 305/745-3355) for its pies, but you can also find everything from cookies and candles to marinades and lotions—all made from Key limes—at their main bakery in Cudjoe Key, right near Key West. Otherwise, their pies are available in Key West at 5 Brother Grocery (930 Southard St.; 305/296-5205).

If you prefer tang rather than tart, **Peppers of Key West** (602 Greene St.; 305/295-9333) has hundreds of variations of hot sauce, from mild to brutally spicy. Grab a seat at the tasting bar and be prepared to let your taste buds sizzle. ***Tip:*** Bring beer, and they'll let you taste some of their secret sauces!

with salad, vegetable, and choice of starch. There's also live music nightly and a lively, colorful, and casual crowd. *139 Seaside Ave. at MM 94.5. ☎ 305/852-5956. www.snapperskeylargo.com. Main courses $10–$25. DISC, MC, V. Sun–Thurs 11am–9pm; Fri–Sat 11am–10pm.*

★ **Tavern n Town** KEY WEST *FLORIBBEAN* Call this a hyphenated restaurant, with Tavern featuring tapas and small plates and Town a more world-class dining experience, but both equally good. An open kitchen shows action, but the real show is on your plate. At Tavern, try the tempura short-rib cake with Wasabi *crema*. Over at Town, black grouper in a *miso* ginger or pan-cooked filet of yellowtail are a far cry from Duval Street's chicken fingers and conch fritters. *In the Beachside Resort, 3841 N. Roosevelt Blvd. ☎ 305/296-8100. Reservations highly recommended. Main courses $19–$32. AE, DC, MC, V. Tavern daily 8am–10:30pm; Town 6–11pm.*

★ kids **Turtle Kraals Wildlife Grill** KEY WEST *SEAFOOD* You'll join lots of locals in this out-of-the-way converted warehouse with indoor and dockside seating, which serves innovative seafood at great prices. Try the twin lobster tails stuffed with mango and crabmeat, stone crabs when in season (Oct–May), or any of the big quesadillas or fajitas. Kids will like the wildlife exhibits, the turtle cannery, and the very cheesy menu. Blues bands play most nights. *213 Margaret St. (at Caroline St.). ☎ 305/294-2640. Main courses $10–$20. DISC, MC, V. Mon–Thurs 11am–10:30pm; Fri–Sat 11am–11pm; Sun noon–10:30pm. Bar closes at midnight.*

★ **Upper Crust Pizza** KEY WEST *PIZZA* Simply put, the best slice on Duval Street. *611 Duval St. ☎ 305/293-8890. www.uppercrustkeywest.com. Pizza $5 slice, $13–$16 pie. AE, DISC, MC, V. Daily 11am–2am.*

Hotel Best Bets

Most **Romantic**
★★★ The Gardens Hotel $$$$ *526 Angela St. (p 183)*

Best **Family Hotel**
★★★ Hawk's Cay $$$$ *61 Hawk's Cay Blvd. at MM 61, Duck Key (p 184)*

Best **Views**
★ Ocean Key Resort & Spa $$$$ *0 Duval St. (p 187)*

Most **Historic Hotel**
★★ Curry Mansion Inn $$$ *511 Caroline St. (p 182)*

Best **Bed & Breakfast**
★★★ Simonton Court $$–$$$ *320 Simonton St. (p 188)*

Best **Moderately Priced Hotel**
★★ Southernmost Point Guest House $–$$ *1327 Duval St. (p 189)*

Best **Cheap Bed**
★★ The Grand $ *1116 Grinnell St. (p 183)*

Best **Place to Avoid if You Don't Like Cats**
★★ Island City House Hotel $$$ *411 William St. (p 184)*

Most **Swanky Hotel**
★★★ Marquesa Hotel $$$ *600 Fleming St. (p 186)*

Most **Modern Hotel**
★★★ Key West Marriott Beachside Hotel $$$$ *3841 N. Roosevelt Blvd. (p 185)*

Best **Hotel Away from Duval Street**
★★★ Parrot Key Resort $$$–$$$$ *2801 N. Roosevelt Blvd. (p 187)*

Best **Spa**
★★★ Pier House Resort and Caribbean Spa $$$$ *1 Duval St. (p 187)*

Best **Private Beach**
★★★ The Reach Resort $$$ *1435 Simonton St. (p 188)*

Best **Private Island Hotel**
★★★ Sunset Key Guest Cottages $$$$ *Sunset Key Island (p 189)*

Best **Breakfast Buffet**
★★★ Ambrosia Key West $$ *662 Fleming St. (p 180)*

Best **Hidden Gem**
★★★ Weatherstation Inn $$ *57 Front St. (p 189)*

Most **Luxurious**
★★★ Little Palm Island Resort & Spa $$$$ *U.S. 1 at MM 28.5, Little Torch Key (p 186)*

Hippest Hotel
★★ Casa Morada $$–$$$ *136 Madeira Rd. (p 181)*

Best **Dive**
★★★ Jules Undersea Lodge $$–$$$ *51 Shoreland Dr. (p 146)*

Best Private **Beach**
★★★ The Moorings $$$$ *123 Beach Rd. near MM 81.5 on the ocean side, Islamorada (p 186)*

Most **Comfortable**
★★★ Cheeca Lodge & Spa $$$$ *U.S. 1 at MM 82 (P.O. Box 527), Islamorada (p 182)*

The Gardens Hotel.

Key West Hotels

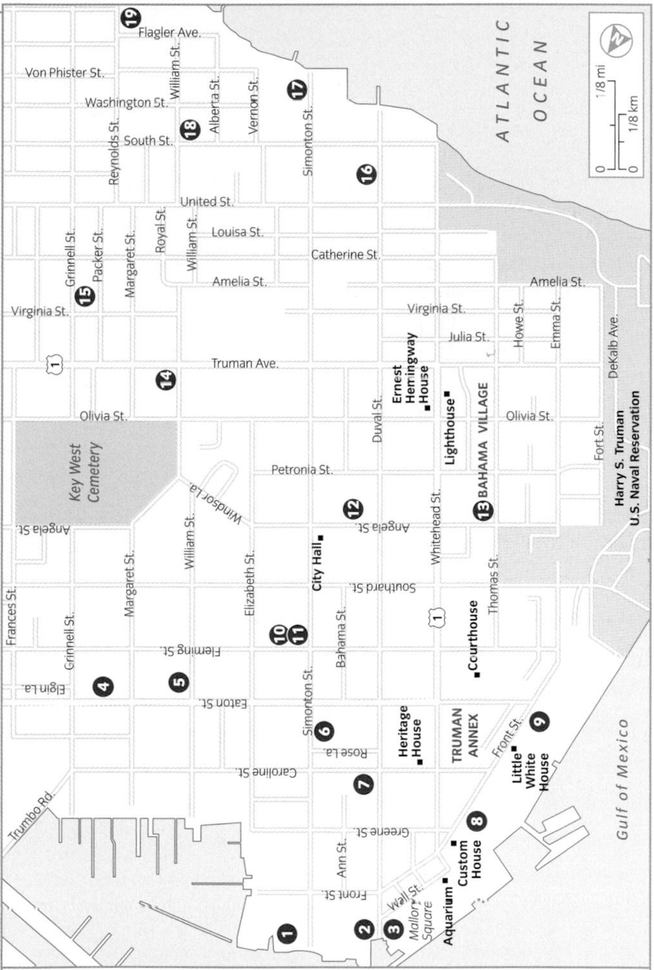

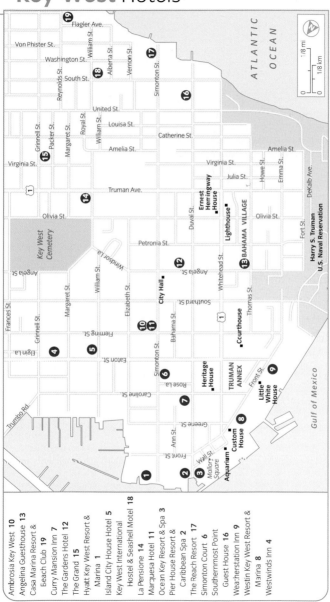

Ambrosia Key West **10**
Angelina Guesthouse **13**
Casa Marina Resort & Beach Club **19**
Curry Mansion Inn **7**
The Gardens Hotel **12**
The Grand **15**
Hyatt Key West Resort & Marina **1**
Island City House Hotel **5**
Key West International Hostel & Seashell Motel **18**
La Pensione **14**
Marquesa Hotel **11**
Ocean Key Resort & Spa **3**
Pier House Resort & Caribbean Spa **2**
The Reach Resort **17**
Simonton Court **6**
Southernmost Point Guest House **16**
Weatherstation Inn **9**
Westin Key West Resort & Marina **8**
Westwinds Inn **4**

Keys Hotels A to Z

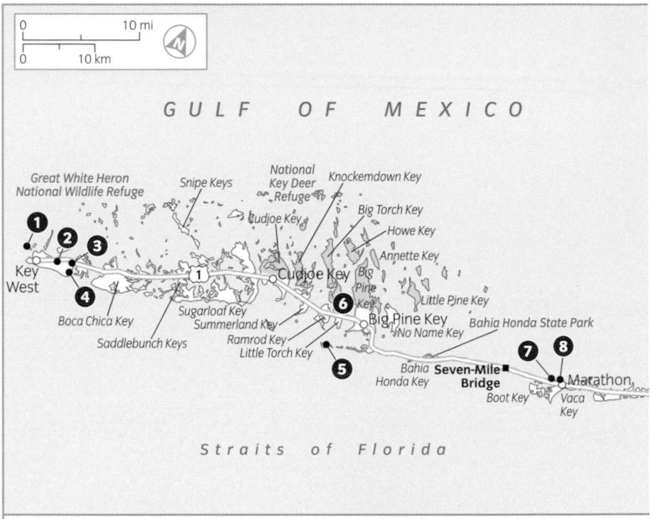

Banana Bay Resort & Marina **8**
Casa Morada **13**
Cheeca Lodge & Spa **12**
Conch Key Cottages **10**
Doubletree Grand Key Resort **4**
Hawks Cay Resort **9**
Key West Marriott Beachside Hotel **3**
Kona Kai Resort & Gallery **15**

★★★ Ambrosia Key West KEY WEST A private compound set on 2 lush acres (1 hectare) just a block from Duval Street. Three lagoon-style pools, suites, town houses, and a cottage are spread around the grounds. Town houses have living rooms, kitchens, and spiral staircases leading to master suites with vaulted ceilings and private decks. All rooms, several of which recently received major renovations, have private entrances, most with French doors opening onto a variety of intimate outdoor spaces, including private verandas, patios, and gardens with sculptures, fountains, and pools. The breakfast buffet rocks. *622 Fleming St. ☎ 800/535-9838 or 305/296-9838. www.ambrosiakeywest.com. 20 units. Suites $179–$609. Rates include breakfast buffet. Pet friendly. AE, DISC, MC, V.*

★★ Angelina Guesthouse KEY WEST This former bordello and gambling hall turned youth hostel–type guesthouse is one of the cheapest in town. Accommodations are furnished in a modest style. Two rooms have full kitchens, one has a microwave and small fridge, and all but three have private bathrooms. A gorgeous lagoon-style heated pool with waterfall and tropical landscaping is an excellent addition. *302 Angela St. (at Thomas St.). ☎ 888/303-4480 or 305/294-4480. www.angelinaguesthouse.com. 13 units. Doubles $69–$199. Rates include continental breakfast. DISC, MC, V.*

★★ Banana Bay Resort & Marina MARATHON This is a beachfront maze of two-story buildings hidden among banyans and palms, with moderately sized rooms, many with private balconies.

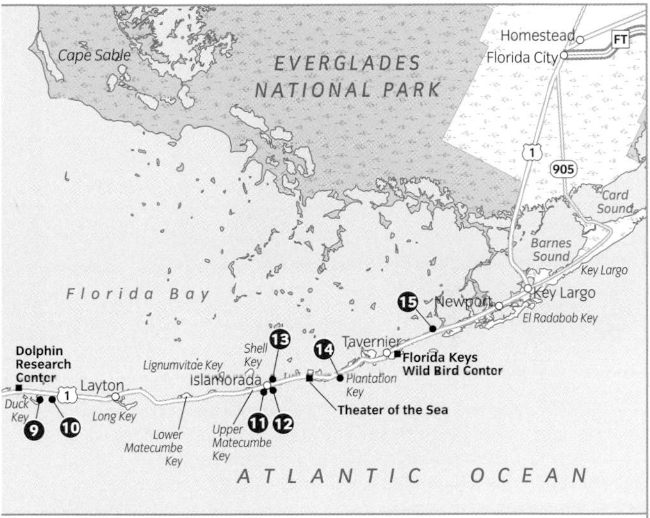

Little Palm Island Resort & Spa **5**
The Moorings **11**
Parmer's Resort **6**
Parrot Key Resort **2**
Ragged Edge Resort **14**
Sunset Key Guest Cottages **1**
Tranquility Bay Beach House Resort **7**

A recreational activity area has horseshoe pits, a bocce court, barbecue grills, and a giant lawn chessboard. The kitschy restaurant serves three meals a day, indoors and poolside. The hotel also rents bikes, boats, WaveRunners, kayaks, day-sailing dinghies, and bait and tackle. Another surprising amenity is Pretty Joe Rock, the hotel's private island, available for long weekends and weekly rentals. ***U.S. 1 at MM 49.5. ☎ 800/BANANA-1 or 305/743-3500. www.bananabay.com. 60 units. Doubles $105–$245. Rates include continental breakfast. AE, DC, DISC, MC, V.***

★ kids **Casa Marina Resort & Beach Club** KEY WEST Supremely located on the south side of the island, spanning more than 1,000 feet (300m) of private beach, the Casa Marina features modern rooms, some with stellar ocean views. In addition to the beach itself, there are also two outdoor pools, a full-service spa, and an outdoor restaurant. Nightly movies shown at the pool with free popcorn and snacks cater to families with kids. ***1500 Reynolds St. ☎ 866/397-6342 or 305/296-3535. www.casamarinaresort.com. 311 units. Doubles $149–$499. AE, DC, MC, V.***

★★ **Casa Morada** ISLAMORADA This 16-suite property is a hipster haven off a sleepy street and radiates serenity and style in an area where serenity is aplenty, but style is elusive. Sitting on almost 2 acres (1 hectare) of prime bayfront, the hotel features a limestone grotto, freshwater pool, and poolside beverage service. Each of the rooms has either a private garden or a terrace—request the one with the open-air Jacuzzi that faces the

Go for the suite with the open-air Jacuzzi at Casa Morada.

bay. While the decor is decidedly island, think St. Barts rather than, say, Gilligan's. *136 Madeira Rd.* ☎ *888/881-3030 or 305/664-0044. www.casamorada.com. 16 units. Doubles $249–$659. Rates include continental breakfast. Friendly pets are welcome. AE, DISC, MC, V.*

★★★ kids **Cheeca Lodge & Spa** ISLAMORADA Located on 27 lush acres (11 hectares) of beachfront, this rambling resort sports one of the only golf courses in the Upper Keys. Rooms have the amenities of a world-class resort in a very laid-back setting, and most feature West Indies–style decor, marble baths, fine linens, plasma TVs, and wireless DSL. The spa offers a variety of treatments, fitness classes, and butler-serviced poolside cabanas. Recreation options include a 9-hole golf course, ecotours, sunset cruises, and snorkel excursions. The $39 daily resort fee may seem steep, but it includes unlimited tennis, golf, fishing rods, bicycles, beach shade cabanas, and sea kayaks. ***Note:*** The resort was closed for renovations at press time, but set to reopen in December 2009. *U.S. 1 at MM 82.* ☎ *305/664-4651. www.cheeca.com. 199 units. Deluxe doubles $269–$369. AE, DC, DISC, MC, V.*

★ **Conch Key Cottages** MARATHON Occupying its own private microisland just off U.S. 1, the Cottages offers solitude, with the exception of one or two interesting eateries. The units, which were built at different times over the past 40 years, overlook their own stretch of natural, but very small, private beach. *Private island off U.S. 1 at MM 62.3.* ☎ *800/330-1577 or 305/289-1377. www.conchkeycottages.com. 12 cottages. Cottages $85–$349. AE, DISC, MC, V.*

★★ **Curry Mansion Inn** KEY WEST This charismatic inn is the former home of the island's first millionaire, a once-penniless Bahamian immigrant who made a fortune as a pirate. The Curry Mansion is now on the National Register of Historic Places, but you won't feel like you're staying in a museum—it's rather like a wonderfully warm home. Rooms are very sparsely decorated, with wicker furniture, four-poster beds, and pink walls. *511 Caroline St.* ☎ *800/253-3466 or 305/294-5349. www.currymansion.com. 28 units. Doubles $195–$300. Rates include breakfast buffet. AE, DC, MC, V. No children 11 & under.*

It's Not Easy Being a Green Hotel

The Gardens (below) is one of the first "Florida Green Lodging Hotels" in the Keys, meaning the hotel has installed energy-efficient light bulbs throughout the property, uses all "green" cleaning products, eliminated plastics and Styrofoam use, educates staff and guests on the importance of recycling, and raises room temperatures to 78°F (26°C) when not in use, among other eco-friendly efforts. For more info on the organization and participating hotels, see www.floridagreenlodging.org.

★ **Doubletree Grand Key Resort** KEY WEST This hotel has been renovated with eco-sensitive materials as well as an interior created to conserve energy, reduce waste, and preserve the area's natural resources. Rooms are clean and comfortable, with some looking onto the spacious pool area, which is surrounded by an unsightly empty lot of mangroves and marshes. Best of all, there's a free shuttle to transport guests to and from Duval Street, which is a considerable walk or cab ride from here. *3990 S. Roosevelt Blvd. ☎ 888/310-1540 or 305/293-1818. www.doubletreekeywest.com. 216 units. Doubles $198–$279. AE, DISC, MC, V.*

Curry Mansion Inn feels more like a home than a hotel.

★★★ **The Gardens Hotel** KEY WEST Once a private residence, The Gardens Hotel (whose main house is listed on the National Register of Historic Places) is hidden amid exotic botanical gardens. Behind the greenery is a Bahamian-style hideaway with luxuriously appointed rooms in the main house, garden and courtyard rooms in the carriage house, and a secluded cottage. A pretty free-form pool is centered in the courtyard, where a Tiki bar serves libations. The Jacuzzi is hidden behind foliage. Guest rooms have hardwood floors, plantation beds with Tempurpedic mattresses, and marble bathrooms. Winding brick pathways lead to secluded seating areas in the private gardens. *526 Angela St. ☎ 800/526-2664 or 305/294-2661. www.gardenshotel.com. 17 units. Doubles $175–$415. Rates include continental breakfast. AE, DC, MC, V.*

★★ **The Grand** KEY WEST Proprietors Jim Brown and Jeffrey Daubman provide any and all services for their appreciative guests. All units have private bathrooms, air-conditioning, and private entrances. The best deal is room no. 2; it's small and lacks a closet, but it has a porch and the most privacy. Suites are a real steal, too: The large two-room units come with kitchenettes. *1116 Grinnell St. (btw. Virginia & Catherine sts.). ☎ 888/947-2630 or 305/294-0590. www.thegrandguesthouse.com. 10 units. Doubles $98–$208. Rates include expanded continental breakfast and free parking. DISC, MC, V.*

★★★ kids Hawks Cay Resort

DUCK KEY Set on its own 60-acre (24-hectare) island in the Middle Keys, Hawks Cay offers sailing, fishing, snorkeling, water-skiing, and the opportunity to interact directly with dolphins in the resort's natural saltwater lagoon. (You'll need to reserve a spot well in advance for this.) Guest rooms are large, with spacious bathrooms, island-style furniture, and private balconies with ocean or tropical views. Organized children's activities include marine- and ecology-inspired programs. *61 Hawks Cay Blvd. at MM 61. ☎ 888/814-9104 or 305/743-7000. www.hawkscay.com. 402 units. Doubles $279–$539. AE, DC, DISC, MC, V.*

★ Hyatt Key West Resort & Marina KEY WEST Ideally situated on the bay, the Hyatt features a waterfront pool, small beach area, and guest rooms with white porcelain-tile floors, flatscreen TVs, and fabulous bathrooms. New spa cabanas allow for outdoor treatments, and a restaurant overlooking the water is great for dinner but spotty on breakfast service. *601 Front St. ☎ 800/55-HYATT or 305/809-1234. www.keywest.hyatt.com. 118 rooms. Doubles $335–$550. AE, DISC, DC, MC, V.*

★★ Island City House Hotel

KEY WEST Island City House consists of three separate buildings that share a common junglelike patio and pool. The first building is a historic three-story wooden structure with wraparound verandas on every floor. The warmly outfitted interiors here include wood floors and many antiques. A shaded brick courtyard and pretty pool are surrounded by lush gardens where, every morning, a delicious continental breakfast is served. ***Note:*** For those who have a fear or dislike of cats, there are several friendly "resident" felines who call Island City House home. *411 William St. ☎ 800/634-8230 or 305/294-5702. www.islandcityhouse.com. 24 units. Doubles $150–$420. Rates include breakfast. AE, DC, DISC, MC, V.*

The pool at Key West Marriott Beachside Hotel has a private tanning beach.

The private Little Palm Island Resort & Spa.

Key West International Hostel & Seashell Motel KEY WEST This well-run hostel is a 3-minute walk to the beach and Old Town. Very busy with European backpackers, it's a great place to meet people. The dorm rooms are dark, grimy, and sparse, but livable if you're desperate for a cheap stay. There are all male, all female, and coed dorm rooms for couples. The higher-priced private motel rooms are a good deal, especially those equipped with kitchens. Amenities include a pool table under a Tiki roof; bike rentals; cheap food at breakfast, lunch, and dinner; and discounted prices for snorkeling, diving, and sunset cruises. There's also free wireless Internet access throughout the property. *718 South St. ☎ 800/51-HOSTEL or 305/296-5719. www.keywesthostel.com. 92 dorm beds, 10 motel rooms. Dorm room $34; motel room $55–$105. MC, V.*

★★★ Key West Marriott Beachside Hotel KEY WEST The resort has superluxe one-, two-, and three-bedroom suites, as well as king bedrooms, all adorned with oversize balconies with waterfront views, open gourmet kitchens, marble Jacuzzi tubs, and, on the third floor, private sun decks. At the tropical waterfront pool, you'll find private cabanas, a private tanning beach, and the Blue Bar. *3841 N. Roosevelt Blvd. ☎ 800/546-0885 or 305/296-8100. www.beachsidekeywest.com. 222 units. Doubles $299–$539. AE, DC, MC, V.*

★★★ Kona Kai Resort & Gallery KEY LARGO This is an exquisite, adults-only waterfront property right on Florida Bay—a choice location that offers a stunning sunset view overlooking Everglades National Park. Highly stylized, modern rooms and suites dot the lush 2-acre (1-hectare) property, brimming with native vegetation and fruit-bearing trees from which you're free to sample. An orchid house has more than 350 flowers. It also has one of the largest private beaches on the island. *97802 Overseas Hwy. (U.S. 1 at MM 97.8). ☎ 800/365-7829 or 305/852-7200. www.konakairesort.com. 11 units. Doubles & 1-bed suite $211–$561. AE, DISC, MC, V. Closed Sept.*

★★ **La Pensione** KEY WEST This classic B&B, set in a stunning 1891 home, is a total charmer. The comfortable rooms all have air-conditioning, ceiling fans, and king-size beds. Many also have French doors opening onto spacious verandas. Although the rooms have no TVs, the distractions of Duval Street, only steps away, should keep you adequately occupied. ***809 Truman Ave. (btw. Windsor & Margaret sts.). ☎ 800/893-1193 or 305/292-9923. www.lapensione.com. 9 units. Doubles $118–$328. Rates include breakfast. AE, DC, DISC, MC, V. No children.***

★★★ **Little Palm Island Resort & Spa** LITTLE TORCH KEY This exclusive island escape—host to presidents, royalty, and even Howard Stern—is not just a place to stay while in the Lower Keys; it's a destination all its own. Built on a private 5½-acre (2-hectare) island, it's accessible only by boat or seaplane. Guests stay in thatched-roof duplexes amid lush foliage, flowering tropical plants, and gentle Key deer. Many villas have ocean views and private decks with hammocks. Inside, the romantic suites have all the comforts of a swank beach cottage, but without phones, TVs, or alarm clocks. ***Launch is on the ocean side of U.S. 1 at MM 28.5. ☎ 800/343-8567 or 305/872-2524. www.littlepalmisland.com. 30 units. Doubles $640–$1,695. Rates include transportation to and from the island and unlimited (nonmotorized) watersports. AE, DC, DISC, MC, V. No children 15 & under.***

★★★ **Marquesa Hotel** KEY WEST The exquisite Marquesa encompasses four buildings, two pools, and a three-stage waterfall that cascades into a lily pond. Two of the hotel's buildings are luxuriously restored Victorian homes outfitted with plush antiques and contemporary furniture. The rooms in the two newly constructed buildings are even more opulent; many have four-poster wrought-iron beds with bright floral spreads. ***600 Fleming St. (at Simonton St.). ☎ 800/869-4631 or 305/292-1919. www.marquesa.com. 27 units. Doubles $220–$395. AE, DC, MC, V. No children 11 & under.***

★★★ **The Moorings** ISLAMORADA You'll never see another soul on this 18-acre (7-hectare) resort, a former coconut plantation, if you choose not to. There isn't even maid

All rooms at Pier House Resort and Caribbean Spa have either a balcony or patio.

The Reach Resort's rooms were recently renovated.

service unless you request it. The romantic whitewashed units, from cozy cottages to three-bedroom houses, are spacious with fully equipped kitchens and rustic, yet modern, decor. Most have washers and dryers, and all have CD players and DVD players; ask when you book. The real reason to come to this resort is to relax on the 1,000-plus-foot (300m) beach (one of the only real beaches around). ***123 Beach Rd. near MM 81.5 on the ocean side. ☎ 305/664-4708. www.mooringsvillage.com. 18 units. Small cottages $250–$325; 2-night minimum. AE, MC, V.***

★ **Ocean Key Resort & Spa** KEY WEST You can't beat the location of this 100-room resort, at the foot of Mallory Square, the epicenter of the sunset ritual. Ocean Key also features a Gulf-side heated pool and the lively Sunset Pier, where guests can wind down with cocktails and live music. Guest rooms are huge and luxuriously appointed, with living and dining areas, oversize Jacuzzis, and views of the Gulf, the harbor, or Mallory Square and Duval Street. ***0 Duval St. (near Mallory Docks). ☎ 800/328-9815 or 305/296-7701. www.oceankey.com. 100 units. Doubles $239–$679. AE, DC, MC, V.***

★★★ **Parmer's Resort** LITTLE TORCH KEY This downscale resort offers modest but comfortable cottages, each of them unique. Some are waterfront, many have kitchenettes, and others are just a bedroom. The Wahoo room (no. 26), a one-bedroom efficiency, is especially nice, with a small sitting area that faces the water. All units have been recently updated and are very clean. ***565 Barry Ave. near MM 28.5. ☎ 305/872-2157. www.parmersresort.com. 45 units. Doubles $99–$194. Rates include continental breakfast. AE, DISC, MC, V.***

★★★ **Parrot Key Resort** KEY WEST Parrot Key's conch-style beach homes are the epitome of luxury, with gourmet kitchens, first- and second-level private porches with waterfront views, 42-inch plasma TVs, premium cable service, and DVD/stereo systems. ***2801 N. Roosevelt Blvd. ☎ 305/809-2200. www.parrotkeyresort.com. 74 units. Doubles $189–$489. AE, DC, DISC, MC, V.***

★★★ **Pier House Resort and Caribbean Spa** KEY WEST Set back from the busy street, on a short strip of private beach, this place is a welcome oasis of calm. The accommodations vary tremendously, from simple business-style rooms to romantic quarters complete with stereos and whirlpool tubs. Although every unit has either a balcony or a patio, not all overlook the water. ***1 Duval St. (near Mallory Docks). ☎ 800/327-8340 or***

305/296-4600. www.pierhouse.com. 142 units. Doubles $229–$529. AE, DC, MC, V.

★★ **Ragged Edge Resort** ISLAMORADA This small oceanfront property's Tahitian-style units are spread along more than half a dozen gorgeous, grassy waterfront acres. All are immaculately clean and comfortable, and most are outfitted with full kitchens and tasteful furnishings. There's no bar, restaurant, or staff to speak of, but the retreat's affable owner is happy to lend bicycles and give advice on the area's offerings. *243 Treasure Harbor Rd. ☎ 800/436-2023 or 305/852-5389. www.ragged-edge.com. 11 units. Doubles $69–$99. AE, MC, V.*

★★★ **The Reach Resort** KEY WEST Fresh from a $37 million renovation, the boutique-style Reach Resort features gingerbread balconies, tin-roof accents, and shaded Spanish walkways characteristic of historic Key West. Newly refurbished guest rooms are large, with modernized decor and custom furnishings that are vibrant and crisp. A new pool deck and 450-foot (135m) natural-sand beach are perfect settings to enjoy a massive array of watersports. *1435 Simonton St. ☎ 866/397-6427 or 305/296-5000. www.reachresort.com. 150 units. Doubles $149–$499. AE, DC, DISC, MC, V.*

★★★ **Simonton Court** KEY WEST Once a cigar factory, Simonton Court features meticulously appointed restored historic cottages and suites amid sparkling pools and luxuriant private gardens. There are several options to choose from: bed-and-breakfast, cottage, guesthouse, mansion, and inn. Some cottages even have their own pools. *320 Simonton St. ☎ 800/944-2687 or 305/294-6386. www.simontoncourt.com. 30 units. Doubles $145–$515. Rates include continental breakfast. AE, DISC, MC, V.*

★★ kids **Southernmost Point Guest House** KEY WEST One of the few inns that actually welcomes children and pets, this romantic guesthouse is a real find. Every unit comes with fresh flowers, wine, and a full decanter of sherry. Mona Santiago, the kind, laid-back owner,

Accommodations at Sunset Key Guest Cottages are spacious and homey.

Sleeping Under the Stars

Bahia Honda State Park (☎ 800/326-3521; www.abfla.com/parks/bahiahonda/bahiahonda.html) offers some of the best camping in the Keys, with more than 500 acres of land, 80 campsites spread throughout three areas, and three spacious and comfortable duplex cabins. Cabins hold up to eight guests each and come complete with linens, kitchenettes, wraparound terraces, barbecue pits, and rocking chairs. For one to four people, camping costs about $26 per site. Depending on the season, cabin prices range from $75 to $120.

The Oceanside KOA Sugarloaf Key Resort ★★, near MM 20, has 200 fully equipped sites, with water, electricity, and sewer, which rent for about $94 a night (no-hookup sites cost about $84). Or you can pitch a tent on the 5 acres of waterfront property. In addition, the resort rents travel trailers: The 25-foot Dutchman sleeps six and costs about $120 a day. For details, contact the resort at P.O. Box 420469, Summerland Key, FL 33042 (☎ 800/562-7731 or 305/745-3549; fax 305/745-9889; www.koa.com).

provides chairs and towels for the beach, which is just a block away. Guests can help themselves to free wine as they soak in the 14-seat hot tub. Kids will enjoy the backyard swings and the pet rabbits. *1327 Duval St. ☎ 305/294-0715. www.southernmostpoint.com. 6 units. Doubles $75–$200. Rates include breakfast. AE, MC, V.*

★★★ **Sunset Key Guest Cottages** KEY WEST This Westin resort is just a 10-minute boat ride from Key West and a 10-minute launch ride to the secluded island of Sunset Key, where there's a white sandy beach, free-form pool with whirlpool jets, two tennis courts, and Latitudes Beach Cafe. Cottages are equipped with full kitchens, high-tech entertainment centers, and one, two, or three bedrooms. *Sunset Key Island. ☎ 800/221-2424 or 305/294-4000. www.sunsetkeyisland.com. 215 units, including cottages. $595–$2,225 up to 5 people. Pets up to 40 lbs. allowed. AE, DC, DISC, MC, V.*

★★ **Tranquility Bay Beach House Resort** MARATHON You'll feel like you're in your own beach house, with gorgeous two- and three-bedroom homes all with water views. All of the subtly decorated beach houses come equipped with everything a techno-savvy beach bum needs—even washers and dryers. Best of all, every beach house has a spacious porch with French doors, wooden deck chairs, and 180-degree views of the water. *2600 Overseas Hwy. ☎ 305/259-0888. www.tranquilitybay.com. 87 units. Doubles $279–$539. AE, DC, MC, V.*

★★★ **Weatherstation Inn** KEY WEST Originally built in 1912 as a weather station, this beautifully restored, meticulously maintained, Renaissance-style inn is just 2 blocks from Duval Street but seems worlds away. It's situated on the tropical grounds of the former Old Navy Yard, now an exclusive and private gated community. Spacious and uncluttered, each guest room is uniquely furnished to complement

Alternative Accommodations

Vacation Key West (☎ 800/595-5397 or 305/295-9500; www.vacationkw.com) is a wholesaler that offers discounts of 20% to 30% and is skilled at finding last-minute deals. It represents mostly larger hotels and motels, but can also place visitors in guesthouses. The phones are answered Monday through Friday from 9am to 6pm, and Saturday from 11am to 2pm. **Key West Innkeepers Association** (☎ 800/492-1911 or 305/292-3600) can also help you find lodging in any price range from among its members and affiliates.

Gay travelers may want to call the **Key West Business Guild** (☎ 305/294-4603), which represents more than 50 guesthouses and B&Bs in town, as well as many other gay-owned businesses. Be advised that most gay guesthouses have a clothing-optional policy. One of the most elegant and popular is Big Ruby's, 409 Applerouth Lane (☎ 800/477-7829 or 305/296-2323; www.bigrubys.com), located on a little alley just off Duval Street. Rates start at $125 double. A low cluster of buildings surrounds a lush courtyard where a hearty breakfast is served each morning and wine is poured at dusk. The all-male guests hang out by the pool, tanning in the buff.

For women only, Pearl's Rainbow, 525 United St. (☎ 800/74-WOMYN or 305/292-1450; www.pearlsrainbow.com), is a large, fairly well-maintained guesthouse with lots of privacy and amenities, including two pools and two hot tubs. Rates range from $89 to $369.

the interior architecture: hardwood floors, tall sash windows, and high ceilings. *57 Front St.* ☎ *800/815-2707 or 305/294-7277. www.weatherstationinn.com. 8 units. Doubles $180–$335. Rates include continental breakfast. AE, DISC, MC, V.*

★★ **Westin Key West Resort & Marina** KEY WEST Ideally situated in the heart of Old Town, the Westin Key West Resort & Marina is next to Mallory Square and within walking distance of famous Duval Street. It features large, well-appointed rooms with all the modern conveniences and the signature Westin Heavenly Bed. Most of the rooms and suites have ocean views and balconies. Bistro 245 serves ample breakfasts and a huge Sunday brunch. *245 Front St. (at the end of Duval St.).* ☎ *800/221-2424 or 305/294-4000. www.westin.com/keywest. 215 units, Doubles $229–$550. Pets up to 40 lbs. allowed. AE, DC, DISC, MC, V.*

★ **Westwinds Inn** KEY WEST A close second to staying in your own private 19th-century, tin-roofed clapboard house is this tranquil inn, just 4 blocks from Duval Street in the historic seaport district. Lush landscaping keeps the place extremely private and secluded; at times, you'll feel as if you're alone. Two pools, one heated in winter, are offset by alcoves, fountains, and the well-maintained whitewashed inn, which is actually composed of five separate buildings. *914 Eaton St.* ☎ *800/788-4150 or 305/296-4440. www.westwindskeywest.com. 22 units. Doubles $90–$220. Rates include continental breakfast. DISC, MC, V. No children 11 & under.*

Key West Nightlife Best Bets

Best for **Key West Party Politics**
★ Captain Tony's Saloon, *428 Greene St. (p 193)*

Best Place to **Get Lost In**
Durty Harry's, *208 Duval St. (p 194)*

Best for **Live Music**
★★★ Green Parrot, *601 Whitehead St. (p 194)*

Best **Biker Bar**
★★★ Hog's Breath Saloon, *400 Front St. (p 193)*

Best **Sports Bar**
★★ Island Dogs Bar, *505 Front St. (p 193)*

Best **Karaoke**
★★ Irish Kevin's, *211 Duval St. (p 193)*

The Green Parrot is known for great live music.

Captain Tony's Saloon.

Best **Small Space**
★ The Lazy Gecko, *203 Duval St. (p 194)*

Best **Boater Bar**
★★★ Schooner Wharf, *202 William St. (p 193)*

Best for **Spring Break**
★ Sloppy Joe's, *201 Duval St. (p 193)*

Best **Drag Show**
801 Bourbon Bar/One Saloon, *801 Duval St. & 514 Petronia St. (p 193)*

Best for **Campy Entertainment**
La Terraza de Martí, *1125 Duval St. (p 193)*

Best **Gay Dance Club**
Aqua, *711 Duval St. (p 193)*

Best **Cabaret**
The Crystal Room, *1125 Duval St. (p 194)*

Key West Nightlife A to Z

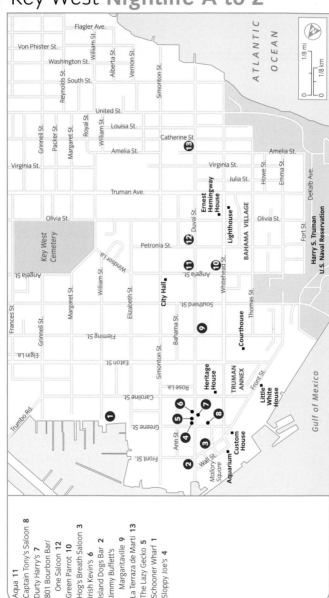

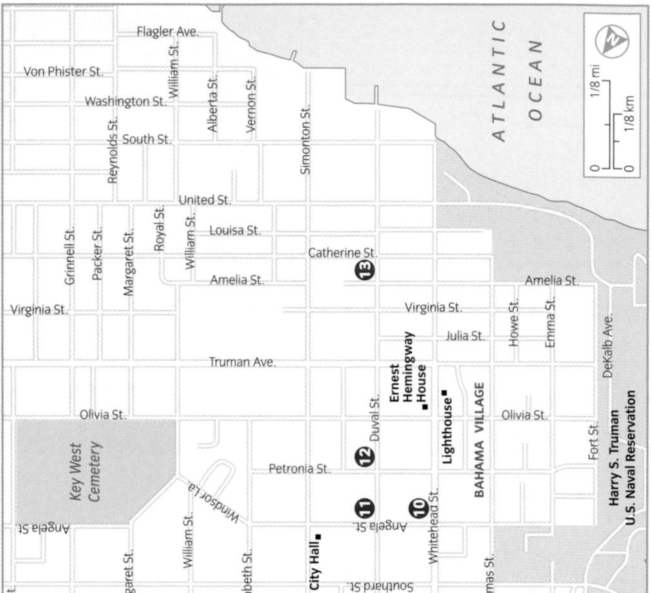

Aqua **11**
Captain Tony's Saloon **8**
Durty Harry's **7**
801 Bourbon Bar/ One Saloon **12**
Green Parrot **10**
Hog's Breath Saloon **3**
Irish Kevin's **6**
Island Dogs Bar **2**
Jimmy Buffett's Margaritaville **9**
La Terraza de Martí **13**
The Lazy Gecko **5**
Schooner Wharf **1**
Sloppy Joe's **4**

Bars

★ Captain Tony's Saloon Just around the corner from Duval's beaten path, this smoky bar is about as authentic as you'll find (they say Hemingway drank, caroused, and even wrote here). *428 Greene St. at Whitehead St. ☎ 305/294-1838. www.capttonyssaloon.com. Mon–Sat 10am–4am; Sun noon–2am.*

★★★ Hog's Breath Saloon The island's most popular biker bar, featuring a decent menu and live music. *400 Front St. ☎ 800/826-6969. www.hogsbreath.com. Mon–Sat 10am–4am; Sun noon–2am.*

★★ Island Dogs Bar This islandy bar is a cool spot to throw back a few while catching a game or a live band. Unlike most bars, the food here is good. Outdoor tables are ideal for watching the crowds stumble—literally—off Duval Street. *505 Front St. ☎ 305/295-0501. Daily 11am–2am.*

★★ Irish Kevin's Irish Kevin's is a must for those who'd like to sing along with the bar's namesake, who sings bawdy, ribald tunes while challenging revelers to drinking contests. *211 Duval St. ☎ 305/292-1262. www.irishkevins.com. Mon–Sat 10am–4am; Sun noon–3am.*

★★★ Schooner Wharf This one's a little off the beaten path, at the Key West Seaport, but worth the walk if you like open-air bars with dirt floors, three daily happy hours, live music, and a colorful Key West cocktail crowd. *202 William St. ☎ 305/292-3302. www.schoonerwharf.com. Daily 9am–4am.*

★ Sloppy Joe's Scholars and drunks debate whether this is the same Sloppy Joe's that Hemingway wrote about. There's live music nightly, as well as a cigar room and martini bar. *201 Duval St. www.sloppyjoes.com. Mon–Sat 10am–10pm; Sun noon–10pm.*

Gay & Lesbian Scene

Aqua Here you might catch drag queens belting out torch songs or judges voting on the best package in the wet-jockey-shorts contest. *711 Duval St. ☎ 305/292-8500. Daily 5:30pm–2am.*

801 Bourbon Bar/One Saloon Get both great drag and lots of disco. A mostly male clientele frequents this hot spot. *801 Duval St. & 514 Petronia St. ☎ 305/294-9349. Daily 10am–4am; Sun noon–4am.*

La Terraza de Marti Sunday nights are fun at this spot, also known as La-Te-Da. A great spot to gather poolside for the best martini in town—but don't bother with the

Bikers hang out at Hog's Breath Saloon.

Sloppy Joe's features live music, a cigar room, and a martini bar.

food. Just upstairs is the **Crystal Room** (☎ 305/296-6706), with a high-caliber cabaret performance. *1125 Duval St. ☎ 305/296-6706.*

Live Music

Durty Harry's This large complex features live rock bands almost every night. You can wander to one of the many outdoor bars or head to Upstairs at Rick's, an indoor/outdoor dance club that gets going late. There's also Red Garter, a pocket-size strip club. *208 Duval St. ☎ 305/296-4890. Mon–Sat 10am–4am; Sun noon–2am.*

Drag queens put on a show at 801 Bourbon.

★★★ **Green Parrot** Dating back to 1890, Green Parrot looks as old as it is but is the island's most popular local bar featuring excellent live music and a lively crowd. *601 Whitehead St. (at Southard St.). ☎ 305/294-6133. www.greenparrot.com. Mon–Sat 10am–4am; Sun noon–4am.*

★ **The Lazy Gecko** For an unabridged frozen-daiquiri menu and some excellent live music, The Lazy Gecko is the place to be. The space, however, is on the small side. *203 Duval St. ☎ 305/292-1903. www.thelazygecko.com. Mon–Sat 10am–4am; Sun noon–3am.* ●

Tip

The **Key West Pub Crawl** (☎ 305/744-9804; www.keywestwalkingtours.com) gives you a 2½-hour tour of the island's most famous bars Tuesday and Friday nights at 8pm. $30 (includes five drinks).

The
Savvy Traveler

Before You Go

Government Tourist Offices

Miami: Greater Miami Convention and Visitors Bureau, 701 Brickell Ave., Miami, FL 33131. ☎ **800/933-8448;** www.miamiandbeaches.com. Greater Miami and The Beaches Hotel Association, 407 Lincoln Rd., Miami Beach, FL 33139; ☎ **800/531-3553;** www.gmbha.org.

Because Miami is such a vast city, some of the more popular neighborhoods have their own chambers of commerce:

- **Miami Beach Chamber of Commerce,** 420 Lincoln Rd., Miami Beach, FL 33139; ☎ **305/672-1270;** www.miamibeachchamber.com.
- **Coral Gables Chamber of Commerce,** 2333 Ponce de León Blvd., Suite 650, Coral Gables, FL 33134; ☎ **305/446-1657;** www.gableschamber.org.
- **Coconut Grove Chamber of Commerce,** 2820 McFarlane Rd., Coconut Grove, FL 33133; ☎ **305/444-7270;** www.coconutgrovechamber.com.
- **Fort Lauderdale:** Greater Fort Lauderdale Convention & Visitors Bureau, 1850 Eller Dr., Suite 303, Fort Lauderdale, FL 33316; ☎ **954/765-4466;** www.sunny.org.
- **Palm Beach:** Palm Beach County Convention and Visitors Bureau, 1555 Palm Beach Lakes Blvd., Suite 204, West Palm Beach, FL 33401; ☎ **561/471-3995;** www.palmbeachfl.com.
- **Florida Keys:** The best place for information is at www.florida-keys.fl.us/chamber.htm, where you can get information for each individual Florida Keys chamber of commerce.
- **Everglades:** Tropical Everglades Visitor Center, 160 U.S. 1, Florida City, FL 33034; ☎ **305/245-9180;** www.tropicaleverglades.com.

Previous page: The Key Lime Pie Factory (p 177).

The Best Times to Go

Contrary to popular belief, the notion of sunny Florida isn't always 100% correct. When it comes to weather, Florida undergoes major mood swings. While it may be pouring rain on the ocean side of Miami Beach, on the bay side, the only thing pouring down may be UV rays. Rain showers aside, the most pressing concern for every South Florida visitor is the unpredictable, unstoppable hurricane. Official hurricane season is June to November, and while the hurricane's actual pattern is unpredictable, the meteorologists at the National Hurricane Center in Coral Gables are able to give fair enough warning so that people can take proper precautions. One of the safest places during a hurricane happens to be in a hotel, because most are sturdy enough to withstand high winds and have generators in case of power failures. For many people, the worst time to come to South Florida is during the summer, when temperatures are usually scorching, humidity is oppressive, and rain at 4pm is a daily occurrence. Wintertime in South Florida is spectacular—not too hot, not too cool. Temperatures can, however, dip down into the low 50s (teens Celsius) during a cold front.

Peak season in South Florida means more tourists, snowbirds, and models—and the influx of celebrities, who also call South Florida their winter home.

In the summer, South Florida practically comes to a standstill as far as special events, cultural activities, and overall pace is concerned. If you can brave the temperatures, you will not have to face the long lines at restaurants and attractions that you will encounter during peak season.

Festivals & Special Events

JAN. Football fanatics flock to the **FedEx Orange Bowl Championship** on New Year's Day, featuring two of the year's best college football teams. Call ☎ **305/341-4700** for tickets, or go to www.orangebowl.org, but do so early—they sell out quickly. In the second week of January, the 3-day **Key West Literary Seminar** (☎ **888/293-9291;** www.keywestliteraryseminar.org) features a different theme every year, along with a roster of incredible authors, writers, and other literary types. The event is so popular it sells out well in advance, so call early for tickets.

FEB. The first full weekend of the month is a feeding frenzy at the **Everglades City Seafood Festival** (☎ **239/695-2561;** www.evergladesseafoodfestival.com), where you'll find everything from stone crab to gator tails. Free admission, but you pay for the food you eat, booth by booth. The **Miami International Film Festival** (☎ **877/888-MIFF;** www.miamifilmfestival.com) features world premieres of Latin American, domestic, and other foreign and independent films at the end of February to early March. The **Miami International Boat Show** (☎ **954/441-3231;** www.miamiboatshow.com) draws a quarter of a million boat enthusiasts to the Miami Beach Convention Center in mid-February. The last weekend of the month hosts the **South Beach Wine & Food Festival** (☎ **877/762-3933;** www.sobewineandfoodfest.com), featuring some of the Food Network's best chefs. There are tastings, lectures, seminars, and parties.

MAR. The gay and lesbian community gathers in early March for the **Winter Party** (☎ **305/538-5908;** www.winterparty.com), a weekend-long series of parties and events benefiting the Dade Human Rights Foundation. Miami's version of Carnival, the **Calle Ocho Festival** (☎ **305/644-8888;** www.carnavalmiami.com), features a lengthy block party spanning 23 blocks.

APR. The **PGA Seniors Golf Championship** (☎ **561/624-8400**) is the oldest and most prestigious of the senior golf tournaments. Mid-April.

JUL. The **Lower Keys Underwater Music Fest** (☎ **800/872-3722**) in early July is an amusing aural aquatic event in which boaters head out to the underwater reef at the Looe Key Marine Sanctuary, drop speakers into the water, and pipe in all sorts of music, creating a disco-diving spectacular.

OCT. The **Columbus Day Regatta** takes place the second week of the month and encourages patrons, like Columbus, to discover—their birthday suits. Strip down to the bare necessities and party at the sandbar in the middle of Biscayne Bay. You'll need a boat to get out to where all the action is. Consider renting one on Key Biscayne, which is the closest to the sandbar. The craziness continues the last week of the month with **Fantasy Fest** (☎ **305/296-1817;** www.fantasyfest.net), when the streets are overtaken by wildly costumed revelers who have no shame (not for those under 18).

MIAMI'S AVERAGE MONTHLY HIGH/LOW TEMPERATURES & RAINFALL

	JAN	FEB	MAR	APR	MAY	JUNE
Avg. High (°F)	76	77	80	83	86	88
Avg. Low (°F)	60	61	64	68	72	75
Avg. High (°C)	24.4	25	26.7	28.3	30	31.1
Avg. Low (°C)	15.6	16.1	17.8	20	22.2	23.9
Avg. Rain (in.)	2.0	2.1	2.4	3.0	5.9	8.8
	JULY	AUG	SEPT	OCT	NOV	DEC
Avg. High (°F)	89	90	88	85	80	77
Avg. Low (°F)	76	76	76	72	66	61
Avg. High (°C)	31.7	32.2	31.1	29.4	26.7	25
Avg. Low (°C)	24.4	24.4	24.4	22.2	18.9	16.1
Avg. Rain (in.)	6.0	7.8	8.5	7.0	3.1	1.8

NOV. Bibliophiles, literati, and some of the world's most prestigious and prolific authors gather mid-month for **Miami Book Fair International** (☎ **305/237-3258**), the largest book fair in the United States. All lectures are free but fill up quickly, so get there early. **White Party Week** (www.whiteparty.org) benefits AIDS research, with the main event taking place at Villa Vizcaya.

DEC. Switzerland's **Art Basel** comes to Miami Beach (www.artbaselmiami beach.com) the first or second weekend of the month. At the **Seminole Hard Rock Winterfest Boat Parade** (☎ **954/767-0686;** www. winterfestparade.com), the boats are decked out in magnificent holiday regalia as they glide up and down the water. If you're not on a boat, the best views are from waterfront restaurants or anywhere you can squeeze in along the water. Mid-December.

Useful Websites

- **www.gomiami.about.com**: A collection of websites regarding Miami, all with links to other relevant websites.
- **www.miami.citysearch.com**: Listings and reviews for Miami arts and entertainment events, restaurants, shopping, and attractions.
- **www.key-west.com**: A well-rounded guide to Key West, including an events calendar and extensive listings for attractions, sightseeing and ecotours, theater, art galleries, dining, lodging, fishing, and shopping.
- **www.gaykeywestfl.com**: A guide to gay-friendly Key West.
- **www.miamiherald.com**: Local news and up-to-date information on events and entertainment options from the *Miami Herald.* The *Herald* also produces a fantastic website covering events, nightlife, dining, and entertainment at www.miami.com.
- **www.timeout.com/miami**: Reviews and listings for attractions, entertainment, restaurants, hotels, and shopping; includes categories for kids and gays and lesbians.
- **www.miaminewtimes.com**: Miami's leading alternative weekly includes features and listings for music, theater, film, and more.

Car Rentals

If you're planning on just staying on South Beach, we recommend that you don't rent a car. And even if you do plan on leaving the city limits during your stay, rent a car only for the day you'll need one. You're far better off sticking to taxis and your own two feet. Parking in Miami is scarce and expensive, and gasoline (petrol) isn't cheap.

If you still want to rent a car, the best deals are usually found at rental-car company websites, although all the major online travel agencies also offer rental car reservations services.

Getting **There**

By Plane

Miami International Airport (MIA) has become second in the United States for international passenger traffic and tenth in the world for total passengers. Despite the heavy traffic, the airport is quite user-friendly and not as much of a hassle as you'd think. Visitor information is available 24 hours a day at the **Miami International Airport Main Visitor Counter**, Concourse E, second level (☎ **305/876-7000**). Information is also available at **www.miami-airport.com**. Because MIA is the busiest airport in South Florida, travelers may want to consider flying into the less crowded **Fort Lauderdale Hollywood International Airport** (**FLL;** ☎ **954/359-1200**), which is closer to north Miami than MIA, or the **Palm Beach International Airport** (**PBI;** ☎ **561/471-7420**), which is about 1½ hours from Miami.

Several regional airlines fly nonstop (about 55 min.) from Miami to **Key West International Airport**, South Roosevelt Boulevard (☎ **305/296-5439**), on the southeastern corner of the island. Fares are about $120 to $300 round-trip.

By Car

Although four major roads run to and through Miami—I-95, S.R. 826, S.R. 836, and U.S. 1—chances are you'll reach Miami and the rest of South Florida by way of I-95. This north-south interstate is South Florida's lifeline and an integral part of the region. The highway connects all of Miami's different neighborhoods, the airport, the beaches, and all of South Florida to the rest of the country. Miami's road signs are notoriously confusing and notably absent when you most need them. Think twice before you exit from the highway if you aren't sure where you're going: Some exits lead to unsavory neighborhoods. Other highways that will get you to Florida include I-10, which originates in Los Angeles and terminates at the tip of Florida in Jacksonville, and I-75, which begins in North Michigan and runs through the center of the state to Florida's west coast.

Florida law allows drivers to make a right turn on a red light after a complete stop, unless otherwise indicated. In addition, all passengers are required to wear seat belts, and children younger than 3 must be securely fastened in government-approved car seats. If you plan to be in your car quite a bit during your visit, you may want to join the **American Automobile Association** (**AAA;** ☎ **800/596-2227; www.aaa.com**), which has hundreds of offices nationwide. Members receive excellent maps, emergency road service, and, upon request, planned, detailed itineraries.

By Train

Amtrak (☎ **800/USA-RAIL;** www.amtrak.com) is an option if you don't want to fly or drive down to South Florida. Two trains leave daily from New York. They both take from 26½ to 29 hours to complete the entire journey to Miami.

Getting **Around**

By Public Transportation

Officially, Miami-Dade County has opted for a "unified, multimodal transportation network," which basically means you can get around the city by train, bus, and taxi. However, in practice, the network doesn't work very well. Things have improved somewhat thanks to the $17 billion Peoples' Transportation Plan, which has offered a full range of transportation services at several community-based centers throughout the county, but unless you are going from downtown Miami to a not-too-distant spot, you are better off in a rental car or taxi.

With the exception of downtown Coconut Grove and South Beach, Miami is not a walker's city. Because it's so spread out, most attractions are too far apart to make walking between them feasible. In fact, most Miamians are so used to driving that they do so even when going just a few blocks.

By Rail

Two rail lines, operated by the **Metro-Dade Transit Agency** (☎ **305/770-3131** for information; www.co.miami-dade.fl.us/transit), run in concert with each other. **Metrorail,** the city's modern high-speed commuter train, is a 21-mile (34km) elevated line that travels north-south between downtown Miami and the southern suburbs. Locals like to refer to this semi-useless rail system as Metro*fail*. If you are staying in Coral Gables or Coconut Grove, you can park your car at a nearby station and ride the rails downtown. However, that's about it. There are plans to extend the system to service Miami International Airport, but until those tracks are built, these trains don't go most places tourists go, with the exception of Vizcaya (p. 68) in Coconut Grove. Metrorail operates daily from about 6am to midnight. The fare is $2. **Metromover,** a 4½-mile (7km) elevated line, circles the downtown area and connects with Metrorail at the Government Center stop. Riding on rubber tires, the single-car train winds past many of the area's most important attractions and its shopping and business districts. You may not go very far on the Metromover, but you will get a beautiful perspective from the towering height of the suspended rails. System hours are daily from about 6am to midnight, and the ride is free.

By Bus

In short, a bus ride in Miami is grueling. Miami's suburban layout is not conducive to getting around by bus. Lines operate and maps are available, but instead of getting to know the city, you'll find that relying on bus transportation will acquaint you only with how it feels to wait at bus stops. You can get a bus map by mail, either from the Greater Miami Convention and Visitors Bureau (see "Government Tourist Offices," earlier in this chapter), or by writing the **Metro-Dade Transit System,** 3300 NW 32nd Ave., Miami, FL 33142. In Miami, call ☎ **305/770-3131** for public-transit information. The fare is $1.50 plus 50¢ for a transfer. To its credit, the **South Beach Local** bus shuttles you around various points of South Beach. On Monday through Saturday the shuttle operates from 8am to 1am, Sundays and holidays from 10am to 1am. Fare is 25¢.

By Car

Tales circulate about vacationers who have visited Miami without a car, but they are very few indeed. If you are counting on exploring the city, even to a modest degree, a car is essential. Miami's restaurants, hotels, and attractions are far from one another, so any other form of transportation is relatively impractical. You won't need a car, however, if you are spending your entire vacation at a resort, are traveling directly to the Port of Miami for a cruise, or are here for a short stay centered on one area of the city, such as South Beach, where everything is within walking distance and parking is a costly nightmare.

When driving across a causeway or through downtown, allow extra time to reach your destination because of frequent drawbridge openings. Some bridges open about every half-hour for large sailing vessels to make their way through the wide bays and canals that crisscross the city, stalling traffic for several minutes.

Fast **Facts**

AIRPORT See "By Plane," earlier in this chapter.

AMERICAN EXPRESS You'll find American Express offices in downtown Miami at 100 N. Biscayne Blvd. (☎ **305/358-7350;** Mon–Fri 9am–5pm); 9700 Collins Ave., Bal Harbour (☎ **305/865-5959;** Mon–Sat 10am–6pm); and 32 Miracle Mile, Coral Gables (☎ **305/446-3381;** Mon–Fri 9am–5pm and Sat 10am–4pm). To report lost or stolen traveler's checks, call ☎ **800/221-7282.**

AREA CODE The original area code for Miami and all of Dade County is 305. That is still the code for older phone numbers, but all phone numbers assigned since July 1998 have the area code 786 (SUN). For all local calls, even if you're just calling across the street, you must dial the area code (305 or 786) first. Even though the Keys still share the Dade County area code of 305, calls to there from Miami are considered long-distance and must be preceded by 1-305. (Within the Keys, simply dial the seven-digit number.) The area code for Fort Lauderdale is 954; for Palm Beach, Boca Raton, Vero Beach, and Port St. Lucie, it's 561.

BUSINESS HOURS Banking hours vary, but most banks are open weekdays from 9am to 3pm. Several stay open until 5pm or so at least 1 day during the week, and most banks feature automated teller machines (ATMs) for 24-hour banking. Most stores are open daily from 10am to 6pm; however, there are many exceptions. As far as business offices are concerned, Miami is generally a 9-to-5 town.

CONSULATES & EMBASSIES All embassies are located in the nation's capital, Washington, D.C. If your country isn't listed below, call for directory information in Washington, D.C. (☎ **202/555-1212**), or log on to www.embassy.org/embassies.

The embassy of **Australia** is at 1601 Massachusetts Ave. NW, Washington, DC 20036 (☎ **202/797-3000;** www.usa.embassy.gov.au). The embassy of **Canada** is at 501 Pennsylvania Ave. NW, Washington, DC 20001 (☎ **202/682-1740;** www.canadianembassy.org). The embassy of **Ireland** is at 2234 Massachusetts Ave. NW, Washington, DC 20008 (☎ **202/462-3939;** www.embassyofireland.org). The embassy of **New Zealand** is at 37 Observatory Circle NW, Washington, DC 20008 (☎ **202/328-4800;** www.nzembassy.com). The embassy of the **United Kingdom** is at 3100 Massachusetts Ave. NW, Washington, DC 20008 (☎ **202/462-1340;** http://ukinusa.fco.gov.uk/en).

CURFEW Although not strictly enforced, there is an alleged curfew in effect for minors after 11pm on weeknights and midnight on weekends in all of Miami-Dade County. After those hours, children younger than 17 cannot be out on the streets or driving unless accompanied by a parent or on their way to work.

CUSTOMS **What You Can Bring into the United States** Every visitor more than 21 years of age may bring in, free of duty, the following: 1 liter of wine or hard liquor; 200 cigarettes, 100 cigars (but not from Cuba), or 3 pounds of smoking tobacco; and $100 worth of gifts. These exemptions are offered to travelers who spend at least 72 hours in the United States and who have not claimed them within the preceding 6 months. It is altogether forbidden to bring into the country foodstuffs (particularly fruit, cooked meats, and canned goods) and plants (vegetables, seeds, tropical plants, and the like). Foreign tourists may carry in or out up to $10,000 in U.S. or foreign currency with no formalities; larger sums must be declared to U.S. Customs on entering or leaving, which includes filing form CM 4790. For details regarding U.S. Customs and Border Protection, consult your nearest U.S. embassy or consulate, or **U.S. Customs** (☎ **202/927-1770;** www.cbp.gov).

What You Can Take Home from the United States:

Canadian Citizens: For a clear summary of Canadian rules, write for the booklet *I Declare,* issued by the **Canada Border Services Agency** (☎ **800/461-9999** in Canada, or 204/983-3500; www.cbsa-asfc.gc.ca).

U.K. Citizens: For information, contact **HM Customs & Excise** at ☎ **0845/010-9000** (from outside the U.K., 020/8929-0152), or consult their website at **www.hmce.gov.uk**.

Australian Citizens: A helpful brochure available from Australian consulates or Customs offices is *Know Before You Go.* For more information, call the **Australian Customs Service** at ☎ **1300/363-263,** or log on to **www.customs.gov.au**.

New Zealand Citizens: Most questions are answered in a free pamphlet available at New Zealand consulates and Customs offices: *New Zealand Customs Guide for Travellers, Notice no. 4.* For more information, contact **New Zealand Customs,** The Customhouse, 17–21 Whitmore St., Box 2218, Wellington (☎ **04/473-6099** or 0800/428-786; www.customs.govt.nz).

DENTISTS **A&E Dental Associates,** 11400 N. Kendall Dr., Mega Bank Building (☎ **305/271-7777**), offers round-the-clock care.

DOCTORS In an emergency, call an ambulance by dialing ☎ **911** (a free call) from any phone. The Dade

County Medical Association sponsors a **Physician Referral Service** (☎ **305/324-8717**) weekdays from 9am to 5pm. **Health South Doctors' Hospital,** 5000 University Dr. (☎ **305/666-2111**), is an acute-care hospital with a 24-hour physician-staffed emergency department.

EMERGENCIES To reach the police, an ambulance, or the fire department, dial ☎ **911** from any phone. No coins are needed. Emergency hotlines include **Crisis Intervention** (☎ **305/358-HELP [4357]** or 305/358-4357) and the **Poison Information Center** (☎ **800/222-1222**).

EYEGLASSES **Pearle Vision Center,** 7901 Biscayne Blvd. (☎ **305/754-5144**), can usually fill prescriptions in about an hour.

GAY & LESBIAN TRAVELERS The **Miami-Dade Gay and Lesbian Chamber of Commerce** (www.gogaymiami.com) has a great site full of information for gay travelers. The **International Gay and Lesbian Travel Association** (IGLTA; ☎ **800/448-8550** or 954/776-2626; www.iglta.org) is the trade association for the gay and lesbian travel industry. Its website offers an online directory of gay- and lesbian-friendly travel businesses.

HOLIDAYS Banks, government offices, and post offices are closed on the following legal national holidays: January 1 (New Year's Day), the third Monday in January (Martin Luther King, Jr., Day), the third Monday in February (Presidents Day), the last Monday in May (Memorial Day), July 4 (Independence Day), the first Monday in September (Labor Day), the second Monday in October (Columbus Day), November 11 (Veterans Day), the fourth Thursday in November (Thanksgiving Day), and December 25 (Christmas). Also, the Tuesday following the first Monday in November is Election Day and is a federal government holiday in presidential-election years (held every 4 years, and next in 2012). Stores, museums, and restaurants are open most holidays, except for Thanksgiving, Christmas, and New Year's Day.

INSURANCE **For Domestic Visitors:** Trip-cancellation insurance helps you get your money back if you have to back out of a trip, if you have to go home early, or if your travel supplier goes bankrupt. Allowed reasons for cancellation can range from sickness to natural disasters to the State Department declaring your destination unsafe for travel. (Insurers usually won't cover vague fears, though.) In this unstable world, trip-cancellation insurance is a good buy if you're getting tickets well in advance. Insurance policy details vary, so read the fine print—and especially make sure that your airline is on the list of carriers covered in case of bankruptcy. For information, contact one of the following insurers: **Access America** (☎ **866/807-3982;** www.accessamerica.com), **Travel Guard International** (☎ **800/826-4919;** www.travelguard.com), **Travel Insured International** (☎ **800/243-3174;** www.travelinsured.com), or **Travelex Insurance Services** (☎ **888/457-4602;** www.travelex-insurance.com).

Medical Insurance: Although it's not required of travelers, health insurance is highly recommended. Unlike many European countries, the United States does not usually offer free or low-cost medical care to its citizens or visitors. Doctors and hospitals are expensive, and in most cases will require advance payment or proof of coverage before they render their services. Though lack of health insurance may prevent you from being admitted to a hospital in nonemergencies, don't worry about being left on a street corner to die: The American way is to fix you now and bill the living daylights out of you later.

Insurance for British Travelers: Most big travel agents offer their own insurance and will probably try to sell you their package when you book a holiday. Think before you sign. **The Association of British Insurers** (☎ **020/7600-3333;** www.abi.org.uk) gives advice by phone and publishes *Holiday Insurance,* a free guide to policy provisions and prices. You might also shop around for better deals: Try **Columbus Direct** (☎ **020/7375-0011;** www.columbusdirect.net).

Insurance for Canadian Travelers: Canadians should check with their provincial health plan offices or call **Health Canada** (☎ **613/957-2991;** www.hc-sc.gc.ca) to find out the extent of your coverage and what documentation and receipts you must take home in case you are treated in the United States.

Lost-Luggage Insurance: On domestic flights, checked baggage is covered up to $3,000 per ticketed passenger. On international flights (including U.S. portions of international trips), baggage is limited to approximately $9 per pound (1kg), up to approximately $635 per checked bag. If you plan to check items more valuable than the standard liability, see if your valuables are covered by your homeowner's policy, or get baggage insurance as part of your comprehensive travel-insurance package. Don't buy insurance at the airport, as it's usually overpriced. Be sure to take any valuables or irreplaceable items with you in your carry-on luggage, since many valuables (including books, money, and electronics) aren't covered by airline policies.

If your luggage is lost, immediately file a lost-luggage claim at the airport, detailing the luggage contents. For most airlines, you must report delayed, damaged, or lost baggage within 4 hours of arrival. The airlines are required to deliver luggage, once found, directly to your house or destination free of charge.

INTERNET ACCESS Internet access is available at Kafka's Cyber Cafe, 1464 Washington Ave. (☎ **305/673-9669**); the South Beach Internet Cafe, 1106 Collins Ave. (☎ **305/532-4331**); and the swanky all-in-one Mobil gas station, 2500 NW 87th Ave. (☎ **305/477-2501**).

LAUNDRY & DRY CLEANING Clean Machine Laundry, 226 12th St. (☎ **305/534-9429**), is convenient to South Beach's Art Deco hotels and is open 24 hours a day. Coral Gables Laundry & Dry Cleaning, 250 Minorca Ave. (☎ **305/446-6458**), offers same-day service and is open weekdays from 7am to 7pm and Saturday from 8am to 3pm.

LIQUOR LAWS Only adults 21 or older may legally purchase or consume alcohol in the state of Florida. Minors are usually permitted in bars, as long as the bars also serve food. Liquor laws are strictly enforced; if you look young, carry identification. Beer and wine are sold in most supermarkets and convenience stores. The city of Miami's liquor stores are closed on Sunday. Liquor stores in the city of Miami Beach are open daily.

LOST & FOUND Be sure to notify all your credit card companies the minute you discover your wallet has been lost or stolen, and file a report at the nearest police precinct (☎ **311**). Your insurance company may require a police report before covering any claims. Most credit card companies have an emergency toll-free number to call if your card is lost or stolen; they may be able to wire you a cash advance immediately or deliver an emergency credit card in a day or two. Visa's U.S. emergency number is ☎ **800/847-2911** or 410/581-9994. American Express cardholders and traveler's check holders should call ☎ **800/221-7282.** MasterCard holders should call ☎ **800/307-7309** or 636/722-7111. For other credit cards, call the toll-free number directory at ☎ **800/555-1212.** If you need emergency cash over the weekend, when all banks and American Express offices are closed, you can have money wired to you via **Western Union** (☎ **800/325-6000;** www.westernunion.com).

If you lost something at the airport, call the **Airport Lost and Found** (☎ **305/876-7377**). If you lost something on the bus, Metrorail, or Metromover, call **Metro-Dade Transit Agency** (☎ **305/770-3131**). If you lost something anywhere else, phone the **Dade County Police Lost and Found** (☎ **305/375-3366**). You may also want to fill out a police report for insurance purposes.

LUGGAGE STORAGE & LOCKERS In addition to the baggage check at Miami International Airport, most hotels offer luggage-storage facilities. If you are taking a cruise from the Port of Miami, bags can be stored in your ship's departure terminal.

NEWSPAPERS & MAGAZINES The *Miami Herald* is the city's only English-language daily. It is especially known for its extensive Latin American coverage and has a decent Friday "Weekend" entertainment guide. The most respected alternative weekly is the giveaway tabloid called *New Times,* which contains up-to-date listings and reviews of food, films, theater, music, and whatever else is happening in town. Also free, if you can find it, is *Ocean Drive,* an oversize glossy magazine that's limited on text and heavy on ads and society photos.

For a large selection of foreign language newspapers and magazines, check with any of the large bookstores or try News Café, 800 Ocean Dr. (☎ **305/538-6397**); the newsstand adjacent to the Van Dyke Cafe, 846 Lincoln Rd. (☎ **305/534-3600**); Eddie's News, 1096 Normandy Dr. (☎ **305/866-2661**); or Worldwide News, 1629 NE 163rd St. (☎ **305/940-4090**).

PARKING Always keep plenty of quarters on hand to feed hungry meters, most of which have been removed in favor of parking payment stations where you feed a machine and get a printed receipt to display on your dash. Or, on Miami Beach, stop by the chamber of commerce at 1920 Meridian Ave. or any Publix grocery store, to buy a magnetic parking card in denominations of $10, $20, or $25. Parking is usually plentiful (except on South Beach and Coconut Grove), but when it's not, be careful: Fines for illegal parking can be stiff. In addition to parking garages, valet services are commonplace and often used. Because parking is at such a premium in bustling South Beach as well as in Coconut Grove, prices tend to be jacked up—especially at night and when there are special events (day or night). You can expect to pay an average of $5 to $15 for parking in these areas.

PASSPORTS **For Residents of Australia:** You can pick up an application from your local post office or any branch of Passports Australia, but you must schedule an interview at the passport office to present your application materials. Call the **Australian Passport Information**

Service at ☎ **131-232,** or visit the government website at **www.passports.gov.au**.

For Residents of Canada: Passport applications are available at travel agencies throughout Canada or from the central **Passport Office,** Department of Foreign Affairs and International Trade, Ottawa, ON K1A 0G3 (☎ **800/567-6868;** www.ppt.gc.ca). ***Note:*** Canadian children who travel must have their own passport. However, if you hold a valid Canadian passport issued before December 11, 2001, that bears the name of your child, the passport remains valid for you and your child until it expires.

For Residents of Ireland: You can apply for a 10-year passport at the **Passport Office,** Setanta Centre, Molesworth Street, Dublin 2 (☎ **01/671-1633;** www.irlgov.ie/iveagh). Those under age 18 and over 65 must apply for a 3-year passport. You can also apply at 1A South Mall, Cork (☎ **021/272-525**), or at most main post offices.

For Residents of New Zealand: You can pick up a passport application at any New Zealand Passports Office or download it from their website. Contact the **Passports Office** at ☎ **0800/225-050** in New Zealand or 04/474-8100, or log on to **www.passports.govt.nz**.

For Residents of the United Kingdom: To pick up an application for a standard 10-year passport (5-yr. passport for children under 16), visit your nearest passport office, major post office, or travel agency, or contact the **United Kingdom Passport Service** at ☎ **0870/521-0410,** or search its website at **www.ukpa.gov.uk**.

International visitors should always keep a photocopy of their passport with them when traveling. If your passport is lost or stolen, having a copy significantly facilitates the reissuing process at a local consulate or embassy. Keep your passport and other valuables in your room's safe or in the hotel safe.

PHARMACIES **Walgreens** has dozens of locations all over town, including 8550 Coral Way (☎ 305/221-9271); 1845 Alton Rd. (☎ 305/531-8868); and 6700 Collins Ave. (☎ 305/861-6742). The branch at 5731 Bird Rd., at SW 40th Street (☎ 305/666-0757), is open 24 hours, as is **CVS,** 6460 S. Dixie Hwy. (☎ 305/661-0778).

PHOTOGRAPHIC NEEDS **One Hour Photo,** in the Bayside Marketplace (☎ **305/377-FOTO [3686]**), is pricey (about $20 to develop and print a roll of 36 pictures), but they're open Monday to Saturday from 10am to 10pm, and Sunday noon to 8pm. Walgreens (see above, under "Pharmacies") or Rite-Aid will develop film by the next day for about $10.

POST OFFICE The Main Post Office, 2200 Milam Dairy Rd. (☎ **800/275-8777**), is located west of the Miami International Airport. Conveniently located post offices include 1300 Washington Ave. in South Beach and 3191 Grand Ave. in Coconut Grove. There is one central number for all post offices: ☎ **800/275-8777.**

At press time, domestic postage rates were 28¢ for a postcard and 44¢ for a letter. For international mail, a first-class letter of up to 1 ounce costs 98¢ (75¢ to Canada and 79¢ Mexico); a first-class postcard costs the same as a letter. For more information, go to www.usps.com and click on "calculate postage."

SAFETY As always, use your common sense and be aware of your surroundings at all times. Don't walk alone at night, and be extra wary when walking or driving though downtown Miami and surrounding areas. Reacting to several highly publicized crimes against tourists several years ago, both local and state governments have taken steps to help protect visitors. These measures include special police units patrolling the airport and surrounding neighborhoods, and better signs on the state's most tourist-traveled routes.

TAXES A 6% state sales tax (plus 1% local tax, for a total of 7% in Miami-Dade County [from Homestead to North Miami Beach]) is added on at the register for all goods and services purchased in Florida. In addition, most municipalities levy special taxes on restaurants and hotels. In Surfside, hotel taxes total 10.5%; in Bal Harbour, 9.5%; in Miami Beach (including South Beach), 11.5%; and in the rest of Dade County, a whopping 12.5%. In Miami Beach, Surfside, and Bal Harbour, the resort (hotel) tax also applies to hotel restaurants and restaurants with liquor licenses.

TELEPHONES For directory assistance ("information"), dial 411. Hotel surcharges on long-distance and local calls are astronomical, so you're usually better off using a cell or public pay telephone. Local calls made from public pay phones in Miami usually cost 50¢. Pay phones do not accept pennies, and none will take anything larger than a quarter.

TIPPING In hotels, tip bellhops at least $1 per bag and tip the chamber staff $1 to $2 per day (more if you've left a disaster area). Tip the doorman or concierge only if he or she has provided you with some specific service (for example, calling a cab for you). Tip the valet-parking attendant $1 every time you get your car.

In restaurants, bars, and nightclubs, tip service staff 15% to 20% of the check, tip bartenders 10% to 15%, tip checkroom attendants $1 per garment, and tip valet-parking attendants $1 per vehicle.

As for other service personnel, tip cab drivers 15% of the fare; tip skycaps at airports at least $1 per bag; and tip hairdressers and barbers 15% to 20%. Beware of tips already added to your bill, usually 15% to 18% gratuity in many South Beach restaurants. However, you are free to adjust that amount as needed.

TOILETS You won't find public toilets or restrooms on the streets. Your best bet for good, clean facilities are hotel lobbies, bars, fast-food restaurants, museums, and department stores. If possible, avoid toilets at parks and beaches, which tend to be dirty.

TOURIST TRAPS & SCAMS If you're planning on attending sporting or concert events, beware of ticket scalpers. Buy your tickets in advance from a legitimate source, as many of the tickets sold by scalpers are counterfeit (and scalping can get you unwanted attention from police officers who patrol stadiums before events).

TRAVELERS WITH DISABILITIES The America the Beautiful—National Park and Federal Recreational Lands Pass—Access Pass (formerly the Golden Access Passport) gives visually impaired or permanently disabled persons (regardless of age) free lifetime entrance to federal recreation sites administered by the National Park Service (such as Everglades National Park), including the Fish and Wildlife Service, the Forest Service, the Bureau of Land Management, and the Bureau of Reclamation. This may include national parks, monuments, historic sites, recreation areas, and national wildlife refuges. The America the Beautiful Access Pass can only be obtained in person at any NPS facility that charges an entrance fee. You need to show proof of medically determined disability. Besides free entry, the pass also offers a 50% discount on some federal-use fees charged for such facilities as camping, swimming, parking, boat launching, and tours. For more information, go to www.nps.gov/fees_passes.htm or call ☎ **888/467-2757.**

Organizations that offer a vast range of resources and assistance to travelers with disabilities include **MossRehab** (☎ **800/CALL-MOSS;** www.mossresourcenet.org); the **American Foundation** for the Blind (AFB; ☎ **800/232-5463;** www.afb.org); and **SATH** (Society for Accessible Travel & Hospitality; ☎ **212/447-7284;** www.sath.org). AirAmbulanceCard.com is now partnered with SATH and allows you to preselect top-notch hospitals in case of an emergency. **Access-Able Travel Source** (☎ **303/232-2979;** www.access-able.com) offers a comprehensive database on travel agents from around the world with experience in accessible travel; destination-specific access information; and links to such resources as service animals, equipment rentals, and access guides.

Many travel agencies offer customized tours and itineraries for travelers with disabilities. Among them are **Flying Wheels Travel** (☎ **507/451-5005;** www.flyingwheelstravel.com) and **Accessible Journeys** (☎ **800/846-4537** or 610/521-0339; www.disabilitytravel.com).

British travelers should contact **Holiday Care** (☎ **0845-124-9971** in U.K. only; www.holidaycare.org.uk) to access a wide range of travel information and resources for seniors and travelers with disabilities.

WEATHER Hurricane season in Miami runs June through November. For an up-to-date recording of current weather conditions and forecast reports, call ☎ **305/229-4522.**

Miami and South Florida: **A Brief History**

MIAMI It wasn't long after Florida became the 27th state in the union that Miami began to emerge as a city. During the war, the U.S. created Fort Dallas on the north bank of a river that flowed through southern Florida. When the soldiers left, the fort became the base for a small village established by William H. English, who dubbed it Miami, from the Indian word Mayami, meaning big water.

In 1822, the Homestead Act offered 160 acres (64 hectares) of free land to anyone who would stay on it for at least 5 years. Edmund Beasley bit, and in 1868 moved into what is now Coconut Grove. Two years later, William Brickell bought land on the south bank of the Miami River, and Ephraim Sturtevant took over the area called Biscayne. In 1875, his daughter, Julia Tuttle, visited him and fell in love with the area, not returning for another 16 years, when she would further transform the city.

In the meantime, Henry Flagler, who made a $50 million fortune working with John Rockefeller in the Standard Oil company, came to Florida in the late 1800s. He built a railroad all the way down the east coast of Florida, stopping in each major town to build a hotel. Another railway honcho, Henry Plant, laid his tracks on the opposite coast, from Jacksonville to Tampa.

When her husband died in 1886, Julia Tuttle decided to leave Cleveland for Florida, and asked Plant to extend his railroad to Miami. Plant declined, so Tuttle went to Flagler, whose own railroad stopped 66 miles (106km) away in what is now known as Palm Beach. Flagler laughed at Tuttle's request, saying he didn't see what Miami had to offer in terms of tourism.

After a devastating winter that killed all crops north of the state, Tuttle sent Flagler a bounty of orange blossoms to prove that Miami did, indeed, have something to offer. After agreeing to give Flagler some of her land along with William Brickell's, Flagler agreed to extend the railway. When the first train arrived in Miami on April 15, 1896, all 300 of the city's residents showed up to see it. Miami had arrived, and newspapers and magazines began touting the city as "the sun porch of America, where winter is turned to summer."

FLORIDA KEYS No one knows exactly when the first European set foot on one of the Florida Keys, but as exploration and shipping increased, the islands became prominent on nautical maps. The nearby treacherous coral reefs claimed many lives. The chain was eventually called "keys," attributed to the Spanish *cayos,* meaning "small islands."

In 1763, when the Spanish ceded Florida to the British in a trade for the port of Havana, an agent of the King of Spain claimed that the islands, rich in fish, turtles, and mahogany for shipbuilding, were part of Cuba, fearing that the English might build fortresses and dominate the shipping lanes. The British realized the treaty was ambiguous, but declared that the Keys should be occupied and defended as part of Florida. The British claim was never officially contested. Ironically, the British gave the islands back to Spain in 1783, to keep them out of the hands of the United States, but in 1821 all of Florida, including the necklace of islands, officially became American territory.

Many of the residents of Key West were immigrants from the Bahamas, known as Conchs (pronounced "conks"), who arrived in increasing numbers after 1830. In the 20th century, many residents of Key West started referring to themselves as "Conchs," and the term is now applied to all residents of Key West. In 1982, Key West, and the rest of the Florida Keys, briefly declared its "independence" as the Conch Republic in a protest over a United States Border Patrol blockade. This blockade was set up on U.S. 1 where the northern end of the Overseas Highway meets the mainland at Florida City. This blockade was in response to the Mariel Boatlift. A 17-mile (27km) traffic jam ensued while the Border Patrol stopped every car leaving the Keys supposedly searching for illegal aliens attempting to enter the mainland United States. This paralyzed the Florida Keys. The Conch Republic Independence Celebration—including parades and parties—is April 23.

THE EVERGLADES Thanks to the work of the Everglades' foremost supporter, Ernest F. Coe, Congress passed a park bill in 1934. Dubbed by opponents as the "alligator and snake swamp bill," the legislation stalled during the Great Depression and World War II. Finally, on December 6,

1947, President Harry S. Truman dedicated the Everglades National Park. In that same year, Marjory Stoneman Douglas first published *The Everglades: River of Grass*.

FORT LAUDERDALE Fort Lauderdale is named after a series of forts built by the United States during the Second Seminole War. However, development of the city did not begin until 50 years after the forts were abandoned at the end of the conflict. Three forts named "Fort Lauderdale" were constructed; the first was at the fork of the New River, the second at Tarpon Bend, and the third near the site of the Bahia Mar Marina. The forts took their name from Major William Lauderdale, who was the commander of the detachment of soldiers who built the first fort.

The area in which the city of Fort Lauderdale would later be founded was inhabited for more than 1,000 years by the Tequesta Indians. Contact with Spanish explorers in the 16th century proved disastrous for the Tequesta, as the Europeans unwittingly brought with them diseases to which the native populations possessed no resistance, such as smallpox. For the Tequesta, disease, coupled with continuing conflict with their Calusa neighbors, contributed greatly to their decline over the next two centuries. By 1763, there were only a few Tequesta left in Florida, and most of them were evacuated to Cuba when the Spanish ceded Florida to the British in 1763, under the terms of the Treaty of Paris (1763), which ended the Seven Years' War. Although control of the area changed between Spain, England, the United States, and the Confederated States of America, it remained largely undeveloped until the 20th century. It was not until Frank Stranahan arrived in the area in 1893 to operate a ferry across the New River, and the Florida East Coast Railroad's completion of a route through the area in 1896, that any organized development began. The city was incorporated in 1911, and in 1915 was designated the county seat of newly formed Broward County.

Fort Lauderdale's first major development began in the 1920s. The 1926 Miami Hurricane and the Great Depression of the 1930s caused a great deal of economic dislocation. When World War II began, Fort Lauderdale became a major U.S. Navy base. After the war ended, service members returned to the area, spurring an enormous population explosion that dwarfed the 1920s boom. Today, Fort Lauderdale is a major yachting center, one of the nation's largest tourist destinations, and the center of a metropolitan division with 1.8 million people.

PALM BEACH Palm Beach County was created in 1909. It was named for its first settled community, Palm Beach, in turn named for the palm trees and beaches in the area. The county was carved out of what was then the northern half of Dade County. The southern half of Palm Beach County was subsequently carved out to create the northern portion of Broward County in 1915. Henry Flagler was instrumental in the county's development in the early 1900s with the extension of the Florida East Coast Railway through the county from Jacksonville to Key West. You can blame or thank architect Addison Mizner for all those pink houses. As Palm Beach became a haven for the rich, it also became a political focal point as one of the counties at the center of the 2000 U.S. Presidential election recount controversy, and ended up turning the state in favor of George W. Bush by 537 votes. ●

Index

See also Accommodations and Restaurant indexes, below.

Y

Z

Accommodations

Restaurants

Photo **Credits**

p viii: © Ken Ross / Viestiphoto.com; p 3 top: © Steve Vidler/Photolibrary.com; p 3 bottom: © Ken Ross / Viestiphoto.com; p 4 top: © Greg Johnston Photography; p 4 bottom: © Joe Viesti / Viestiphoto.com; p 5 top: © Alex Segre / Alamy Images; p 5 bottom: © Greg Johnston Photography; p 6 top: © Ken Ross / Viestiphoto.com; p 6 bottom: © Ken Ross / Viestiphoto.com; p 7: © Andrew Itkoff Photography; p 9: © Greg Johnston Photography; p 10 top: © Ken Ross / Viestiphoto.com; p 10 bottom: © Ken Ross / Viestiphoto.com; p 11 top: © Jeffrey Greenberg / Alamy Images; p 11 bottom: © Ken Ross / Viestiphoto.com; p 13: © Ken Ross / Viestiphoto.com; p 14 top: © Marjorie Ochstein/Courtesy Heritage Schooner Cruises; p 14 bottom: © Joe Viesti / Viestiphoto.com; p 16: © Joe Viesti / Viestiphoto.com; p 17: © Ken Ross / Viestiphoto.com; p 19: © Ken Ross / Viestiphoto.com; p 20 top: © Greg Johnston Photography; p 20 bottom: © Joe Viesti / Viestiphoto.com; p 21: © Greg Johnston Photography; p 22: © Joe Viesti / Viestiphoto.com; p 23: © Jeffrey Greenberg / Alamy Images; p 25: © Andrew Itkoff Photography; p 27: © Ken Ross / Viestiphoto.com; p 28 top: © Ken Ross / Viestiphoto.com; p 28 bottom: © Ken Ross / Viestiphoto.com; p 29: © Ken Ross / Viestiphoto.com; p 31: © Joe Viesti / Viestiphoto.com; p 32 top: © Richard l'Anson / Lonely Planet Images; p 32 bottom: © Joe Viesti / Viestiphoto.com; p 33 top: © Joe Viesti / Viestiphoto.com; p 33 bottom: © Joe Viesti / Viestiphoto.com; p 35: © Ken Ross / Viestiphoto.com; p 36: © Joe Viesti / Viestiphoto.com; p 37: © Ken Ross / Viestiphoto.com; p 39 top: © Joe Viesti / Viestiphoto.com; p 39 bottom: © Joe Viesti / Viestiphoto.com; p 40 top: © Andrew Itkoff Photography; p 40 bottom: © Andrew Itkoff Photography; p 41 top: © Andrew Itkoff Photography; p 41 bottom: © Andrew Itkoff Photography; p 42 top: © Joe Viesti / Viestiphoto.com; p 42 bottom: © Joe Viesti / Viestiphoto.com; p 43: © Joe Viesti / Viestiphoto.com; p 44: © Joe Viesti / Viestiphoto.com; p 48: © Andrew Itkoff Photography; p 49 top: © Andrew Itkoff Photography; p 49 bottom: © Joe Viesti / Viestiphoto.com; p 50: © Andrew Itkoff Photography; p 51: © Joe Viesti / Viestiphoto.com; p 52 top: © Andrew Itkoff Photography; p 52 bottom: © Jeffrey Greenberg / Alamy Images; p 53: © Joe Viesti / Viestiphoto.com; p 54 top: © Joe Viesti / Viestiphoto.com; p 54 bottom: © Ken Ross / Viestiphoto.com; p 55: © Joe Viesti / Viestiphoto.com; p 56: © Ken Ross / Viestiphoto.com; p 58: © Ken Ross / Viestiphoto.com; p 59 top: © Ken Ross / Viestiphoto.com; p 59 bottom: © Ken Ross / Viestiphoto.com; p 61 top: © Ken Ross / Viestiphoto.com; p 61 bottom: © Ken Ross / Viestiphoto.com; p 63: © Ken Ross / Viestiphoto.com; p 64 top: © Ken Ross / Viestiphoto.com; p 64 bottom: © Ken Ross / Viestiphoto.com; p 65: © Ken Ross / Viestiphoto.com; p 67: © Joe Viesti / Viestiphoto.com; p 68: © Ken Ross / Viestiphoto.com; p 69: © Ken Ross / Viestiphoto.com; p 70: © Ken Ross / Viestiphoto.com; p 71: © Courtesy Andrew Meade / Meat Market Restaurant; p 72: © Joe Viesti / Viestiphoto.com; p 75: © Joe Viesti / Viestiphoto.com; p 77: © Courtesy Michael Katz Photography / Blue Door at Delano; p 78: © Joe Viesti / Viestiphoto.com; p 79 top: © Ken Ross / Viestiphoto.com; p 79 bottom: © Ken Ross / Viestiphoto.com; p 82: © Joe Viesti / Viestiphoto.com; p 83: © Ken Ross / Viestiphoto.com; p 84: © Ken Ross / Viestiphoto.com; p 85: © Joe Viesti / Viestiphoto.com; p 87 top: © Ken Ross / Viestiphoto.com; p 87 bottom: © Jeffrey Greenberg / Alamy Images; p 88: © Ken Ross / Viestiphoto.com; p 89: © Ken Ross / Viestiphoto.com; p 90: © Ingolf Pompe 9 /Alamy Images; p 92: © Ken Ross / Viestiphoto.com; p 94: © Ken Ross / Viestiphoto.com; p 95: © Courtesy Mokai; p 96: © Ken Ross / Viestiphoto.com; p 97: © Ken Ross / Viestiphoto.com; p 98: © Ken Ross / Viestiphoto.com; p 99: © Courtesy Jonas Grabarnick / SET; p 100: © Ken Ross / Viestiphoto.com; p 102: © Ken Ross / Viestiphoto.com; p 103: © Larry French / Getty Images; p 104: © Robin Hill/Courtesy Ballet Flamenco La Rosa; p 107 top: © Ken Ross / Viestiphoto.com; p 107 bottom: © Courtesy Gary T'To / New World Symphony, Miami; p 108: © Ken Ross / Viestiphoto.com; p 109: © Ken Ross / Viestiphoto.com; p 110: © Ken Ross / Viestiphoto.com; p 111: © Clive Brunskill / Getty Images; p 112 top: © Jeffrey Greenberg / Alamy Images; p 112 bottom: © Lynne Sladky / AP Wide World Photos; p 113: © Courtesy Viceroy, Miami; p 114: © Ken Ross / Viestiphoto.com; p 119: © Ken Ross / Viestiphoto.com; p 120: © Joe Viesti / Viestiphoto.com; p 121: © Joe Viesti / Viestiphoto.com; p 122: © Ken Ross / Viestiphoto.com; p 123: © Ken Ross / Viestiphoto.com; p 124 top: © Courtesy The Raleigh; p 124 bottom: © Andrew Itkoff Photography; p 125 top: © Jeffrey Greenberg / Alamy Images; p 125 bottom: © Ken Ross / Viestiphoto.com; p 126: © Ken Ross / Viestiphoto.com; p 127: © Courtesy The Standard, Miami; p 129: © Greg Johnston Photography; p 131 top: © Joe Viesti / Viestiphoto.com; p 131 bottom: © Joe Viesti / Viestiphoto.com; p 132 top: © Joe Viesti / Viestiphoto.com; p 132 bottom: © Andrew Itkoff Photography; p 133: © Joe Viesti / Viestiphoto.com; p 135: © Flagler Museum; p 136: © Joe Viesti / Viestiphoto.com; p 137: © Joe Viesti / Viestiphoto.com; p 139: © Ken Ross / Viestiphoto.com; p 140: © Witold Skrypczak / Lonely Planet Images; p 141: © Ken Ross / Viestiphoto.com; p 143: © Greg Johnston Photography; p 145:

© Greg Johnston Photography; p 146: © Joe Viesti / Viestiphoto.com; p 147: © Greg Johnston Photography; p 149: © Greg Johnston Photography; p 150: © Joe Viesti / Viestiphoto.com; p 151: © Greg Johnston Photography; p 153: © Greg Johnston Photography; p 154 top: © Greg Johnston Photography; p 154 bottom: © Greg Johnston Photography; p 155: © Greg Johnston Photography; p 156 top: © Greg Johnston Photography; p 156 bottom: © Greg Johnston Photography; p 157: © Greg Johnston Photography; p 159: © Greg Johnston Photography; p 160: © Greg Johnston Photography; p 161: © Greg Johnston Photography; p 163: © Greg Johnston Photo-graphy; p 164: © Greg Johnston Photography; p 165: © Greg Johnston Photography; p 166: © Greg Johnston Photography; p 170: © Joe Viesti / Viestiphoto.com; p 171: © Greg Johnston Photography; p 172 top: © Greg Johnston Photography; p 172 bottom: © Greg Johnston Photography; p 173: © Joe Viesti / Viestiphoto.com; p 174 top: © Greg Johnston Photography; p 174 bottom: © Joe Viesti / Viestiphoto.com; p 175: © Joe Viesti / Viestiphoto.com; p 176: © Joe Viesti / Viestiphoto.com; p 178: © Greg Johnston Photography; p 182: © Greg Johnston Photography; p 183: © Greg Johnston Photography; p 184: © Greg Johnston Photography; p 185: © M. Timothy O'Keefe / Alamy Images; p 186: © Joe Viesti / Viestiphoto.com; p 187: © Courtesy Tom Hart Shelby / Reach Resort; p 188: © Courtesy Sunset Key Cottages, A Westin Resort; p 191 top: © Greg Johnston Photography; p 191 bottom: © Joe Viesti / Viestiphoto.com; p 193: © Joe Viesti / Viestiphoto.com; p 194 top: © Greg Johnston Photography; p 194 bottom: © Greg Johnston Photography; p 195: © Greg Johnston Photography